Setting the
PACE

Managing Transition
to Patient-Centered Care

Setting the

PACE

Managing Transition
to Patient-Centered Care

Edited by
Phyllis B. Risner
Claire Blust Rodehaver
Robin G. Bashore

Health Administration Press
Ann Arbor, Michigan   1995

99 98 97 96 95   5 4 3 2 1

Library of Congress Cataloging-in-Publication Data

Setting the PACE : managing transition to patient-centered care / edited by Phyllis B. Risner, and Claire Blust Rodehaver, Robin G. Bashore.
    p.   cm.
  ISBN 1-56793-024-7 (Softbound : alk. paper)
  1. Nursing services—Administration.   2. Organizational change.   3. Health care teams.   4. Patient satisfaction.   I. Risner, Phyllis B.   II. Rodehaver, Claire Blust.   III. Bashore, Robin G.
  [DNLM: 1. Pace 2000 (Program)   2. Hospital Administration.   3. Patient Care Team—organization & administration.   4. Patient Satisfaction. 5. Quality Assurance, Health Care—organization & administration. 6. Models, Organizational.
WX 150 S495 1995]
RT89.S475   1995   362.1'73'068—dc20   94-43730 CIP

The paper used in this publication meets the minimum requirements of American National Standard for Information Sciences—Permanence of Paper for Printed Library Materials, ANSI Z39.48-1984. ∞™

Health Administration Press
A division of the Foundation of the
   American College of Healthcare Executives
1021 East Huron Street
Ann Arbor, Michigan 48104
(313) 764-1380

*To the dedicated health care providers and
support personnel of Miami Valley Hospital.*

Contents

vii

List of Tables

List of Figures and Exhibits

Figures

xiii

Exhibits

Foreword

In these days of health care reform, many providers are taking the lead and reforming their own organizations first. In 1991, Miami Valley Hospital (MVH) leadership had the vision to take a serious look at how to redesign their organization's operations. Today, the hospital is reaping the considerable benefits of its staff's cutting-edge efforts. Members of the multidisciplinary team that led MVH's redesign have decided to share their experiences with others interested in operational restructuring and have written a practical, first-hand account of how to change patient care delivery.

Nursing leaders played an important role in MVH's *Positive Actions for Care Excellence (PACE) 2000* program, of course, but it was the involvement of all health care disciplines in the process that made the difference. Disciplines that were only indirectly involved in past change efforts were totally integrated into PACE 2000 and were instrumental in the implementation of the new patient care delivery system. This multidisciplinary involvement is reflected in the project's outcomes as well as this book's authorship.

Another key ingredient of MVH's redesign success was its comprehensive, holistic approach. No stone was left unturned and no sacred cows were honored. Because they focused on streamlining patient care delivery processes instead of departments, team members were able to eliminate many redundancies, wasted time, and unnecessary work that otherwise would have remained hidden. This how-to book outlines the way they applied practical concepts and explains the structures, processes, issues, and outcomes of PACE 2000. It also includes examples of forms, curricula, and job descriptions that are applicable in many health care settings.

As a leader of the APM Incorporated consulting team that worked with MVH on Operational Excellence (OE), I can attest to the quality of the hospital's internal resources and the staff's enthusiasm for aggressively investigating new technologies and developing creative solutions to bottlenecks and internal barriers. Their experiences will be invaluable to their health care colleagues across the country.

It's never too late to begin a patient care delivery process redesign. Fortunately for today's readers, this book goes a long way in making the process a smoother, richer experience.

Connie R. Curran, RN, Ed.D., FAAN
National Director, Patient Care Services
APM Incorporated

Preface

Nursing care delivery systems affect patient quality and costs in acute care organizations. The changing health care environment in the 1990s demands that administrators and staff evaluate how and by whom care is provided while balancing cost-effectiveness with the maintenance or improvement of quality patient care. The role of the Registered Nurse (RN) is essential, but what nurses do and the percent of time spent in direct patient care must be examined. The purpose for this how-to book is to share one organization's successful transition from an RN-focused, primary nursing patient care delivery system to a partnership model with nurse extenders.

This book addresses structure (the players), processes (the strategies), issues (barriers), and outcomes (what worked and did not work), beginning with the strategic plan through implementation and evaluation of the new patient care delivery model. The book will be helpful to hospital executives, administrators, managers, and staff who are anticipating changing the patient care delivery system or those who have recently changed. Examples of checklists, tools, and forms are provided in many of the chapters and appendixes.

The book is divided into five parts: Strategic Planning, Operational Planning, Implementation, Evaluation, and Future Directions. Part I, Strategic Planning, begins with a brief historical background. Concepts and theories used as theoretical foundations for the project are discussed and applied in Chapter 2. Chapter 3 describes preliminary planning and unfreezing within the organization. It includes an explanation of the organization structure and timeline for changes, an evaluation of new paradigms for patient care delivery and the formation of the Operational Excellence (OE) Project Team who led the effort. The authors include a list of pros and cons for cost reduction using internal resources, as well as a scoring model for evaluating consulting firms. Chapter 3 also addresses an evaluation of nursing and nonnursing activities performed by RNs, plus a discussion of different care delivery models. The concluding appendix for Chapter 3 describes characteristics of the new patient-centered care delivery model.

Part II, Operational Planning, includes Chapters 4 and 5. Chapter 4 examines design issues in planning for the new model. The authors describe the development of OE subcommittees with a focus on the Patient Care Task Force and subgroups. A discussion of skill mix trends is also included. Chapter 5 describes the transition from the OE process to the new Patient Care Model Committee, which was entitled Positive Actions for Care Excellence (PACE) 2000. The authors present a diagram and explanation of the committee structure. They also discuss foundation/philosophical components and implementation plans for the new PACE 2000 model.

Part III, the Implementation Phase, includes five chapters about specific components of the model. Chapters 6, 7, and 8 address role analysis and curricular requirements for (1) the registered and licensed practice nurse; (2) the patient care technician (PCT); and (3) the service associate (SA). Chapter 6 also includes a helpful list of 63 care activities differentiated by professional level of caregivers. Chapter 7 describes process flowcharts for employing PCTs internally and externally. The authors also include a skills self-evaluation checklist for the new role. Chapter 8 focuses on the evolution of the new role, SA, from the housekeeping and dietary departments, as well as addressing the fiscal impact to various departments.

Chapter 9 describes the Documentation Subcommittee structure and processes for revising patient documentation. The authors provide an environmental analysis that identifies key issues that are similar throughout acute care settings. They discuss a three-stage plan that prioritizes the relevant changes. The chapter concludes with results of the implementation and lessons learned. Chapter 10 provides an analysis of three subgroups: pharmacy, respiratory therapy, and clinical laboratory, whose functions impact patient care. Their functions were labeled *enabling* to the new model of care delivery. Changes were made in these three enabler groups prior to the implementation of the new PACE 2000 model.

Part IV, Evaluation of Model, includes two chapters about evaluation of the model. The authors of Chapter 11 provide a frank discussion of the financial impact of all cost-reduction activities during the OE process, including the new model for patient care delivery. The chapter outlines how ideas moved from suggestions through quantification to implementation and evaluation. The authors include nursing cost calculator and variance report forms in addition to several useful worksheets related to skill mix and staffing. Chapter 12 focuses on evaluation of stakeholder satisfaction. The authors include sections about patient, employee, and physician satisfaction; patient outcomes; community response; cost-effectiveness; and clinical efficiency. They share preimplementation and postimplementation results of a Work Characteristics Inventory (adapted from Simms and Erbin-Roesemann 1989). Examples for the SA Survey, the PCT, and RN Evaluation of PACE 2000 are included in the chapter appendixes.

Part V, Future Directions, includes chapters about case management and clinical benchmarking, which are currently under development for a possible concurrent phase-in. Chapter 13 examines the historical background of case management. The authors also address the relationship between OE and quality assurance. They provide a discussion of key steps in case management and flow sheets describing the process of case management and documentation. Chapter 14 explains the concept and describes the benchmarking steps for the diagnosis of pneumonia, diagnosis-related group (DRG) 89.

The Epilogue by Patricia Sue Fitzsimons summarizes the gains and ongoing programmatic changes. She presents a realistic conclusion to the effects of work restructuring and cost containment in a dynamic health care organization.

Acknowledgments

The efforts described in this book could never have been accomplished without the vision, the commitment, and the contributions of the entire staff of Miami Valley Hospital. All departments and every level of personnel were involved in this tremendous effort.

Our deepest thanks to Sue Fitzsimons for the vision and the energy to move us forward and encourage the risk-taking associated with a change of this magnitude.

Our thanks also to the contributing authors who put their efforts into writing so that others could learn from their experiences.

For her perseverance, patience, and expertise, we are greatly indebted to Christine Alley for preparation of the manuscript.

Part I

Strategic Planning

Part I, Strategic Planning, provides the context for the development of a new patient care delivery model. Chapter 1 describes the setting, addresses the historical background of the organization, and includes a brief overview of the restructuring process. Chapter 2 explains theories and concepts that were applied to effectively plan and implement the redesign process. Concepts discussed include strategic planning, leadership, empowerment, change, and organizational culture. Chapter 3 offers a detailed explanation of the organizational structure and timeline for change for the reengineering project. The authors describe preliminary planning that helped prepare the system for change. The OE Project team structure and process are described. The chapter is organized according to steps in the preliminary process of unfreezing for change: getting started, analyzing care delivery systems, including the roles of RNs and NAs, identifying limitations, and reviewing the literature. The chapter concludes with the conceptual framework for the new patient-centered care model. Helpful tables and checklists are included.

1

Historical Perspective

Patricia Sue Fitzsimons

Early in 1990, Miami Valley Hospital (MVH), Dayton, Ohio, initiated a strategic planning process designed to ensure the hospital's success over the coming decade. Analysts from a national planning agency assisted MVH in the strategic planning process. The collaborative effort took four months, resulting in a comprehensive, multiyear plan.

The hospital undertook its strategic planning in the midst of increasing pressure on inpatient volumes and a squeeze on profit margins. Like other acute care institutions, MVH felt the effects of payers bidding for hospital business. In this increasingly competitive environment, the hospital's overriding strategic challenge was to protect and strengthen its market, especially its inpatient business. In addition, for the hospital to compete effectively in the managed care market, as well as to maintain its financial stability, it had become imperative for MVH to achieve a lower-cost position while maintaining excellence in care delivery.

As the management team approached implementation of the strategic plan, it focused on maintaining patient-care leadership and considered the efficacy of restructuring the hospital's care delivery system. At the root of the discussion was the question, "Should the hospital's primary care nursing system be evaluated and the role of the nurse be restructured concurrently with an organizationwide effort to reduce costs?" The outcome of this discussion prompts this book.

Background

MVH is a 772-bed, tertiary-care teaching hospital located in Dayton, Ohio. Recognized for its Level I Trauma Center and Level III Perinatal Center, the institution also offers programs in rehabilitation, psychiatry, dialysis, oncology, chemical dependency, burn care, and infertility care in addition to traditional inpatient and outpatient services. The hospital supports a strong commitment to education. MVH is the largest affiliate of Wright State University School of Medicine, sponsors numerous medical residency programs, and has a joint arrangement with Wright State University to sponsor its School of Nursing.

Through its 100-year history, MVH gained distinction among physicians and consumers alike as a leader in medical care delivery, culminating in its recognition as "The Region's Leader." Its strong tradition of high-quality physician and nursing staff created an environment where nursing and nurses could flourish and led to its image as a leader in professional nursing practice.

By 1990, the hospital's division of nursing had become recognized as a trailblazer in the implementation of primary nursing and also for the development of a clinical ladder and nursing empowerment through implementation of shared governance. The division of nursing also initiated a unique education-service collaboration with Wright State University–Miami Valley School of Nursing. These factors, plus the hospital's excellent reputation and its respect and support for nursing, were reflected in nursing's 1 percent vacancy rate and 9 percent turnover rate. These percentages were well below the national average of 5.0 percent vacancy and 12 percent turnover rates (Springhouse Corporation 1992).

Nursing Undergoes Evaluation

Following the institution's strategic planning process in 1990, the hospital's policymaking team debated a course of action for implementing the strategic plan. This team was led by the president and chief executive officer (CEO) and included the chief operating officer (COO), the chief financial officer (CFO), and the chief nursing officer (CNO).

Thomas G. Breitenbach, hospital president and CEO (Breitenbach 1993), said

> Our goal in these discussions was to develop a plan for embarking on a formal program of cost containment and cost reduction. As part of our

discussions, we debated whether to include in the process a review of the hospital's overhead and its patient care paradigm, which would mean restructuring the role of the nurse. With a number of tough questions on the table, we agreed to get some expert advice.

The policy team invited several consultant firms to present various approaches to cost cutting. They specifically sought approaches that included overhead reduction, with and without a paradigm shift in nursing. The policy team spent many hours during the initial planning days discussing the merits of each approach. Meanwhile, a project team was appointed to submit request for proposals (RFP) to major firms.

Numerous firms responded to the RFPs. Upper management evaluated each of the firms for approach, past experience, success record, and fit with MVH values. Ultimately, a national consulting firm, was hired to implement a formal, cost-savings program that would position MVH as a successful player in the Dayton market into the year 2000. Their approach would involve the development of a new patient care paradigm that would reduce costs through staff mix change and work restructuring. This was the beginning of the organizational process, Operational Excellence (OE).

Concurrent with these discussions at the policy level, nurse leaders at MVH were evaluating this future direction. Clinical nurse specialists (CNSs) reviewed the literature on patient-focused care and evaluated the hospital's care delivery system. Working from the hospital's strengths in clinical areas of excellence and its primary nursing program, the CNSs presented a proposal for significant change. Their work became the foundation for the new patient care model at MVH.

In the initial stages of the change process, the majority of decision making was done by the hospital's policymaking team. This group spent many hours in review, analysis, and discussion of the impact of change on patient care and staff, as well as on physician satisfaction and morale.

Values, philosophy, vision, and the future were common topics for discussion. Meanwhile, in another part of the hospital, the consultants, along with the hospital's analyst staff, initiated comparisons of MVH statistics with benchmark institutions. Data were retrieved about hours per day, skill mix, and salary expense per patient day. The consultants were able to provide one data base from their client hospitals; a second data base was available through the Voluntary Hospitals of America Data Comparison Reporting System. A very deliberate approach to decision making was used.

The CNO, along with directors of nursing and nurse managers, spent many hours considering philosophical and practical issues. At the core of their final plan was a firm belief that quality would be maintained and/or improved. Additionally, considerable weight was given to the satisfaction levels of patients, physicians, and staff.

As the decision-making process continued, other administrative staff and a steering committee, composed of staff and physicians, debated the appropriateness and attainability of the financial targets. After many weeks of analysis, everyone reached a degree of comfort with the financial targets for the institution as well as for nursing.

Clearly, the analysis called for an examination of skill mix through work redesign and role restructuring. The process began with identifying the structure that would allow for maximum participation by all stakeholders. Ultimately, a Patient Care Task Force composed of four major subgroups was developed: nursing model, patient flow, nursing support, and perinatal/ neonatal (Berry Group) (See Figure 4.1). Each of these major groups was broken down into numerous subgroups to tackle process and work-redesign issues. Weekly meetings were held by a steering committee to coordinate and monitor the work of all groups. (See Chapter 3 for an overview of the OE process.)

The outcome of the process is described in the chapters that follow. The success is clearly a tribute to commitment and teamwork.

References

Breitenbach, T. G. 1993. Personal Communication, July.
Springhouse Corporation. 1992. *National Association of Healthcare Recruitment Survey*. Springhouse, PA: The Corporation.

2

Empowering Change

Patricia Sue Fitzsimons and
Phyllis Baker Risner

Change is process and not a destination. It never ends. . . . empowerment creates change.

—Belasco 1990

Managing complex change in any organization involves knowledge and integration of organizational theories and concepts. Empowerment, partnership, and commitment were overriding themes at MVH that helped set the tone for employee involvement and responsibility throughout the change process. The purpose of this chapter is to provide an overview of one hospital's move from an existing successful system to a new vision for a restructured system integrating the concepts of strategic planning, leadership, empowerment, change, and organizational culture.

Strategic Planning

The impetus for change evolved from the strategic planning process in 1990. The Board of Trustees and the Hospital Policy Committee (comprised the CEO, CFO, COO, and the CNO) directed a strategic planning team to assess the organization for its readiness for the future. The overall purpose at the start of the process was to ensure the economic success of the organization and to identify the fit of a caregiving paradigm.

7

The strategic planning process involved assessment and analysis of internal and external environments, which included strengths, weaknesses, threats, opportunities, priorities, and strategies for the organization (Beckhard and Harris 1987; Hernandez 1988; Hernandez, Fottler, and Joiner 1988; Johnson 1992; Pegels and Rogers 1988). The framework for the internal assessment at MVH was based on three major components: the mission, objectives (priorities), and outputs (MedAmerica 1990). Within the framework, six additional factors were assessed: physical structure, organizational structure, system (including financial resources), staff, skills, and strategies.

An internal environmental assessment identified strengths and weaknesses. Strengths included a cadre of committed and effective leaders with credibility, leadership visibility, a progressive organization with shared governance, a clinical ladder, an active nursing research department, staff stability (small amount of turnover), longevity and loyalty of employees, high-quality patient care, competent staff with a large percentage prepared at the baccalaureate and master's degree level, and solid financial base. Weaknesses included departmental territoriality, a belief that "if it ain't broke, don't fix it", the power of tradition, too many levels in the organizational chart, and a trend toward decreased revenues.

Assessment of internal stakeholders was an important task that helped set the stage for empowerment and ultimate buy-in. Internal customers were identified as board of trustee members, physicians, hospital administrators, hospital employees, staff nurses, nurse managers, nurse directors, and other departmental managers. Identification of internal stakeholders established the foundation for bottom-up participation in the process of developing organizational priorities and outputs.

An external environmental assessment provided data about external stakeholders and the political climate. The major external customers were patients (both inpatients and ambulatory), third party payers, and local large businesses. Vendors and suppliers, neighbors, and the metropolitan community were also considered. An analysis of the market and service segments identified the trend toward decreased lengths of stay, increased need for ambulatory and home health care, plus creative alternatives to emergency room care (where an increased use trend led to an increase in uncompensated care costs). Although the hospital was perceived as the region's leader, this group of stakeholders became a major external driving force for organizational change.

The strategic planning team also reviewed the organizational mission. It remained unchanged and was determined to be appropriate for the present as well as the future. The objectives and priorities identified by the team as most critical were to maintain and improve the quality of patient care, decrease costs, recruit primary care physicians, and remain competitive. A crucial decision was whether to plan a two-phase process for cost reduction focusing on overhead first, then adding nursing, or to include a nursing paradigm shift in one major project. At this point, the nursing leadership group became involved. This process is described in Chapter 3.

Leadership

Manthey (1993, 1) states that "leaders are people who influence others by what they say and how they say it. Leadership skills include creativity, influence, and the ability to apply vision to practice." Wilson (1992, 17–18) adds that to develop the organization of the future, nurse leaders must "challenge the status quo, adventure into unknown territory, and take risks." The nursing leadership group at MVH demonstrated these principles. They understood the effect of the macro forces on the organization and ultimately on nursing practice. The leaders used their skills and knowledge to involve others in assessing the existing patient care delivery system, identifying its strengths and liabilities, reviewing literature about alternative delivery systems, and interviewing leaders in organizations where successful restructuring had occurred. The nursing leadership group provided the energy and commitment that helped design the vision for a new nursing care delivery paradigm. It was their ability to effectively communicate and empower others that provided the impetus and reinforcement for the project. The nursing leadership group was an effective driving force for organizational change.

Empowerment

According to Belasco (1990, 238), "The process is the product." Focusing on the processes of team building and participatory decision making while fostering responsibility and accountability provided a sound basis for effecting change. The nursing leadership group shared their ideas for new visions as well as stimulated others from the unit level upwards to think creatively about improved patient care delivery models and processes. The output of the empowering process was the design of a new patient care delivery system by the people who would be implementing the changes.

How MVH Established and Maintains Empowerment

Manthey's (1993, 14) four essential elements for successful change-through-empowerment process were helpful in planning and implementing the changes and are as follows:

1. Identifying the core group of informal leaders and other members who will be involved in the project
2. Developing a group with healthy interpersonal relationships
3. Creating a tightly linked network between the core group and the rest of the staff
4. Making consensus-based decisions about aspects of unit operations that affect the entire staff.

Empowerment and commitment to excellence are essential leadership values that permeate the MVH organization. The board of trustees empower the executive leadership who empower the middle- and first-line managers who empower their employees. For the restructuring process, the nurse executive identified a core group of formal and informal leaders with excellent communication, clinical, and team-building skills. They recognized each other as colleagues and worked collaboratively within the discipline of nursing as well as with physicians and other health care providers toward a common vision. The commitment, enthusiasm, and momentum of the core leader group helped motivate staff and encourage them to participate in decision making about the new patient care system.

The empowerment process was embodied in the bottom-to-top approach used in OE, a separate framework that helped "establish the urgency to change" (Belasco 1990, 22) and energize the organization to act. (OE is explained in Chapter 3.)

Change

Lewin (1951) discussed the importance of identifying driving and restraining forces prior to beginning the first of three phases of his change process: unfreezing, moving, and refreezing. At MVH, the unfreezing process included external and internal driving forces that affected the organization. External driving forces included the following: (1) public discontent with quality and costs within the health care system, (2) business and industry concerns with the increasing costs of health care and health care insurance, (3) third party payers' concern with length of stay, (4) increased demographics of aging, (5) increasing acuity level of inpatients, (6) increased uncompensated care, and (7) increasing downward census fluctuations. Internal driving forces included increased costs of nurses' salaries, nurses' increasing discontent with the amount of nonnursing tasks related to primary nursing, and the number of nurses with baccalaureate or higher educational preparation.

Restraining forces included organizational stress from numerous changes occurring daily, many related to external forces such as Joint Commission for Accreditation of Healthcare Organizations, the Occupational Health and Safety Act, the Centers for Disease Control, and both Medicare and Medicaid. Internal restraining forces included a fairly new divisional nursing council without total support and buy-in from all staff nurses, especially at the unit level; employees who wanted to maintain the status quo; turf and territoriality issues between departments and some disciplines; and lack of understanding of each other's role.

During the unfreezing phase, nurse leaders developed strategies for dealing with the restraining forces and resistance. Strategies that were most effective included involving the main resistors in the process; providing multiple methods of information dissemination about issues that needed to be addressed with a rationale (educating for the need for change); planning weekly meetings for a concentrated period of time; encouraging every employee to submit *bright ideas*, each of which would be considered; and creating an atmosphere of openness, flexibility, and acceptance. These strategies along with multiple channels and opportunities for communication helped *unfreeze* the organization and allowed plans to be made for changing.

The planning phase involved all levels of employees and all disciplines participating in the decision-making process. Existing employee groups were also included, such as representatives from the nursing council. Alternative options were brainstormed and evaluated for feasibility. Consultants and a steering committee assisted with the final evaluation and recommendations. The planning phase included asking for volunteer pilot units for different projects and also included educational components. Evaluation was also built into the plan.

The implementation or moving phase occurred in stages depending on the project. During this time, successes were recognized and celebrated. The pilot units were supported by the project directors, the administrators, and the nursing leadership group. Pilot units were allowed flexibility in applying the plan to their specific needs. They were aware that the plan was not written in stone, so variations were allowed. Units were encouraged to help clarify and refine the new roles for their particular needs.

Refreezing occurs on the units that have *gone on line*. The units are monitored regularly by the project directors as well as the nurse managers. Monthly management forums address skill mix, the new roles, and examples of what works and what does not. Administrative support is visible and constant. Regular written communications throughout the organization keep all employees apprised of the progress. Updates and revisions are critical and are also communicated throughout the organization. Successes are celebrated with appreciation and recognition given to those involved. One critical component remains the focus or purpose of the change: to improve quality and patient service while saving costs.

The nurse leaders became the change agents by helping manage the organizational change process. Their knowledge and expertise in leadership, management, empowerment, and organizational behavior contributed to the on-going cycle of change within the system.

Organizational Culture

Changing organization culture takes time. Changing the patient care delivery model, including skill mix, new roles, and new processes affects the culture. New norms and values evolve as the new delivery system progresses. However, during the transition between the old and new model (while both are still in effect), there may be confusion and uncertainty about what is valued. Both formal and informal leaders can facilitate empowerment by reinforcing the purpose of the change and focusing on the commonalities within the organization while helping employees let go of the past. The ultimate goal is to maintain a strong culture with "a high level of integration and congruence of values and beliefs throughout the organization" (Batey 1992, 109).

Summary

This chapter provides a theoretical basis for the book by discussing essential concepts that facilitated change within the entire organization. The processes included strategic planning leadership, empowerment and organizational culture. Organization-specific examples for each of the concepts were given with a discussion of their effectiveness. This book explains the change process from preliminary planning through implementation and evaluation.

References

Batey, M. V. 1992. "Organizational Culture: Analysis of the Concept." In *Nursing Administration: A Micro/Macro Approach for Effective Nurse Executives*, edited by P. J. Decker and E. J. Sullivan, 101–12. Norwalk, CT: Appleton & Lange.

Beckhard, R., and R. T. Harris. 1987. *Organizational Transition: Managing Complex Change*, 2d ed. Reading, MA: Addison–Wesley.

Belasco, J. A. 1990. *Teaching the Elephant to Dance: The Manager's Guide to Empowering Change*. New York: Plume.

Hernandez, S. R. 1988. "Formulating Organizational Strategy." In *Strategic Management of Human Resources in Health Services Organizations*, edited by D. Fottler, S. R. Hernandez, and C. L. Joiner, 20–50. New York: Delmar.

Hernandez, S. R., M. D. Fottler, and C. L. Joiner. 1988. "Strategic Management of Human Resources in Health Services Organizations." In *Strategic Management of Human Resources in Health Services Organizations*, edited by M. D. Fottler, S. R. Hernandez, and C. L. Joiner, 3–19. New York: Delmar.

Johnson, L. 1992. "Strategic Management in Nursing Administration." In *Nursing Administration: A Micro/Macro Approach for Effective Nurse Executives*, edited by P. J. Decker and E. J. Sullivan, 71–100. Norwalk, CT: Appleton & Lange.

Lewin, K. 1951. *Field Theory in Social Science*. New York: Harper & Row.

Manthey, M. 1993. "Empowering Staff to Create a Professional Practice Environment." In American Organization of Nurse Executives, *Nursing Leadership: Preparing for the 21st Century*, 1–17. Chicago: The American Hospital Association.

MedAmerica Health System, and McKinsey & Company. 1990. *Ensuring Success in the 1990s*. Cleveland, OH: McKinsey & Company, Inc.

Pegels, C. C., and K. A. Rogers. 1988. *Strategic Management of Hospitals and Health Care Facilities*. Rockville, MD: Aspen.

Wilson, C. K. 1992. *Building New Nursing Organizations: Visions and Realities*. Gaithersburg, MD: Aspen.

3

Preliminary Planning and Unfreezing

Jayne Lachey Gmeiner, Mary Lou Anderson,
Bonnie Coalt, Therese C. Lupo,
and Deborah Mals

This chapter establishes the need to evaluate cost-effective methods of care delivery by the division of nursing at MVH. The focus of this chapter is cost-reduction analysis and the plan for implementing a new patient care delivery system. It is organized according to steps in the process:

1. Getting started
2. Analyzing care delivery systems, including historical perspectives
3. Identifying limitations
4. Reviewing the literature
5. Developing a conceptual framework.

Figure 3.1 depicts the organizational structure and timeline for change from 1990 through 1993. Key components of this structure will be discussed in this chapter and throughout the text.

Step 1: Getting Started

In 1990, MVH in collaboration with a national planning agency, developed a comprehensive multiyear strategic plan (MedAmerica 1990)

15

Figure 3.1

Organizational Structure and Timeline for Change

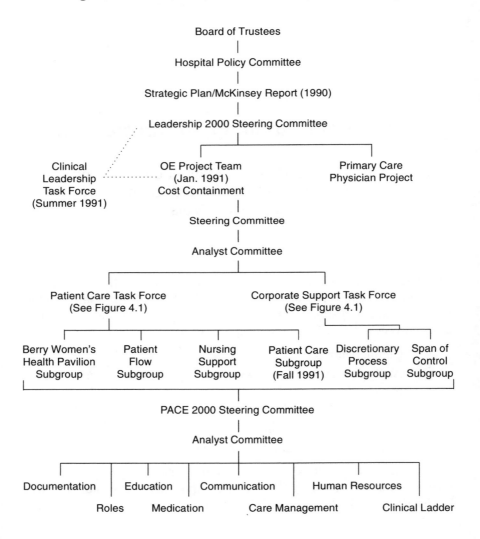

that served as the foundation for work redesign and restructuring efforts. The strategic plan included two major strategies for the future vision of MVH: (1) primary care physician recruitment and retention and (2) cost containment (OE). These strategies were congruent with goals from the Leadership 2000 Task Force, which comprised board members, administrators, physicians, and nurses. The multiyear strategic plan suggested MVH could achieve multiple million dollar savings through overhead cost reductions. A commitment by the MVH Board of Trustees to recommend a course of action to reduce costs was established with a target date of June 1991.

The overall program to evaluate MVH, its systems, and potential cost-reducing ideas was named Operational Excellence (OE). In January 1991, the charter for OE was formulated with the following project team membership:

1. COO, committee chair
2. Vice president, Hospital Operations, project team leader
3. CNO
4. Vice president, Division of Finance
5. Director, Pharmacy Services
6. Director, Purchasing
7. Director, Nursing
8. Director, Management Engineering
9. Director, Human Resources
10. Director, Respiratory Care Services.

Nomination to the OE Project Team was based on several criteria: "cross organizational representation, commitment, past experience, and perhaps most importantly, an orientation to continuous improvement, as well as to 'getting things done' " (Thornton and Boosalis 1991).

The OE Project Team charter was to "recommend an approach to the Leadership 2000 Steering Committee for reducing MVH costs in 1992" (MVH 1991a). The issues requiring resolution included the following:

1. Was there a reasonable chance for payout and sustained savings?
2. Had MVH done well in limiting full-time equivalent (FTE) growth but not done as well in aligning the work?
3. Was there a need to visit with other organizations that have participated in major cost-containment efforts to identify attitudinal-impact issues?
4. Did MVH have the skills and resources to communicate and implement the recommended approach internally?

5. What operational issues would be affected by utilizing existing management resources to facilitate the project?
6. Should only overhead be included? If so, how should it be defined?

The OE Project Team attended a three-day quality planning session to promote optimal group process and develop skills to facilitate technical and behavioral elements of quality planning (Juran 1989). The OE Project Team also became familiar with Juran's brainstorming techniques listed as follows:

1. Generate as many ideas as possible.
2. No ideas are challenged, criticized, or ridiculed.
3. Free thinking is encouraged.
4. Everyone has an opportunity to contribute.
5. No one, particularly an expert, is allowed to dominate the procedure.
6. Combine and adapt ideas. Put ideas to other uses, adapt them, magnify them, minify them, rearrange them, reverse them, combine them, and modify them.
7. Allow incubation (the work of the unconscious or subconscious) to occur between sessions. Often sudden insight and spurts of creativity result. (Juran 1989, 10)

Early meetings focused on the multiyear strategic plan and two key messages: (1) operating margins are threatened if expense growth continues to outpace net revenue growth, and (2) the future looks more challenging than the past (MedAmerica 1990). The OE Project Team asked several major questions during initial meetings, which are as follows:

1. Did the members agree with the strategic plan recommendations that MVH needed to undertake a cost containment effort?
2. Did the members value the data collection methods and the analysis of the consulting group?
3. Did members believe that the cost containment effort could be accomplished utilizing resources within MVH?
4. Did the members believe that there was a benefit to have an external consultant group facilitate the cost-containment effort?

As work continued by the OE Project Team, it became evident that the major cost savings that occur in corporations is an end result of a reduction in personnel. The division of nursing represented 40 percent of the total operational budget, and for the hospital to meet its target cost savings, nursing would be required to contribute to the overall cost savings target. It soon became evident that a cost savings in nursing would require work redesign, elimination of unnecessary tasks, and reassigning tasks to lower-paid individuals.

The team focused on evaluating strategies to promote cost containment through blending internal resources with external consulting firms expertise. A timetable of two months was established to review an initial list of 22 consulting firms by announcing a request for proposal (MVH 1991b). MVH's leadership stressed that whatever the structure or process proposed, the following principles would be essential:

1. Most important, any cost reductions must not come at the expense of MVH's highest goal of quality.
2. Any cost reductions must not sacrifice the improvements made in the last several years in physician and employee satisfaction.
3. While short-term reductions may be achieved, processes and structure must be provided to build the necessary skills and capabilities necessary for ongoing cost management. (MVH 1991b)

The project team developed a list of the pros and cons for an internal approach to cost containment (Table 3.1). The analysis was based on historical institutional reactions to change and the impact this process could impose on employees at all levels. The internal approach was not recommended because of the following major concerns pertaining to the internal approach: excessive length of time to accomplish, higher risk, fragmentation, lack of experience, lack of objectivity, and the ability to sustain momentum. The list was presented to the OE Steering Committee, that comprised OE Project Team members, physicians, representatives, board members, and the CEO of MVH. The project team reached the conclusion that the internal option would not be feasible.

Each project team member was assigned to inquire about one or more consulting firms, including follow-up and reference checking. A scoring method was developed by Management Engineering (Table 3.2) to rate the firms in the areas of organizational impact, breadth of organizational involvement, characteristics of savings, hospital experience, cost, proposal clarity, and reference checks to provide a consistent method of evaluation between group members. The group continually debated the idea of internal versus external approaches to cost containment while

Table 3.1

Operational Excellence Project Team: Pros and Cons for Doing Cost Reductions Using Internal Resources

Pros

Cost: Est. one-tenth, less cuts to achieve same target (net reductions)

Knowledge (of approaches):
- Exists—internal Mgt. Systems Staff & OE Team
- Have list of hundreds of industry applied opportunities

Data Base:
- Competitors cost position, done annually
- DRG Analysis—1989 Dayton hospitals top 150 Medicare
- DRG Analysis—internal benchmarking using MedisGroups & TSI
- Transition Sys—department cost detail, August 1991
- Transition Sys—clinical prog. cost detail, 1989 & 90 data, July 91
- VHA–DCRS, Benchmarking 601+ bed peer group

Proj. Mgt: Initial successes achieved with O.E. & P.C.P.P.

Facilitation: Build experience level of internal staff

Credibility: Clear show of confidence in internal knowledge and skills required

Communications Plan: Dependent on internal communications staff

Human Res. Plan: Dependent on internal H.R. policy decision processes

Control Mechanisms: Currently under implementation (See TSI)

Physician Involvement: Internal mgt. exposure will increase

Catalyst for Mgt. Decision Making: Defined structure & process

Cons

Timing:
- Would require shutting down other projects to meet deadline
- Could req. timely search for new positions if no projects are shut down

Experience:
- Of using approach; possibly no significant difference
- Lacking in implementation; especially clinical areas

Data Base: Learning Curve, many under pros are new; external experience

Proj. Mgt: Ability to sustain urgency over 6–9 months

Facilitation: Difficult role to play in politically sensitive issues (objectivity)

Credibility: Lack of name recognition that external would bring

Communications Plan: Timing–lack of pre-prepared and tested approach

Human Res. Plan: Timing–external could provide jump-start

Control Mechanisms: External will emphasize they're not currently used

Physician Involvement: Lack of any involvement to date in the O.E. effort

Catalyst for Mgt. Decision Making: Unknown capabilities

narrowing the consulting firm bids to six. Six firms were interviewed four to five months into the project. The interview process resulted in narrowing the gap for consulting firm bids to two and another round of questioning to determine fit with the culture of MVH.

Human resource issues became a topic for the project team and resulted in the following important questions:

1. Was there a reasonable chance for pay-out and sustained savings?
2. How ingrained in the MVH culture was the idea of job security?
3. If the answer was "yes" to question number 1, was pay-out worth organizational upheaval or change?
4. Was it possible to look at a single source for cost savings (for example, supplies or overhead)?
5. The literature review indicated that the majority of organizations did unit-specific reductions; was it preferable to use this approach versus one organizationwide?
6. Was attrition more attractive from a long-range cultural perspective despite the longer time frame (18–24 months)?
7. What communication approach and timing were preferable, assuming an outside firm was selected?

These questions were considered by the project team as consulting firms presented their approach to cost reductions. Through calculations, the OE Project Team members' weighted scores were totaled and the consulting firm was chosen. A presentation was planned and given to the Leadership 2000 Steering Committee based on an internal versus external approach six months into the process. The steering committee reached the decision to commit to the external approach for cost containment. Simultaneously, the emphasis and commitment continued for the OE Project Team to maintain quality and the hospital's reputation as "the region's leader."

There was consensus that work redesign would be essential to gain any cost reductions for the division of nursing. Historically, the division of nursing at MVH had been providing excellent care as demonstrated through annual surveys of patients and physicians. The primary challenge would be to continue to deliver excellent care after work redesign.

Another challenge would be to create a positive atmosphere for change within a highly satisfied nursing staff. A multiphase ongoing research study had demonstrated a history of satisfaction with nursing

Table 3.2 Operational Excellence Scoring Model Re-cap Sheet

*** Due: To Tim Collins by 4 p.m., Friday, April 12th, 1991 ***

DIRECTIONS: Rate each category for each consulting firm using the following whole number scale:

1	VERY Unfavorable
2	Unfavorable
3	Average
4	Favorable
5	VERY Favorable

IMPORTANT: PLEASE USE ONLY WHOLE NUMBERS, NO DECIMAL PLACES.

COMPLETED BY: Total Team Re-cap

DATE: _____

Category Wt. -->	10%	20%	5%	15%	5%	20%	25%	100%
Category -->	Breadth Org. Inv.	Charact. Savings	Budget Cost	Exp: Cost Red. Proj.	Proposal Clarity	Reference Check	Org. Impact	Overall Wt. Score
						See Note Below*		
1						3		0.60
2						3		0.60
3						3		0.60
4						3		0.60
5						3		0.60
6						3		0.60
7						3		0.60
8						3		0.60
9						3		0.60
10						3		0.60
11						3		0.60
12						3		0.60
13						3		0.60
14						3		0.60
15						3		0.60
16						3		0.60
17						3		0.60
18						3		0.60

Note: At the April 1, 1991 Team Meeting, it was decided to rate this category after the firms are cut to the Top 6. Therefore, round 1 evaluation all firms will receive an average rating (3).

personnel in the areas of job satisfaction, professional autonomy, organizational climate, professional practice climate, power orientation, and centralization power.

Step 2: Analyzing Care Delivery Systems

The division of nursing in collaboration with hospital operations established a need to redefine the current care delivery system in the spring of 1991. This opportunity was given to an ad hoc clinical leadership task force consisting of clinical nurse specialists (CNS) and nurse educators from all specialities in the institution. Membership included representatives from the following areas: medical-surgical, cardiovascular, obstetrical, neonatal, oncology, neurological, critical care, pain, and orthopedics. The task force was charged with the following objectives:

1. To review the current care delivery system.
2. To review the literature about care delivery systems and consider the potential effect on the organizational culture.
3. To contact colleagues regionally and nationally to assess the current status of care delivery systems.
4. To evaluate pros and cons of various models in relation to a "fit" at MVH.
5. To provide recommendations for a future care delivery system.

The Clinical Leadership Task Force was facilitated by the acting chairperson(s) of the CNS and nurse educator groups. Principles of shared governance such as clinical practice accountability, autonomy, collaboration, collegiality, and consensus-based decision making were applied from the initial starting point during the group discussions. "Shared governance, through the contribution of different roles to a common endeavor, provides the glue and energy that motivates and moves the system toward success" (Porter-O'Grady 1990). A common belief was that if the Clinical Leadership Task Force accepted the responsibility for decision making, it would also acknowledge ownership of the problem with the current care delivery system and create ideas for possible solutions. Analysis of the existing care delivery system, plus brainstorming and dream sessions about a future care delivery system resulted in a formal presentation to a permanent organizational group, the Clinical Nursing Management Group, in September 1991. This presentation focused on the following topics: historical perspectives, limitations of current care delivery system, literature review, and recommendations for the future. Each topic will be further discussed in this chapter.

Historical Perspectives

Primary nursing

MVH incorporated the philosophy and practice of primary nursing as its nursing care delivery system in the mid-1970s. Primary nursing is a mode of nursing care delivery whose purpose is both to maximize the benefits of care to patients and to ensure maximum utilization and development of nursing staff (Sigmon 1981). According to Sigmon (1981), this model indirectly improves the nurse's work satisfaction through the nurse's responsibility and accountability for care. Improved patient satisfaction was a major outcome from primary nursing through an increase in nurse-patient contact as evidenced by the patient satisfaction scores and nurse satisfaction scores at MVH in 1991. Patient satisfaction scores compiled through the internal marketing department in the fall of 1991 confirmed the positive perceptions of care delivered and care received. MVH also had a 2 percent registered nurse (RN) staff vacancy rate for the five years prior to restructuring with the average length of staff nurse employment being approximately eight years and four months. Nurses reported a high degree of satisfaction with care delivered.

The earliest interpretation of primary nursing was designed to have the professional nurse perform clinical functions with minimal or no delegation of tasks to others. Nurses who are individually responsible for patient's comprehensive nursing care are able to enter into a collegial relationship with physicians who provide the patient's medical care (Goodwin, Long, and Nassif 1981). In primary nursing, the clinical nurse is responsible for initiating the nursing process, formulating a plan of care, and evaluating outcomes of that care for a set of patients. Primary nursing leads the nurse to a clear collaborative role with the physician, since both the physician and primary nurse have an in-depth, firsthand knowledge of the patient.

Clinical ladder

MVH historically combined the clinical ladder with primary nursing to facilitate indirect outcomes and improve the quality of patient care. Historically, the need to develop a system of promotion for the professional practitioner comparable with the nurse administrator was identified by Creighton (1964). The first proposal for a clinical ladder as a concept for nursing practice was presented by Zimmer (1972). This ladder was designed to address the failure of traditional nursing organizations to (1) provide a working environment that would nurture and challenge professional growth, and (2) recognize excellence in clinical practice (Sanford 1987). According to Merker, Mariak, and Dwinnels (1985), a clinical ladder is a system that provides benefits and recognition for staying in the clinical area equal to promotion into administrative or educational tracks. Understanding what motivates nurses and how to reduce staff turnover by providing career paths can help administration increase productivity and reduce personnel costs (Gibson and Dewhirst 1986). Murray (1993, 46) noted that "Nursing leaders search for new and creative ways to increase the productivity of experienced bedside professional nurses to handle the increased acuity of today's hospitalized patients". The search has resulted in the need to reevaluate and redefine existing promotional systems.

MVH has had four levels of promotion in the clinical ladder system. The functions of each level of the clinical ladder have evolved over the past few years as a reflection of higher acuity, outpatients, flexible patient census, and increasing fiscal demands within the hospital environment. Direct care is provided to patients by all four levels of the clinical ladder, although the majority of staff nurses are primary I or II. The nurse educator (primary III) and CNS (primary IV) spend 20–40 percent of their time in direct patient care. The remainder of their time is devoted to nondirect care functions, including unit/division quality assurance, patient education, nursing education, consultation, unit/division nursing committees, research, publication, and community service.

Nursing assistants

As patient acuity continued to increase on the medical-surgical units between 1983 and 1986, nursing assistants (NAs) were added to the care delivery system. NAs were usually assigned to a wing and were shared by all RNs. The NA reported to each RN on the unit and generally completed tasks per routine assignment. A ladder for NAs was introduced in the late 1980s to distinguish between skill levels of NAs and to provide a formal method of monetary compensation and title recognition. The NA I or II assisted the RN by performing assigned patient care tasks. The NA was also responsible for unit activities that maintain an environment to promote safety and comfort for the patient. The NA ladder was based on two skill levels and the ability to perform certain tasks:

- NA I. Performs basic activities under the following performance areas according to their job description: direct patient care, therapeutic procedures, environment, job knowledge/development, customer relations, and requirements/qualifications (See Appendix 3.A for a checklist of skills).
- NA II. Performs all responsibilities outlined above with the following additional tasks: applies heat and cold, applies binders, assists with procedures, dressings, wound and decubitus care, etc., catheterizes patients, discontinues foley catheters, suctions patients, performs wound care, applies oxygen cannula, collects sterile specimens, and records chest tube drainage (See Appendix 3.B for a checklist of skills).

The NA I attended lectures and completed a skills checklist before receiving a promotional raise and the title of NA II.

Historical synthesis

The organization has been recognized as the region's leader by both patient and physician consumer satisfaction surveys. The blend of primary nursing and the clinical ladder created an atmosphere that increased autonomy, professional growth, and most of all, high quality patient care. The blending of clinical ladders and primary nursing produced a positive climate that defined and promoted professional nursing while supporting knowledgeable nurses with expertise at the bedside (Sigmon 1981).

The Clinical Leadership Task Force recognized the impact of total primary nursing on an institution from the cost perspective of an all RN staff and the potential effect of a nursing shortage on a primary care delivery system. MVH was fortunate to have weathered the most recent nursing shortage in the late 1980s and early 1990s without significant nurse turnover. A Voluntary Hospitals of America (VHA) (1990) report stated hospital nursing care delivery systems evolved through the years in response to changes in institutional goals and an ever continuing search by nurse executives to improve patient care. The Clinical Leadership

Task Force believed MVH would be able to evolve into an expanded method of care delivery keeping the premise of primary nursing and the clinical ladder as its foundation for expansion.

Step 3: Assessing Limitations of Existing Care Delivery System

The Clinical Leadership Task Force spent many hours assessing the existing care system and identified multiple opportunities for improvement. The task force recognized that an overall care delivery system change would require total involvement of the institution. The application of shared governance with representatives from all levels of MVH would provide the framework to fulfill this goal. The Clinical Leadership Task Force through discussion and brainstorming sessions developed a list of limitations or opportunities for improvement in the current primary nursing care delivery system as identified by role and type of system. Opportunities were identified related specifically to the RN role, evaluating those responsibilities that affected continuity and quality of care and nonnursing duties performed by RNs. Limitations were identified for the RN role, the care delivery system, and the NA role.

Limitations of the RN role

1. The RNs lacked delegation skills that impacted NAs' ability to maintain NA II skills.
2. The RNs were not comfortable with supervising or confronting NAs regarding performance and skill issues.
3. The RNs spent considerable time doing nonnursing tasks; time that could be spent on patient and family teaching was lost.

Limitations of care delivery system

1. There was no standardized report mechanism for RN/NA communication.
2. Change of shift reports were sometimes lengthy and inconsistent.
3. RNs were not knowledgeable about standards of care.
4. Important patient history was lost in the existing documentation or care planning system (Nursing Information Management System).

5. The documentation system was too time-consuming. RNs were performing nondirect patient care activities that should have been performed by dietary, pharmacy, laboratory, transportation, and unit clerk personnel (Table 3.3).

Limitations of the NA role

1. A standardized NA unit orientation was not in place.
2. The NA orientation process on the unit was not long enough.
3. A formalized NA preceptor program was not in existence.
4. RNs were not appropriately involved in precepting NAs.
5. Many NA II skills were applicable to only a few units.
6. NAs were not utilized to their potential capacity (e.g., Accuchecks).

Table 3.3

Current Nonnursing Duties Performed by RNs

Dietary
Filling out menus
Passing/picking up trays
Errands for food (salt, coffee)
Distributing water pitchers

Pharmacy
Intravenous tubing changes
Running for medications
Counting narcotics

Housekeeping
Emptying trash
Cleaning rooms
Making unoccupied beds
Cleaning equipment

Transportation
Taking patients to clinics
Taking patients to Perinatal building
Taking patients to psychiatric
  evaluations

Laboratory
Drawing specimens from central
  lines

Unit Clerk
Answering call lights
Answering telephones
Finding personnel/staff
Deciphering physician orders
Noting/entering physician orders

Other
Finding equipment
Going to dumbwaiter
Running errands

7. NAs commitment to role and the institution was a concern due to a perceived high turnover and different work ethic.

Also, new nursing personnel were unfamiliar with the NA role due to a long history of primary nursing at the institution. A mechanism to validate the competency of the NAs was not in place. And last, NAs were hired from within MVH when a more qualified applicant may have been available outside.

Limitations and opportunities gave the Clinical Leadership Task Force valuable information and ideas to create the energy to move forward to evaluate potential new care delivery systems. Analysis continued by reviewing the literature and networking with nurse colleagues throughout the nation.

Step 4: Reviewing the Literature

The Clinical Leadership Care Delivery Task Force wanted to establish support and affirmation for the need to change the existing method of providing patient care. Initial buy-off for change from this task force would be very important to the overall success of redefining a care delivery system. The literature review revealed several articles (Glandon, Colbert, and Thomasama 1989; Manthey 1988; Prescott et al. 1991) that cited rationale for changing present care delivery models based on appropriate utilization of nursing expertise, cost containment, survival during periods of nursing shortages, and the need to retain experienced and motivated staff. Other strategies examined to reduce costs and to consider new paradigms for patient care delivery were based on a national data base and The Healthcare Advisory Board's million-dollar cost savings ideas (The Healthcare Advisory Board 1989). The new paradigms feature cross education of staff, creative staffing patterns, documentation changes, elimination of management levels and centralization of distribution (Table 3.4). The resurgence of nonnurse personnel into acute care hospitals resurfaced on a national scale in the late 1980s as units closed, surgeries were canceled, and unmeasured reductions in both quality and quantity of nursing care for individual patients were brought to the forefront (American Hospital Association 1987). The need to understand and manage nursing costs has become increasingly important to hospitals since the introduction of diagnosis-related group (DRG) based payment systems in the early 1980s (Glandon, Colbert, and Thomasama 1989).

The Secretary's Commission on Nursing (1988) also responded with several recommendations to alleviate the nursing shortage of the late 1980s including

1. Raising nursing wages relative to other professions
2. Encouraging part-time nurses to work more hours
3. Encouraging nurse employers to use scarce RN resources in an efficient and effective manner, thereby enhancing the adequacy of the existing RN supply. (U.S. Department of Health and Human Services 1988)

Table 3.4

Theoretical Approaches to Patient Care Cost Management

Tactic	Advisory Board Grade	Possible Annual Savings
Cross-training nurses in ancillary skills	A	$ 2,200,000–2,400,000
Cross-training nurses in specialties	A	1,300,000–1,500,000
Cross-training ancillary and support staff	B	450,000–500,000
Renaissance of LPNs, nurse's aides	B	825,000–925,000
Deprofessionalizing ancillary services	B–	425,000–475,000
Charting by exception	B–	300,000–350,000
Just-in-time nurse staffing	A	1,500,000–1,700,000
Computerized scheduling	B+	1,225,000–1,325,000
Mini-shifts	B (savings estimated)	550,000–600,000
100% on-time delivery	B (savings estimated)	600,000–650,000
Reduced hours of operation	B	525,000–575,000
Seasonal staffing	D	< 50,000
"Best Cost" standards engineering	A+	10,000,000–11,000,000
Eliminating management layers	A+	3,500,000–4,000,000
Centralizing hospital distribution	B–	125,000–175,000
Consolidating patient admission	B	425,000–475,000
Eliminating satellites	D	< 50,000
Super nursing units	A+	10,000,000–11,000,000

Adapted from: "Million Dollar Cost Saving Ideas," the Healthcare Advisory Board, 1989. The Governance Committee, Washington, DC, the Advisory Board Company, with permission.

As patient acuity continued to rise, the RNs felt overtaxed and frustrated with patient assignments and the completion of nonnursing tasks. Prescott et al. (1991) identified that RNs spent their time in four major categories, which are as follows:

1. Direct care: nursing care performed in the presence of patient/ family
2. Indirect care: nursing care done away from but on the patient's behalf (i.e., charting)
3. Unit related: activities related to the general maintenance of the nursing unit
4. Personal: activities related to RN meals, personal phone calls.

Prescott et al. (1991) reported minimal time being spent on personal activities, but time spent on unit activities was fairly high and could be performed more effectively by others. Time might be substantially decreased by computers and other ways to streamline information flow. Prescott and associates also proposed improving delivery of nursing care in four ways:

1. Developing assistive nursing personnel
2. Developing new types of workers to provide nonclinical support
3. Implementing labor savings devices
4. Restructuring RN roles. (Prescott et al. 1991)

Increasing assistive personnel (nurse extenders) could result in the RN being pulled away from direct patient care and needing more time to mentor, manage, or assist in the development of new types of workers. Changes in care delivery systems should be evaluated in terms of improvement of patient care services in respect to providing quality care in a timely, appropriate, and cost-effective manner.

Lengacher and Mabe (1993) summarized 29 articles regarding nurse extenders reported in the literature. Four major categories and definitions of models were seen in the five-year review of literature:

- Traditional Extender Model (26 percent). Assistive personnel to the RN, including the NA, unit assistant, ward clerk, orderly, housekeeping, and dietary aide.
- Nontraditional Extender Model (16 percent). Assistive positions to the RN that require extra training; includes the electrocardiogram

(EKG) technician, monitor technician, phlebotomy technician, and corpsmembers.

- Traditional Extender in Partnership Model (26 percent). Assistive personnel to the RN, including the traditional extender as a partner in patient care with an RN (NAs and licensed practical nurses).
- Nontraditional Extender in Partnership Model (32 percent). Assistive personnel to the RN, including the use of a nontraditional extender partner in patient care with a RN (primarily patient care and critical care technicians). (Lengacher and Mabe 1993)

Four different models of care were consistently found through review of the literature as identified below:

1. *Team*: Team nursing consists of RN leaders to oversee the care to others such as LPNs and trained attendants. This model of care utilizes the least number of RNs per unit and is commonly used in extended care facilities or nursing homes.

2. *Modular nursing*: Modular nursing consists of a staff being paired or tripled together into a care unit to provide nursing care for their set group of patients. These care units are assigned a geographic area of the unit. A care unit example may be two RNs and one trained attendant to care for 10 to 12 patients. Modular nursing is less costly than primary nursing.

3. *Primary nursing*: Primary or total nursing care had the highest cost, highest number of RNs, and highest acuity level. Primary nursing views the primary nurse as having 24-hour accountability for patient care.

4. *Total patient care*: Total patient care reflects 8-hour accountability, instead of the 24-hour accountability found in primary nursing. Total patient care is a case method way to organize nursing care. (Hegyvary 1977)

Glandon and partners (1989) analyzed the average cost of nursing dollars per patient day for each of the models utilizing Medicus Systems Corporation's National Comparative Data Base. This study utilized nursing information from 392 medical and surgical nursing units in 62 hospitals for three months in 1977. The average cost of nursing dollars per patient day was identified as follows: *Team*—$58.73, *Modular*—$60.55, *Total*—$63.83, and *Primary*—$68.22 (Glandon, Colbert, and Thomasama 1989).

The Clinical Leadership Care Delivery Task Force knew that economic forces in the 1990s would drive care delivery systems and nursing practice in hospital situations. The commitment to change became focused on promoting a care delivery system that would improve quality, promote collegiality of all hospital departments, minimize institutional limitations, provide cost efficient and effective patient care.

The idea of combining the concepts of primary nursing, case management, partnerships, and patient-family centered care into one delivery system became a group vision. Manthey (1988) suggests the development of primary practice partners to maintain the integrity of primary nursing. Manthey (1988) also states that by assigning the NA to an RN instead of patients, many of the potential problems experienced in the past could be avoided. The focus of change needed to revolve around an overall system review with total involvement of all levels of employees.

Step 5: Developing a Conceptual Framework

Through review of the literature and consideration of the philosophy and culture at MVH, ideas for change began to take shape. Four assumptions formed the conceptual framework to provide support to change the existing care delivery system in the organization. These assumptions were identified by the clinical leadership group based on Maslow's hierarchy of needs (Maslow 1954) in relationship to patient care needs adapted from Kirby and Garfink (1991), and are as follows:

1. Two factors influence the extent to which patient care needs are met: the number of caregivers and the way the care is distributed among those caregivers (Garfink et al. 1990). Figures 3.2 and 3.3 are adaptations of Kirby and Garfink's (1991) model using Maslow's hierarchy of needs to categorize patient care needs. Traditional care delivery systems result in higher level patient care needs not being met. The RN and NA spend their time meeting the infinite number of basic physical and safety needs as demonstrated in Figure 3.2. Lack of direct RN communication and delegation result in poor utilization of NAs. The focus of caregivers toward basic needs results in decreased time to meet self-actualization, esteem, and love needs.

   Care delivery systems that feature NAs or partners to assist directly with patient care delivery can result in all levels of needs being met (Figure 3.3). The RN directs patient care in an environment

Figure 3.2

Traditional Care Model

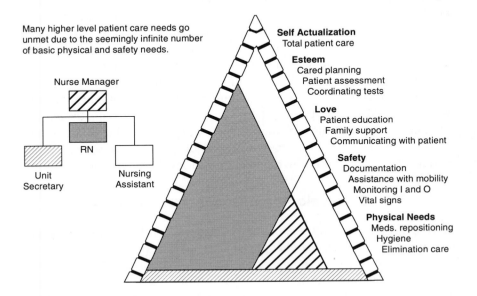

Many higher level patient care needs go unmet due to the seemingly infinite number of basic physical and safety needs.

Nurse Manager

RN

Unit Secretary

Nursing Assistant

Self Actualization
Total patient care

Esteem
Cared planning
Patient assessment
Coordinating tests

Love
Patient education
Family support
Communicating with patient

Safety
Documentation
Assistance with mobility
Monitoring I and O
Vital signs

Physical Needs
Meds. repositioning
Hygiene
Elimination care

Reprinted with permission from Kirby, K., and C. M. Garfink. 1991. "The University Hospital Nurse Extender Model." *Journal of Nursing Administration* 21 (1): 25–30.

to meet physical, safety, love, esteem, and self-actualization needs. Mutual trust is required to ensure that the nurse delegates sufficiently and appropriately. Therefore, nurses must develop delegation skills and be willing to focus their time on higher level needs. Additionally, it is required that NA IIs have the skills to carry out the assigned tasks consistently and accurately as well as a commitment to meet the patient care needs.

2. By allowing the nurses to achieve more collegiality, professional autonomy, and experience greater job satisfaction, they will most likely mentor and influence the NAs they work with more consistently.

3. The program must be cost-effective. If nurses spend more time planning and coordinating patient care, hospital length of stay will be lowered and costs reduced. In addition, redefining roles, implementing

Figure 3.3

Partners in Professional Practice

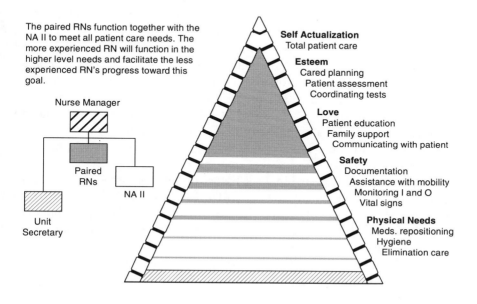

The paired RNs function together with the NA II to meet all patient care needs. The more experienced RN will function in the higher level needs and facilitate the less experienced RN's progress toward this goal.

Nurse Manager

Paired RNs

NA II

Unit Secretary

Self Actualization
Total patient care

Esteem
Cared planning
Patient assessment
Coordinating tests

Love
Patient education
Family support
Communicating with patient

Safety
Documentation
Assistance with mobility
Monitoring I and O
Vital signs

Physical Needs
Meds. repositioning
Hygiene
Elimination care

Reprinted with permission from Kirby, K., and C. M. Garfink. 1991. "The University Hospital Nurse Extender Model." *Journal of Nursing Administration* 21 (1): 25–30.

enablers (Chapter 10), and shifting work previously performed by RNs to lower paid NAs reduces the cost of care by providing the opportunity for RNs to stretch their care caseload.

4. Quality of patient care will improve with the model presented in Figure 3.3. More patient needs will be met and patient care will be enhanced.

After consideration of these assumptions, the review of the literature and the organizational culture, extensive discussion ensued regarding *primary practice partner* (Manthey 1988) and the formation of dyads or triads to deliver care. The clinical leadership group was intrigued with the concept of a partnered system integrated with the clinical ladder in which an experienced nurse teams up with a less experienced nurse and an NA II. Members of the partnership would be assigned consistently to a module to maintain continuity of care. This also allows partners to have a vested interest in each other's performance and in mentoring each other. A partnered system works within the context of primary nursing because nurses assigned to a module are responsible and accountable for all the care delivered to their patients.

The term *partners in professional practice* was utilized to promote collegiality and cohesiveness among work groups and results in many benefits. The system was proposed to foster increased job satisfaction of the RN and the NA. In addition, there may be a decreased orientation time since a formal mentoring system is established between the experienced and novice nurse. Finally and most important, the partners model should have increased patient satisfaction because patient needs should be met more effectively.

The Clinical Leadership Task Force formally presented the concept of partners in professional practice to the Clinical Nursing Management Group and external consultants in the fall of 1991. This presentation consisted of a formal paper and a verbal overview of concepts and theories relevant to future care delivery systems. The CNO and the Clinical Leadership Task Force shared ideas for the future. The Clinical Leadership Task Force summarized the recommendations and developed characteristics of the proposed model.

Patient-Centered Care Model

The division of nursing at MVH chose to implement a patient-centered care model that

- Enhances quality of care
- Maximizes professional and ancillary staff talents
- Cultivates patient independence and encourages/supports active participation of patients and significant others as members of the health care team
- Provides cost-effective care that maximizes reimbursement.

This is an integrated care model that is based on elements from the following philosophies:

- The RN plans and evaluates the nursing care plan
- Use of nurse extenders

- Identifying specific managed care guidelines that are developed collaboratively with physicians and health care team members for specific patient case types
- Effective communication to ensure collaboration, collegiality, and professionalism
- Research utilization and evaluation research are processes inherent in continuous quality improvement necessary in nursing practice, education, and administration.

This care delivery system is organized to deliver patient-centered care. All systems, policies, and procedures serve to make the services to the patient and his or her family as simple and sensitive as possible. This new setting is characterized by the following:

- Increased patient and family participation in the care as a means to facilitate a smooth transition to the home or posthospitalization setting
- Fewer caregivers who interact with patients in order to strengthen the care-team relations with the patient and family
- Respect for the patient in all communication and decisions concerning him or her
- Increase in the percentage of patient care activities that are accomplished/delivered on the unit or in the patient's room
- Documentation systems are streamlined to reduce time spent charting
- Case management systems are driven by protocols developed by physician and nursing staff
- Cross-trained staff are used for clinical and support service roles
- Scheduling of all off-unit services is done centrally on the unit and through a centralized scheduling service in the hospital
- Patient care units operating fairly autonomously with authority to plan, make decisions, and act to make them responsive to patient and physician needs
- Unit is integrated with other elements of the hospital and the continuum of services in the hospital network
- Staff and physicians using the unit are continuously seeking alternatives to improve the quality of care rendered

- Computers are used to simplify documentation, speed communication, reduce unit congestion, and support the delivery of care to patients
- All of the above will be done in order to optimize the value of the service to the patient.

Recommendations

In the process of analyzing the current care delivery system and the development of the conceptual framework for the new patient care delivery system, many strategies worked. An outline of those strategies that worked and those that could have worked better is as follows:

What worked

- Hospital administration communications, which provided the information and the enthusiasm for change to occur
- Early involvement of the staff from all hospital departments, which facilitated the trust and bonding necessary to have a creative working environment
- Multidisciplinary committees assessing the potentials of a new patient care system, which prevented bias and enhanced brainstorming
- A timeline that was realistic but on the fast track, which required a constant focus on the goals
- The literature search conducted by the nurse educators and CNSs prior to project development
- A hospitalwide nursing council and many unit-based nursing councils
- A stable satisfied nursing staff.

What could have worked better

- Convincing the nursing staff that they would not lose their jobs because the implementation of the new patient care model would be by attrition.

Summary

This chapter presented Leadership 2000's step-by-step planning, beginning with the results from the national planning agency. Following review of the strategic plan, Leadership 2000 established OE (MVH cost reduction program) in January 1991, and the selection of a consulting firm to assist MVH staff in identifying the potential cost reductions. Simultaneously, the Clinical Leadership Task Force focused on the assessment of the current care delivery system and review of the care delivery literature, concluding with the identification of limitations in the current system and recommendations for a new nursing system. The chapter that follows will discuss design issues and implementation strategies for the new care delivery system utilizing staff participation.

References

American Hospital Association. 1987. *The Nursing Shortage: Facts, Figures, and Feelings*. Chicago: AHA.

Creighton, H. 1964. "Nurse Clinician Needs Special Line of Advancement." *Modern Hospitals* 103 (1): 106–7.

Gibson, L. W., and H. D. Dewhirst. 1986. "Using Career Paths to Maximize Nursing Resources." *Health Care Management* 11 (2): 73–82.

Glandon, G. L., K. W. Colbert, and M. Thomasama. 1989. "Nursing Delivery Models and RN Mix: Cost Implications." *Nursing Management* 20 (5): 30–33.

Goodwin, P., S. Long, and L. Nassif. 1981. "A Report on Collaborative Practice." Paper presented at the Primary Nursing Symposium, Dallas, Texas, 5–7 October.

The Healthcare Advisory Board. 1989. *The Governance Committee Preliminary Study*. Washington, DC: The Advisory Board Company.

Hegyvary, S. 1977. "Foundations of Primary Nursing," *Nursing Clinics of North America* 12 (6): 187–96.

Juran, J. M. 1989. *Juran on Planning for Quality*. New York: The Free Press.

Kirby, K., and C. M. Garfink. 1991. "The University Hospitals Nurse Extender Program." *Journal of Nursing Administration* 21 (1): 25–30.

Lengacher, C. A., and R. R. Mabe. 1993. "Nurse Extenders: Review of Literature." *Journal of Nursing Administration* 23 (3): 15–19.

Manthey, M. 1988. "Primary Practice Partners: A Nurse Extender System." *Nursing Management* 19 (3): 58–59.

Maslow, A. H. 1954. *Motivation and Personality*. New York: Harper.

MedAmerica Health Systems, and McKinsey & Company, Inc. 1990. *Ensuring Success in the 1990s*. Cleveland, OH: McKinsey & Company, Inc.

Merker, L., K. Mariak, and D. Dwinnels. 1985. *The Clinical Career Ladder*. New York: Springer Publishing Company.

Miami Valley Hospital. 1991a. "Operational Excellence Charter." Unpublished intrahospital document.

———. 1991b. *Request for Proposal*. Dayton, OH. Unpublished intrahospital document.

Murray, M. 1993. "Where Are Career Ladders Going in the '90s?" *Nursing Management* 24 (6): 46–48.

Porter-O'Grady, T. 1990. *Reorganization of Nursing Practice*. Rockville, MD: Aspen.

Prescott, P. A., C. Y. Phillips, J. W. Ryan, and K. O. Thompson. 1991. "Changing How Nurses Spend Their Time." *Image: Journal of Nursing Scholarship* 23 (1): 23–28.

Sanford, R. C. 1987. "Clinical Ladders: Do They Serve Their Purpose?" *Journal of Nursing Administration* 17 (5): 34–37.

Sigmon, P. M. 1981. "Clinical Ladders and Primary Nursing: The Wedding of the Two." *Nursing Administration Quarterly* 5 (3): 63–67.

Thornton, W., and M. H. Boosalis. 1991. Personal communication.

U. S. Department of Health and Human Services, Office of the Secretary. 1988. *Secretary's Commission on Nursing, Volume I*. Washington, DC: U.S. Government Printing Office.

Voluntary Hospitals of America. 1990. *Chapter VII*. 24 July: 87–92.

Zimmer, M. 1972. "Rationale for a Ladder for Clinical Advancement." *Journal of Nursing Administration* 11 (6): 18–24.

Appendix 3.A

Nursing Assistant I Skills Checklist

	Date	Date	Comments
A. Assists in Direct Patient Care Activities as Assigned by the Registered Nurse			
1. Admission, Transfer, Dismissal of patients			
a. Cares for patient's belongings and valuables			
b. Orients patient to unit environment			
c. Dispenses admission kit			
d. Explains NA I role to patient and family/significant other			
2. Personal Patient Care			
a. Gives bed baths to selected patients			
b. Shaves and gives shampoos to selected patients			
c. Gives skin care and backrubs			
d. Gives perineal care			
e. Positions patients			
f. Gives and removes bedpan and urinal			
g. Gives mouth care			
h. Prepares patients for meals			
i. Feeds selected patients—may use syringe			
j. Delivers and retrieves meal trays and nourishments			
k. May perform above duties for patients in isolation			
3. Therapeutic Procedures			
a. Gives tub and sitz baths			
b. Administers enemas (tap water, SS, NS, and Fleet)			
c. Measures and applies elastic hose/ace bandage			

	Date	Date	Comments
d. Obtains and records			
(1) T-P-R (oral, rectal, and axillary), BP's			
(2) Height, weight, and records (Obtains weight with bed scales and records)			
(3) I&O—totals and records			
e. Documents on appropriate records			
f. Initiates and assists in CR as directed by RN			
g. Performs S&A urine tests/hemacult			
h. Empties/rinses ostomy appliances			
i. Applies/empties external urinary devices and leg urinal bags			
j. Shaves/preps			
k. Gives nonmedicated douches			
l. Additional duties: Male NA I			
(1) Catheterization of male patients			
(2) Insertion of retention catheters in male patients			
(3) Respond to Code 6			
m. Inserts rectal tubes			
n. Changes drainage bottle on suction machines and records			
o. Empties foley drainage bag			
4. Patient Comfort and Safety Measures			
a. Makes occupied, unoccupied, and special beds			
b. Transfers patients to beds, carts, wheelchair, chair, etc., using appropriate equipment (i.e., slide board, rollers, walkers, etc).			
c. Uses lifting and turning sheet			
d. Ambulates patients			
e. Turns and positions patients			
f. Applies Posey jacket, Swedish belt, and soft restraints			

	Date	Date	Comments
g. Assists with post-mortem care			
h. Answers patient call lights			
i. Reports observed changes in patients to the RN and contributes to care plan by sharing information with the RN			
j. Is courteous and helpful to families and visitors			
k. Assists with care of patients on special-purpose beds			
l. Observes suicide patients & records information on appropriate record			
m. Observes and provides care for the patient in escape precautions			
B. Assists the RN by Performing Patient Care Services			
1. Fills water pitchers			
2. Sorts/distributes mail and flowers			
3. Maintains supply of chart forms at the bedside			
4. Collects (nonsterile) urine, sputum, and feces specimens			
5. Enters Central Services charges			
6. Orders supplies from Central Services			
7. Adds forms and lab sheets to chart			
C. Unit Environment Tasks			
1. Sets up/cleans equipment, identifies and reports defective equipment and unsafe conditions to RN			
2. Maintains a clean, orderly, and safe patient care environment			
3. Distributes/disposes of linen			
4. Prepares/cleans showers and tubs			
5. Cleans unit areas as assigned			

	Date	Date	Comments

D. Escorting and Errands

  1. Accompanies patients to other hospital areas

  2. Picks up and delivers messages, supplies, equipment, and specimens

  3. Obtains blood from the Blood Bank

E. Requirements

  1. Certified in CPR

  2. Attends annual review for fire, safety and infection control

Appendix 3.B

Nursing Assistant II Skills Checklist

	Date	Date	Comments
1. Documents on patient's chart, flow sheet, integrated progress notes, graphic sheet (records T-P-R, BP, Ht, Wt, I&O)			
2. Demonstrates oral and nasal suctioning			
3. Demonstrates aseptic technique			
4. Demonstrates application of O2 cannula and sets O2 flowmeter			
5. Demonstrates application of heat/cold Blanketrol			
6. Records chest tube drainage on I&O			
7. Demonstrates catheterization of male patients			
8. Demonstrates catheterization of female patients			
9. Demonstrates straight catheterization			
10. Discontinues foley			
11. Empties and rinses ostomy appliances			
12. Performs dressing change			
13. Performs decubitus care			
14. Demonstrates sterile specimen collection			
a. Urine culture			
b. Wound culture			

Part II

Operational Planning

Part II, Operational Planning, focuses on the development of the new patient care delivery model. Chapter 4 explains the responsibilities of the OE Task Forces and their contributions to the total project and design issues. It also includes strategies for obtaining maximum staff participation and a discussion about skill mix change. Chapter 5 discusses the transition from the OE process to a new organizational structure for implementing the new patient care delivery model: the Positive Actions for Care Excellence (PACE) 2000 Committee. The authors include a diagram and describe the structure and decision making process of the new committee. The PACE 2000 Steering Committee and each of the eight subcommittees are explained: Human Resources, Care Management, Roles, Education, Communication, Documentation, Clinical Ladder, and Medication Administration. The new patient care delivery model (partners in practice) is discussed, including philosophy, values, roles, and an implementation plan.

4

Building a Patient-Care Model: Design Issues

Jayne Lachey Gmeiner,
Mary Lou Anderson, Bonnie Coalt,
Therese C. Lupo, and Deborah Mals

> It must be remembered that there is nothing more difficult to plan, more doubtful of success, nor more dangerous to manage than the creation of a new system. For the initiator has the enmity of all who would profit by the preservation of the old institutions and merely lukewarm defenders in those who would gain by the new ones.
>
> —Machiavelli 1984

This chapter describes the development of the OE subcommittees. It explains the subcommittee structure utilized to address the implementation of a patient care delivery system. Strategies used to maximize staff participation in the change process will be discussed as well as the impact on the organization.

Resource Allocation to Begin Change

Hospital operations, nursing administration, and the Clinical Leadership Task Force all focused on the same vision to provide cost effective and efficient care while maintaining MVH's highest goal of quality. The next

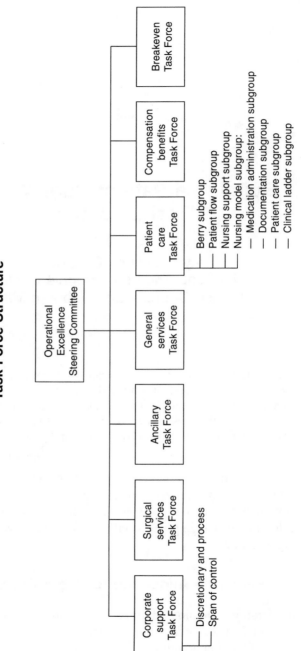

Figure 4.1
Task Force Structure

task considered was resource allocation to allow visions to be created by the employees representing the institution. During this time, the external consultant staff were present setting the stage for the overall hospitalwide effort to reduce MVH costs in 1992.

Seven task forces were created for OE as indicated in Figure 4.1: corporate support, surgical services, ancillary, general services, patient care, compensation and benefits, and breakeven. The purpose of the Corporate Support Task Force was to recommend improvements in management span of control and corporate support services. The purpose of the Surgical Services Task Force was to examine the cost structure and work flows, in all areas related to surgical services, to improve utilization throughout and productivity, while maintaining quality and service standards. The purpose of the Ancillary Task Force was to address nonlabor, skill mix, and scheduling issues and to improve coordination/utilization of ancillary functions within the hospital, while maintaining quality and service standards. The purpose of the General Services Task Force was to improve the supply and service management and delivery while continuing to support the service and quality needs of patients, physicians, and other MVH departments; to streamline process flows, optimize make versus buy decisions, and to maximize utilization of labor and nonlabor resources. The purpose of the Patient Care Task Force was to recommend operational improvements related to the delivery of patient care, the efficiencies of patient flow, the operations of the Berry Women's Health Pavilion (BWHP), and role of nursing support services. The purpose of the Compensation and Benefits Task Force was to identify and implement changes in compensation and benefits packages to reduce costs while maintaining competitiveness in the local market. The purpose of the Breakeven Task Force was to determine overall visibility of select business units within the scope of MedAmerica Health Systems Corporation and to improve their profitability by reducing costs, increasing volume, or developing new, creative means to operate the business. In addition, an OE Steering Committee was established to coordinate the task forces and guide the change. Although all seven task forces were essential to the project, the focus of this book involves the Patient Care Task Force.

The Patient Care Task Force charter goal was "to recommend operational improvements related to the delivery of patient care, the efficiencies of patient flow, the operations of the Berry Women's Health Pavilion, and the role of nursing support services" (Miami Valley Hospital 1991). The target range of cost-savings for the Patient Care Task Force ranged from \$3,795,000 to \$5,550,000, or 11–16 percent of total labor dollars. The Patient Care Task Force was guided by a steering committee that met at least weekly to keep updated on the progress of the subgroups for the Patient Care Task Force and the Corporate Support Task Force. The Patient Care Task Force Steering Committee consisted of the following membership:

1. CNO: leader
2. External analysts (3)
3. Directors of nursing (2)
4. Management engineers (3)
5. Nursing council chairperson
6. External consultants (2)
7. MVH analysts (4)
8. External project manager.

The Patient Care Task Force designed its approach based on the same premise as the OE Project Team (Chapter 3). A key component of this phase was defining and developing the role of the internal and external analysts for the OE project. External analysts and consultants facilitated the project with the expectation that MVH would provide equal participation with internal analysts. The Patient Care Task Force leader (CNO) and the directors of nursing believed the role of the analyst was crucial in the analysis phase of the project and anticipated a rigorous time commitment from the internal analysts.

The need was identified for a full-time employee to serve as internal analyst from the division of nursing. The CNO and directors of nursing appointed two employees from the division of nursing to share the role of internal analyst. The employees chosen for this role included the air ambulance nurse manager and the director of resource systems. It was hoped that each could continue to participate in his or her normal roles within reason to minimize disruption of day-to-day operations in the division of nursing. The analysts were chosen based on previous experience, cross organizational representation, commitment, an orientation to continuous improvement, and their ability to establish time lines and complete a project. The analysts served as the vital communication link between the two major task forces and analysts of all the subgroups.

Membership on the different subgroups of the Patient Care Task Force was a key component to the success of sharing ideas and creating visions and support for change. The CNO leader, directors of nursing, external consultants, and internal OE analysts determined the importance of membership and the need to have participation and representation from as many units and specialities as possible. Discussions also focused on the importance of including as many different job classifications as possible in the subgroup memberships to establish a diverse working group to enhance creativity and promote change.

The Patient Care Task Force was divided into four subgroups coordinated by the Patient Care Task Force leader (CNO), the subgroup leaders, and the OE analysts. The four subgroups included: perinatal/neonatal (BWHP), patient flow, nursing model, and nursing support services. The leader of each subgroup was either a director of nursing or the CNO.

Each director of nursing elicited lists of candidates from unit nurse managers with the goal of obtaining motivated, enthusiastic, energized individuals for membership. After lists were complete for each Patient Care Task Force subgroup, requests were made to ask if members were willing to serve. Then a confirmation letter was sent to each employee member officially notifying them of their appointment.

The Patient Care Task Force included representation from all levels of staff within the institution including: physicians, RNs, NAs, LPNs, respiratory therapists, nurse educators, nurse managers, faculty from Wright State University–Miami Valley School of Nursing, consumer relations, laboratory, nurse discharge planning, health unit coordinators, medical records, management engineering, human resources, environmental services, volunteer services, quality assurance, social services, purchasing, finance, marketing, and pharmacy. Ground rules for participation (Exhibit 4.1) were identified and stressed before every meeting with the main goal of meeting the expectations of the charter within a three-month timeline.

The time commitment was defined with the expectation of a minimum of two to eight hours per week to work on the project. The time commitment impacted patient care hours and required creative scheduling for the patient care units to allow participation of staff members during worked hours. Each task force member was also required to take four classes to provide a foundation to initiate change. Classes were led by the external consultant staff and featured the following topics:

1. Defining customer service requirements
2. Analyzing capacity utilization
3. Staffing to demand analysis

Exhibit 4.1

Nursing Model Subgroup Meeting Rules

1. Attendance at meetings is mandatory.

2. Team Leader should be notified of any absence. If you should miss a meeting, it is expected that you will contact a team member for review of meeting content and assignments.

3. Meetings will start and end on time.

4. Members shall be prepared in advance of the meeting.

5. Agenda and other materials will be generated and distributed prior to the meeting time.

6. Meetings will be opened by stating the purpose. Meetings will be closed by summarizing the results and developing assignments and confirming next steps.

7. Minutes will be kept in simplified form where possible, with information items, decisions, and action items clearly defined (responsible committee member identified). The secretary will assume the role of time keeper to monitor time and facilitate completion of agenda.

8. Group discussion regarding specific topics should be limited to 15 to 20 minutes.

9. Expected behaviors:

   a. Side conversations and outside work is not permitted.

   b. Team members may not dominate/avoid involvement in group activities.

   c. All members are encouraged to clarify, challenge, and conform for the benefit of all.

   d. Positive and/or corrective feedback is encouraged to build/support a team environment.

   e. Information shared outside the task force will be done so prudently. Group members are responsible for how information is shared and the impact to the group and other employees.

   f. Phone calls received from other team members should be considered a priority and returned as soon as possible.

---

4. Charting process flow.

The orientation packet described OE as "a process that involves restructuring the way people do their jobs in order to provide a sustainable competitive advantage; it is quite different from a budget reduction in its purpose and its outcome" (Miami Valley Hospital 1991). The task force members had the following responsibilities as described in the orientation packet:

1. Generate ideas to meet target.
2. Brainstorm for ideas.
3. Solicit ideas from other employees.
4. Explore appropriate ideas.
5. Quantify dollar impact.
6. Work through feasibility of ideas.
7. Document analysis.
8. Meet at least weekly to review progress.

The charter for the BWHP Subgroup (perinatal/neonatal) was to recommend operational improvements in efficiency and effectiveness relating to the BWHP, increasing efficiency within the BWHP and between the BWHP and relevant hospital departments while maintaining quality and service standards. The BWHP Subgroup was further divided into five smaller subgroups to allow for critical analysis: medication administration, documentation, patient care, surgical services, and laboratory.

The charter for the Patient Flow Subgroup was to identify means of facilitating patient flow into and through MVH while maintaining quality and service standards. The Patient Flow Subgroup membership consisted of employees from patient financial services, admitting, division of nursing, respiratory services, consumer relations, medical records, trauma program, medical-surgical health center, volunteer services, orthopedic services, quality assurance, information systems, social services, and environmental services.

The charter for the Nursing Model Subgroup was to examine a variety of nursing models and recommend a model which was consistent with MVH's mission and culture, incorporate such variables as managed care and clinical ladder, and maintain quality and service standards. The Nursing Model Subgroup was further divided into four smaller subgroups: medication administration, documentation, patient care, and clinical ladder.

The charter for the Nursing Support Services Subgroup was to increase the efficiency and effectiveness of nursing support services, while maintaining quality and service standards. The Nursing Support

Services Subgroup membership consisted of employees from the following areas: infection control, human resources, staff resources, division of nursing, Wright State University–Miami Valley School of Nursing, information systems, nursing education, intravenous therapy, consumer relations, discharge planning, and nursing research.

The institution also requested that all employees submit *bright ideas* to improve service and ways to do things better. The bright ideas were prioritized by the OE analysts and identified as high- or low-risk items before being returned to the appropriate subgroup for analysis. The subgroup leaders were expected to consider and respond to every employee idea submitted and report the status of each idea on a weekly basis. The goal was to give every employee the opportunity to participate in this project trusting that those who "do the work" know it best (Boosalis 1991).

More than 4,000 bright ideas were received in the suggestion box system and tracked by the analyst group. The process resulted in many ideas for change in the organization, including the redesign of the current care delivery model based on the initial foundation set by the clinical leadership group. An institution has to be organized so as to bring out the talent and capabilities within the organization to encourage individuals to take initiative, give them a chance to show what they can do, and a scope within which to grow.

Overall, the impact of such a project on the institution was felt in waves. Many departments were given immediate targets by the Hospital Policy Committee and the Board of Trustees for implementation and changes to occur very rapidly. The division of nursing was given a two-year time frame to implement a new care delivery system. This time frame was developed mutually by the CNO, Leadership 2000 Steering Committee, Hospital Policy Committee, and the OE Steering Committee.

Impact on Nursing and Other Departments of MVH

The Nursing Model and BWHP Subgroups recognized that the opportunity for maintaining and improving quality of care while promoting cost-effectiveness would be possible through skill mix changes on the patient care units. The Nursing Model and BWHP Subgroups sorted through 724 bright ideas related to patient care, methods to improve care, and efficiency of care delivery. The ideas submitted resulted in many subgroup discussions revolving around allowing the RN to practice professional nursing and the need to provide supportive services to allow this to occur.

The Patient Care subgroups began analyzing the bright ideas in relation to nonprofessional roles to support the RN. Discussion resulted in the need for an assistant to the RN and the development of another role to perform environmental and basic nutritional aspects of patient care. Due to the very narrow time frames projected by the OE process, the thorough definition of roles was incomplete before the nurse managers were required to take ideas discussed and develop projections for future needs in skill mix and FTE allotment. This period was very difficult for the nurse managers, directors of nursing, and analysts because the future roles in the new care delivery system were not clearly defined. The directors of nursing charged each nurse manager to make projections based on the characteristics of the proposed patient care model and the following premises:

1. Quality of care must be maintained and improved.

2. The RN would be responsible for planning, directing, and evaluating care based on the professional responsibility of the nursing process. Support to the RN could be provided through a direct assistant in many patient care areas and an employee who would assist with maintenance of environmental and nutritional aspects of care.

3. Changes in care delivery and the number of RNs in the institution would occur through natural attrition and over a two-year period.

4. The focus will change evaluation from hours per patient day (HPDs) to cost of operating and improving efficiency of care.

5. The nurse managers would need to pull together a unit working group to discuss these issues if an active nursing council did not exist on a particular unit. The OE process had been designed to incorporate those who "do the work know it best," which directly revolved around the focus of shared governance in the division of nursing.

6. The nurse managers would need to develop targets for skill-mix changes and dollar savings because the directors of nursing believed that the unit leadership was best able to make unit specific changes and drive personnel changes.

The nurse managers worked closely with the directors of nursing and the OE analysts during this time. Targets for unit specific skill-mix changes needed to be completed and returned to the OE analysts within a two-week time frame. At this time the nurse managers voiced many concerns about the unknown and the impact that rapid plans may have on the future of their patient care units and the employees who work on those units. Many of the nurse managers requested targets from the directors of nursing because of the fear of the unknown, and it was soon recognized that communication differences existed at the individual nursing unit levels as a result of involvement or lack of involvement in the OE planning and analysis process. As a result of asking for input from staff, rumors began and staff needed reassurance about positions, roles, and the kind of care delivery system being proposed. Open meetings for staff were facilitated by the CNO, the directors of nursing, and nurse managers. Discussion uncovered the following staff concerns: loss of job, loss of wages, and possible schedule disruption. Staff concerns were addressed directly by the CEO, COO, and CNO through the question and answer section of the OE newsletters. Examples of questions regarding loss of jobs included "Are there plans to lay off nurses during the implementation process of the patient care model?" The CNO responded with the following statement, "We firmly believe all RNs will maintain positions with MVH. Implementation plans are being done in conjunction with attrition" (Fitzsimons 1992). (Appendix 4.A contains questions and answers about PACE 2000.)

The facilitators tried to minimize the impact of changes to employees and emphasized the goal of maintaining/improving quality while being more cost-effective with care delivery. Leaders made every attempt to keep communication open to diffuse rumors and foster an environment to support/promote change.

Simultaneously, the nurse managers still were required to make projections for future needs even though staff concerns required much of their energy. The data submitted by each nurse manager were entered into an external worksheet referred to as the *cost calculator*. The cost calculator was the external consultant's method of analyzing and projecting cost savings as a result of proposed skill mix changes. The managers met with the lead analyst from the consulting firm, the OE analysts, and the directors of nursing to check on unit specific data, but the directors thought the nurse managers had a sense of unrealness about the whole process and the end goal. The cost calculator created anxiety from the internal OE analysts and directors of nursing because of the lack of familiarity with the tool and many questions regarding its validity. At this time the directors of nursing had to balance their desire to understand the data being returned from the cost calculator against possibly appearing resistant to change or failing to critically evaluate patient care units' budgetary accountability. Historically, the institution had a sophisticated method of budget analysis and the OE analysts suggested entering information from the cost calculator into the zero-based budgeting process to recognize skill mix changes and cost savings with the support of management engineering.

The changed format resulted in a much lower projected cost savings; but a savings that the internal OE analysts and directors of nursing believed was realistic and achievable. The directors of nursing continued to struggle with the short time frame to critically evaluate each unit, their individual plans of action, and actual data calculated for cost savings. Frequent meetings between the OE analysts, management engineers, and the directors of nursing assisted in diffusing the concerns, but both groups identified that better communication between Nursing, Finance, and Management Engineering may have improved this process and overall budget planning outcomes.

Significant skill mix changes in the division of nursing were proposed with the overall goal to reduce the existing 80 percent professional RN skill mix to a hospitalwide skill mix of 65 percent professional RN staff over a two-year period. Figure 4.2 shows the hospital RN skill mix varied from 76 percent in 1984 to a high of 86 percent in 1988 followed by 79 percent in 1992. Table 4.1 displays the average skill mix by specialty units between 1984 to 1994. The areas most affected by the skill mix changes have been the medical-surgical areas, the burn unit, and the behavioral science areas. The initial data from the OE analysts documented that overall the division of nursing would actually grow in FTEs, which created some concern in other departments of MVH as their departments were asked to reduce employee numbers and FTEs through the OE process. Figure 4.3 illustrates that although the total number of FTEs in the division of nursing increases, the ratio of professional to nonprofessional staff changes. The increase in FTEs resulted from the environmental services department to accomplish the SA role.

At the same time, working relationships with other departments of MVH became crucial because the proposed change in care delivery would blend the departments of nursing, nutrition services, and environmental

Figure 4.2

MVH Skill-Mix Trends—Hospitalwide

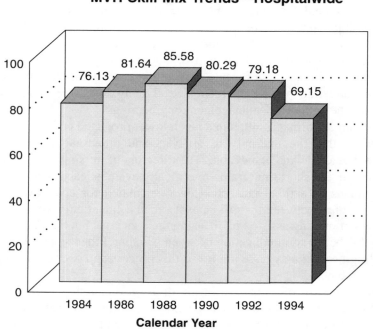

RN skill mix defined as percent of total caregivers. Implementation began 1992.

services through a multiskilled employee. Even though all task forces were multidisciplinary in membership, the distorted information taken back to individual departments added to the confusion and further enhanced the need to break down barriers between departments when the new care delivery system was implemented. Effective methods to break down barriers were facilitated by direct communication, open meetings on an as-needed basis, personal contact by administrative levels, and one-on-one communications.

The scope of the implementation of a new care delivery system was recognized, and the need for project managers was determined by the CNO, directors of nursing, external analysts, and internal OE analysts. The external consultants in their initial proposal offered to plan and direct

Figure 4.3
Planned Skill Mix for Patient Care

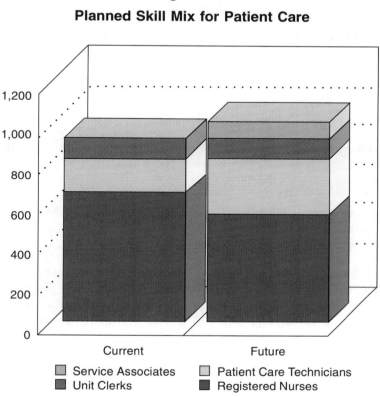

Current full-time equivalents 914.3; future full-time equivalents 998.6.

the implementation phase of the new care delivery system, but the CNO and directors believed this function would best be fostered by an internal implementation team utilizing the principles of shared governance. Plans were set to identify project managers and set committee structure for implementation of the new care delivery system.

During the entire OE process, physician involvement was crucial and promoted by active committee membership. Physician and employee involvement was very important because the institution attempted to bridge original ideas into actual implementation of a new care delivery system resulting in skill mix changes and overall cost savings in

Table 4.1

MVH Skill-Mix Trends over Last Decade (1984–1994)

Area	1984 (%)	1986 (%)	1988 (%)	1990 (%)	1992 (%)	Budgeted 1994 (%)
Medical/surgery	77.46	84.06	83.05	77.13	74.95	61.65
Stepdown areas	77.83	82.36	81.66	78.37	79.38	64.82
Critical care areas	92.37	97.60	97.29	95.82	95.97	86.46
Labor and delivery	79.44	NA	NA	87.27	79.37	71.69
Burn	92.49	70.35	71.89	70.40	74.60	57.75
Behavioral science	71.71	72.52	80.27	67.17	62.78	55.10

Note: Averages by specialty units. Implementation began October 1992.

delivery of care. The OE Analyst Team, the steering committee, and the clinical nursing management groups of MVH were given presentations of the basic group of concepts that would set the stage for the new care delivery system incorporating primary nursing, partners in practice, case management, and patient focused care. The steering committee approved the basic ideas and projected cost savings with the realization that implementation and ongoing evaluation would be vital to the success and transition from primary nursing to a new care delivery method. It became evident that it would be necessary to spend money to save money.

Recommendations

In the process of developing the subcommittees and ideas for the new patient care delivery system, many strategies worked. The following outlines those strategies that worked and those that could have worked better.

What worked

• The generation of bright ideas for change came from all departments and all job categories of employees.

- The communications at open meetings that defused many unfounded rumors.
- Enhanced working relationships between departments.

What could have worked better

- Due to the narrow timeline, the nurse managers were requested to forecast the skill mix and FTE allotment prior to the completion of the model. The nurse managers with very little involvement in the project had little understanding of the philosophy of the new patient care delivery system. This limited understanding of the new patient care delivery system made their forecasting of the skill mix and FTEs nearly impossible.
- Open meetings for nurse managers/shift managers on a biweekly basis would be a strong consideration if time and resources would have allowed to provide direct opportunities for communication from the project team.
- In retrospect, another opportunity for PACE 2000 would have been to recommend partnerships between the nurse managers, making partners of the involved managers with those who were uninvolved. Not only would this have assisted the forecasting process, but it would have enhanced both managers' understanding of the model and removed at least an element of bias from the forecasting.

Summary

This chapter describes the concepts of membership development and staff involvement in the change process. Implementation of the new care delivery emphasizes the need for staff participation. Also, the impact of change on the institution is discussed, as well as the strategies to control disruption caused by the change process.

Implementation strategies for the new care delivery system were designed to maximize staff participation. The patient care delivery and unit council implementation teams will be described in Chapter 5.

References

Boosalis, M. H. 1991. Personal communications.
Fitzsimons, P. S. 1992. Personal communications.

Machiavelli, N. 1513. *The Prince*, translated edition by P. Bondanella and M. Musa. 1984. Oxford, England: Oxford University Press: 21.

Miami Valley Hospital. 1991. *Operational Excellence Task Force Member Orientation, 1991*. Miami Valley Hospital, personal communication.

———. 1991. *Operational Excellence Newsletter*, 11: 2–3.

Appendix 4.A

Questions and Answers about PACE 2000

When will the new patient care model be implemented?

A few units may be ready to implement in September 1992. Confirmation is not complete at this time. We hope to have more definite plans in July 1992.

Will there be any open meetings?

Sue Fitzsimons will hold open meetings for all interested staff to discuss patient care model changes. The meetings are scheduled for:

July 6, 2 - 3 p.m., 6NW 1 & 2
July 7, 7:30 - 8:30 a.m., 6NW 1 & 2
July 8, 10 - 11 a.m., 6NW 1 & 2

When will RNs be salaried?

The issue of RNs being salaried versus hourly is not part of the patient care model implementation. The issue will be discussed at a later date after full implementation of the model.

When will the clinical ladder be implemented?

The Clinical Ladder Subcommittee is investigating levels of practice that will enhance our present system. Potential implementation date is in 1994. Information regarding the subcommittee's progress will be shared as plans are made.

How are LPNs going to be used in the new model?

The job descriptions of RN, NA, and LPN are being revised. The new patient care model is to utilize LPNs according to their Nurse Practice Act and to do so consistently across the organization. LPNs are members of the Roles Subcommittee and are assisting with revisions.

Will more LPNs be hired in the future?

The Emergency and Trauma Center and the Neonatal Intensive Care Unit are trialing the use of LPNs in their patient care model. A decision on whether or not to hire more LPNs will come after evaluation of these trials.

Are there plans to lay off nurses during the implementation process of the patient care model?

We firmly believe all RNs will maintain positions with Miami Valley Hospital. Implementation plans are being done in conjunction with attrition.

What kind of education plans are being made for the RNs, nursing assistants, and service associates?

The Education Subcommittee is establishing a curriculum for RNs and NAs. Education needs of service associates have been determined and the core curriculum is in the planning phases. Look for more information about this in the next issue of the PACE 2000 newsletter.

As the PACE 2000 plans are implemented, how will the hospital ensure that we continue to provide good patient care?

Criteria has been established to monitor patient, family, employee, and physician satisfaction. Other ways to monitor patient care will include system efficiency, patient outcomes, and community response.

Will nurses be spending less time at the bedside with the increased use of nursing assistants?

With an increased number of nursing assistants to assist with bathing and feeding, the goal is for RNs to be able to spend more time with patients in assessments, planning, and education. A survey in October 1991 showed RNs spent 48 percent of their time with patients. The new goal is to increase that time up to 75

percent. We hope that enablers will be in place to allow this to happen.

How can I find out what is happening with PACE 2000?

1) Plan to ask your immediate supervisor for ongoing information and changes.

2) Read the PACE 2000 newsletter, Nursing News, the Insider and Chart to continue to be updated on changes.

3) Attend your staff meetings and open meetings whenever possible.

4) Use the PACE 2000 direct line, 496-6265.

5) Use the PACE 2000 box provided in Rubicon Place to ask questions, share concerns, or make recommendations.

6) Talk with committee members, Nursing Council members, and your unit communication representative.

Remember, the success of PACE 2000 is up to all of us!

PACE 2000 Newsletter Premieres

This is the first of several issues of the PACE 2000 newsletter. As new information is available on the many changes that will take place during the PACE program, additional issues will be published. Also watch for related stories in Insider and Nursing News. Future issues will discuss the changes in the roles of the nurse, nursing assistants, and service associates, and highlight implementation strategies and successes.

5

The Model: Positive Actions for Care Excellence (PACE) 2000

Mary Lou Anderson and
Jayne Lachey Gmeiner

This chapter explains the transition from the OE outcomes to an organizational implementation structure that developed and implemented the new patient care model. The OE process provided the groundwork and foundation for the new Patient Care Model Committee, which was entitled PACE 2000. The structure and decision-making process of the committee will be discussed, as well as a description of the model. Included are the philosophy and values of the new patient care partnership model.

Two nurses, who had served as patient care subgroup leaders during OE, were selected as project managers for planning and implementing the new patient care model on the inpatient units. Hospital administrators directed the project managers to function as facilitators and motivators of the staff, nursing council, unit councils, or unit committees, in their combined efforts to design and implement the new patient care model.

The first steps in organizing and implementing the new patient care system were to review and incorporate the information gained during the OE process. At the beginning of that project, the basic concepts of the new patient care delivery system had been outlined by the Clinical Leadership Task Force. The hospital staff had generated 724 bright ideas about patient care, and information was available about committee structure and performance from the OE process.

Structure

An assessment of the changes needed to incorporate the new patient care model identified the following needs:

1. A name for the new patient-centered care delivery system, which incorporates case management, primary nursing, partners in practice, and patient-centered care
2. Job descriptions for the new roles and revision of current roles
3. Education of current staff and education of staff in new roles
4. Knowledge about hiring, attrition rates of RN staff, and compensations benefits
5. A method to ensure that all divisions are informed regarding the planned changes in skill mix and/or practice
6. Evaluation criteria to monitor the effectiveness and opportunities for improvement concurrently and retrospectively
7. Critical paths for the major diagnostic groups.

In utilizing the above needs list, a contest was established to name the patient care system. Approximately 30 names were submitted by various nursing units and various hospital departments. The Analyst Committee, which consisted of the vice president of nursing, the directors of nursing, the project leaders, the subcommittee chairpersons, financial analysts, and the nursing shared governance council representatives voted on suggested names. The new patient care delivery system was named PACE 2000, an acronym meaning **P**ositive **A**ctions in **C**are **E**xcellence, moving toward the year 2000.

Several committees that were very successful during the OE process continued in the implementation phase of the process, called the patient care model. Four committees continued from OE included the Multidisciplinary Steering Committee and three subcommittees: documentation, clinical ladder, and medication administration (Figure 5.1). In addition, five additional subcommittees were developed to concentrate on specific needs of the model: education, roles, human resources, communications, and case management.

Figure 5.1

Miami Valley Hospital Patient Care Delivery System (PACE 2000) Implementation Approach

The multidisciplinary steering committee served as the focal point to review, debate, modify or accept new ideas, roles or policies about the new patient care model. The membership on this committee and all the patient care committees was multidisciplinary with membership including physicians, RNs, NAs, licensed practical nurses (LPNs), nurse educators, nurse managers, nurse discharge planners, health unit coordinators, respiratory therapists, and representatives from consumer relations, laboratory, environmental services, quality assurance and quality improvement, management engineering, legal services, nutritional services, and human resources. This committee met on a monthly basis to review progress.

Documentation Subcommittee

The Documentation Subcommittee monitored, revised, and evaluated the new documentation system, which started with the OE process. The goal was to implement the documentation changes two to three months prior to implementation of the new care delivery system and provide a more efficient and effective means of documentation. Details of the documentation effort are discussed in Chapter 9.

Clinical Ladder Subcommittee

The Clinical Ladder Subcommittee ensured that concepts of the proposed professional ladder could be integrated into the new patient care model. The current clinical ladder was established in the late 1970s with the transition to the primary nursing care delivery system. The promotional career development ladder was designed as a four-step system but actually allowed for only two levels of promotion due to educational and FTE restrictions. The goal for this committee was to develop a clinical ladder that recognized peak clinical performance and provided incentives for RNs to stay at the bedside.

In May 1994, the proposal for the new professional ladder was approved by Hospital Policy Committee and the MVH Board of Trustees. The new system, known as the Pathway for Advancement in Clinical Excellence (PACE for Quality Program), provides a system for RNs at MVH to advance and grow in the clinical setting. The PACE for Quality Program has been designed over a three-year period (1991–1994) with a committee consisting of energetic and creative nursing representatives from a variety of areas in the hospital and members of the human resources department (HRD). The philosophy of PACE for Quality states that "MVH believes that the development of the professional nurse is critical to the practice of clinical nursing." (MVH 1994, 1) The PACE for Quality Program is intended to reward RNs who attain and maintain a higher level of clinical practice and continue to develop themselves and their profession. The PACE for Quality Program is the link between self-accountability and the professional nurse. The PACE for Quality Program is based on the belief that rewarding expert clinical practice will positively impact patient outcomes and continue to improve our high standard of quality care. The PACE for Quality Program was developed by and for the RN at MVH. The program has identified five major objectives, which are as follows:

1. Provide high-quality care
2. Provide staff RNs who deliver patient care services with recognition/reward associated with their levels of clinical expertise
3. Provide staff RNs with incentives to increase and broaden their current clinical experience levels
4. Provide the hospital's RN staff with a program to attract and retain highly competent RNs in the direct patient care environment
5. Provide a framework for nurses that includes a *vision for nursing* in this challenging health care environment.

The PACE for Quality Program is designed as a clinical advancement program based on a four-level system. The criteria for the PACE for Quality Program are cumulative in that an individual must meet all the criteria for levels 1, 2, and 3 to advance to level 4. Individuals must meet all sets of criteria within each level to achieve that level. The identified domains of the program include experience, education, citizenship, nursing practice, nurse/patient relations, and collaboration. Basic assumptions incorporated into the new PACE for Quality Program system are designed to promote and emphasize the PACE 2000 philosophy and values, including the following:

1. Maintain primary nursing philosophy
2. Utilize case management concepts
3. Maintain expert RNs in the clinical setting
4. Recognize and compensate RNs for their level of practice
5. Show evidence yearly of maintenance of a level on the pathway. Conceivably, an RN may go up or down the pathway.
6. Maintain levels for RNs who have changed positions or moved to a different department at the next review date. At this time the RN must demonstrate proficiency of level in the new department to maintain that current level.
7. Achieve any level on the pathway, for the initial implementation process. After that time, each nurse may advance one level each year.

The PACE for Quality Program was initiated on 1 January 1995, with the first recognition of RNs in May 1995. The incentives for RNs who advance on the pathway have been developed in coordination with the CNO, business manager for the division of nursing, directors of nursing, and the HRD. The communication to the RNs, clinical nursing management, and other departments will occur in the summer and fall of 1994. A celebration was planned for the fall of 1994 to recognize the participants of the previous clinical ladder and their accomplishments. This celebration also served to facilitate the transition period between the old and new system. A method to evaluate the system has been established to monitor staff satisfaction, recognize opportunities for improvement, and determine effectiveness of the new system. Evaluation will also occur through verbal feedback from RNs, nurse managers, and administration.

The PACE for Quality Program, domains of practice, criteria for advancement, and evaluation will be discussed in future publications after system implementation in 1995.

Medication Administration Subcommittee

The Medication Administration Subcommittee ensured completion of the medication enablers accepted in the OE process and examined other more efficient and effective ways to save nursing time and improve patient care. The Pyxis system (computerized medication machine for narcotics and PRN drugs) was introduced in OE as an enabler for nursing. Also the Bard syringe pump for antibiotic delivery was implemented as part of OE. Details of the Medication Administration Subcommittee's activities will be discussed in Chapter 10.

Human Resource Subcommittee

The Human Resource Subcommittee focused on hiring practices, compensation issues, and balancing RN attrition with new staff mix requirements. The committee used a proactive approach to potential employee concerns. The Human Resource Subcommittee was active in developing guidelines for dealing with hiring, failure to complete educational programs, and strategies to work with employees in any position.

Human resource issues and outcomes related to each role change are discussed in Chapters 6, 7, and 8.

Case Management Subcommittee

The Case Management Subcommittee focused on the development of guidelines and critical pathways for high-volume diagnostic groups.

Details of this subcommittee's activities will be featured in Chapter 13, "Case Management," and Chapter 14, "Clinical Benchmarking."

Roles Subcommittee

The Roles Subcommittee developed job descriptions in accordance with the patient care model changes and monitored the trial of the new roles during the developmental stage. Role analysis stimulated conversation and created a natural transition to the creation and revision of the patient care job descriptions.

Education Subcommittee

The Education Subcommittee developed the educational programs for the current staff, as well as the programs to educate new employees in their new roles. Details of the activities from the Roles and Education Subcommittees are outlined in Chapters 6, 7, and 8. These chapters are organized according to the RN role, the patient care technician role, and the service associate role respectively.

Communication Subcommittee

The Communications Subcommittee focused on verbal and written communication to ensure that proper information regarding change within the PACE 2000 project was disseminated throughout the organization in a timely manner. Several avenues of communication had been established during the implementation phase of PACE 2000, including the following:

1. All levels of personnel from all specialties were represented on the Education Subcommittee and Roles Subcommittee, as well as on several other key committees.
2. An information sharing committee composed of unit managers and representatives met monthly for PACE 2000 updates.
3. A PACE 2000 communication newsletter was published periodically for all hospital personnel.

All of the subcommittees and the Steering Committee were instilled with an awareness of the complexity of the internal and external environment. As noted in Figure 5.1, considerations included community response, employee satisfaction, resource utilization, third party responses, patient, family, and physician satisfaction, and most important, quality outcomes. The Communication Subcommittee's efforts through the newsletter and meetings helped promote communication throughout the system. One factor that we realized early on is that communication could have been emphasized tenfold and still may have been deficient. A PACE 2000 hotline was also established to provide a central place for phone call communication. This phoneline system was used frequently, especially by the service associates (SAs) and patient care technicians (PCTs) for questions. Response to questions was delivered by the PACE 2000 program managers within 24 hours if possible. Communication methods are also discussed in the implementation phase (Chapters 6–10).

Decision Process

As indicated in Figure 5.1, all subcommittee recommendations were forwarded to the Analyst Committee. The Analyst Committee met weekly to ensure the flow of each committee's work was in synch with the other committees' efforts. The Analyst Committee served as the decision-making body for issues regarding the conversion to a new delivery system. A steering committee, consisting of all members of the Analyst Committee, nurse managers, physicians, members of ancillary departments, and nursing council representatives, served as the group responsible for developing, implementing, and guiding the conversion to the new patient care delivery system. The Steering Committee provided feedback prior to the implementation of various ideas. It is through this structure (Figure 5.1) that ideas generated in the subcommittees were analyzed, refined, and operationalized.

Philosophy

The PACE 2000 philosophy statement was the combination of the role analysis and clinical leadership vision. PACE 2000 enhances patient care delivery by incorporating the following foundations:

Primary Care

The RN has the responsibility to coordinate and plan patient care based on the patient plan of care. RNs work a variety of shifts/schedules to accommodate unit and personal needs.

Partners in Practice

A partnership is established through mutual agreement and maintained by joint cooperation of the partner(s). The RN is scheduled with an LPN and/or PCT developing this employee through patient assignment, supervision, and evaluation.

Case Management

Specific managed care guidelines are being developed collaboratively through a process called benchmarking with physicians and other key health care members. The end goal of this process is to promote efficient utilization of resources to provide cost-effective care. The case management/benchmarking process is designed to promote utilization of the RN caregiver as the case manager.

Patient and Family-Centered Focus

The delivery system is patient and family-centered in focus, meeting both the acute physiological needs and the activities of daily living. The continuous goal is to facilitate communication between departments and to promote the philosophy that patients are the number one reason for the existence of the organization.

Values of PACE 2000

The implementation of PACE 2000 at MVH allows for development of consistency, collegiality, mutual respect, and empathy for the patient and each other. The integrated training and education provided through PACE 2000 enhances employees' responsiveness to the needs of patients, visitors, staff, and all other departments. The outcomes of the educational process focus on (1) high standards for quality care measured by patient satisfaction scores and patient outcomes via hospital and unit specific quality improvement efforts; (2) satisfaction of all staff facilitated by the PACE 2000 implementation team and MVH's Human Resource and Marketing Departments; and (3) cost-effectiveness monitored by the PACE 2000 implementation team and facilitated by MVH's Management Engineering Department.

Physician satisfaction is very important to the Division of Nursing. Physicians are encouraged to share information regarding patient care with the RN caring for the patient. Historically, the RN reported patient care variances directly to the physician on an as-needed basis, and this concept will not change with PACE 2000. Physician and nurses at MVH continue to strive for close working relationships, which ultimately enhance positive patient outcomes. The roles of the nonlicensed patient caregivers will be discussed in detail in the following chapters, but a brief description of each role will be provided.

Roles

The Registered Nurse

The RN plays a central role in the coordinating, managing, and monitoring of a patient's care and progress. Job responsibilities of the RN include the following:

- Assessing patient needs, planning, delivering, and directing a plan of care
- Mentoring other patient-care employees to promote positive relationships and positive patient outcomes
- Delegating appropriate direct care tasks and responsibilities to the PCT or LPN as outlined in the job description, unit-specific checklists, and MVH policies and procedures
- Evaluating patient care needs continuously and identifying if a change in treatment is needed with appropriate utilization of resources.

The Licensed Practice Nurse

The LPN's practice at MVH is in accordance with the LPN Practice Act governed by the Ohio Board of Nursing. The LPN provides patient care under the direction and guidance of the RN.

The Patient Care Technician

The PCT position consolidated the former NA I and II roles to allow for a consistent level of practice from unit to unit. The PCT job responsibilities include providing patient care under the direction and guidance of the RN as identified by the PCT job description and unit-specific checklists.

The Health Unit Coordinator

The health unit coordinator (HUC) plays a vital role as receptionist and informant at the communication center on each patient care unit. The HUC is responsible for transcription of medical orders, computer data entry for procedures and ordering of supplies, answering of patient care lights via the intercom system, and various other unit specific receptionist activities.

The Service Associate

The SA position combines the aspects of environmental services, nutrition services, and direct clinical services, which maintain efficient functioning of the patient care unit. The service associate's responsibility is to promote and enhance patient comfort, safety, and satisfaction through maintenance of a clean and safe environment.

Implementation

A six-month timeline to develop the roles and education was a constant incentive to keep moving (Table 5.1). In order to meet the timeline, individual bias was kept to a minimum by using humor. Almost everyone has individual bias about issues or ways of doing things (sacred cows). However as a group, the mission was to sacrifice sacred cows for the goal of the project. The international "no" symbol superimposed over a cow was adopted to symbolize the need to focus on the committee goal and not on personal biases. The Analyst and Steering Committees developed the PACE 2000 implementation plan based on readiness of units. This readiness was determined by the following two main factors:

- Human resource issues: (1) the current skill mix, (2) attrition rates for RNs, and (3) skill levels of current NAs, which were evaluated for each patient care unit. Those patient care units with a history of higher attrition rates due to maternity leaves, relocation, or transfers were cited as early implementation units. These data were evaluated historically with the assistance of the human resources and management engineering departments. The current employee job market in the Dayton area was also considered, and annual attrition estimates were revised, which resulted in an adjustment in the implementation timeline.

- Leadership issues: The nurse managers and unit councils became a vital component of the implementation because they determined staffing needs related to the skill mix changes. Unit awareness, patient care trends, and overall hospital program goals were included in the patient care unit implementation plan. Other factors taken into consideration included unit council abilities, experience of the unit leadership at the nurse manager and shift manager levels, and issues beyond the scope of PACE 2000, such as dramatic changes in patient census, remodeling, etc. For example, the neonatal intensive care unit (NICU) and intensive care unit (ICU) had recently hired new nurse managers, and the need was recognized that to be successful, implementation for these areas would need to occur at a later date.

Table 5.1

PACE 2000 Roles and Education Timeline

April 1992—October 1992

	April	May	June	July	Aug.	Sept.	Oct.
Documentation development	XXXXX	XXX					
Committee organization	XXXXX	XXX					
Analysis of current roles	XXXXX	XXX					
Pyxis implemented	XXXXX	XX					
Bard pumps implemented							
Development of new roles	XXXXX	XXXXX	XX				
RN roles defined	XXXXX	XXXXX	XXXXX				
PCT roles defined	XXXXX	XXXXX	XXXXX				
RN education developed	XXXXX	XXXXX	XXXXX	XXXXX			
PCT education developed	XXXXX	XXXXX	XXXXX	XXXXX			
SA role defined		XXXXX	XXXXX	X			
SA education developed			XXXXX	XXXXX	XX		
Documentation implemented					XXXXX		
Classes for PCTs					XXX	XXXXX	XX
Classes for RNs						XXXXX	XXX
Classes for SAs					X	XXXXX	XXX
Cluster I implemented PACE							XX

Recommendations

In the process of synthesizing all the information gained in OE and the clinical leadership group for the PACE 2000 subcommittees, many strategies worked. Strategies that worked and those that could have worked better are as follows:

What worked

- The diversity of the employees on the subcommittees was an advantage. The differences in the group forced analysis of the current system to be investigated and the rationale for change to be justified. It should be noted that the committee members were different in their job descriptions, departments, years of service, as well as their reason for being on the committee.
- Having motivated subcommittee chairpersons who created open communication with their teams.
- Having a charter for each subcommittee helped keep the groups focused.

What could have worked better

- Units with no unit council or one that was not fully established had greater difficulty with the transitions to the new model. Problem-solving and group dynamics should have been offered to these units to assist them in the development of their council to the level necessary to analyze their unit needs.

Summary

In summary, this chapter describes the utilization of information gained through the analysis of the OE process, the clinical leadership visions and the nursing council philosophy of patient care as the foundation for the new patient/family care delivery system. Humor and open communication were utilized to recognize and control for individual bias and barriers to the PACE 2000 goals. Timeline for unit implementation was based on the attrition rate of the RN staff, unit awareness, and unit leadership abilities, which included the managers, unit councils, and staff experience. With each unit implementation, a celebration atmosphere was planned with bundles of PACE 2000 balloons.

The implementation plan and clusters were established by grouping units with similar rates of attrition into the same cluster. Two units chose to implement by shift rather than the entire unit *going up*, which resulted in more confusion in relation to staffing issues, role confusion, and management of the old and new system. Units that chose to implement the concept on all shifts at the same time seemed to have an easier transition.

The efforts of many employees will be described in the following chapters in relation to implementing a new, successful care delivery system.

Reference

Miami Valley Hospital. 1994. "PACE for Quality Philosophy." Unpublished intrahospital document.

Part III

The Implementation Phase

Part III, Implementation Phase, includes chapters about each of the major components in the new partners in practice patient care delivery model. The roles and education are described in detail for the RN and LPN in Chapter 6, PCT in Chapter 7, and the Service Associate in Chapter 8. Chapter 9 discusses the process of streamlining documentation and explains activities and outcomes of the Documentation Subcommittee during the OE process. The authors address an environmental analysis and key issues; they conclude with lessons learned. Chapter 10 describes enabling activities that supported the change to the new partners in practice model. The enabler groups included pharmacy, respiratory care, and clinical laboratory. Each of the enabler groups discuss their efforts and changes to support the organizational redesign. Pharmacy enablers include analysis of a new automated medication dispensing machine, syringe pump purchases, recycling distribution bags, implementation of new orders, interdepartmental communication, and bar coding. Respiratory enablers discussed include decentralization, low flow oxygen, incentive spirometry, arterial blood gas sampling, and resuscitation bags. Clinical laboratory enablers analyzed include consolidating blood draws, patient location, arterial/central lines, and computer process.

6

The Role and Education of the Registered Nurse and Licensed Practical Nurse

Jayne Lachey Gmeiner, Rebecca J. Czachor, Jennifer L. Eddlemon, and Mary Lou Anderson

Evolution is "a process of change in a certain direction; the process of developing" according to the 9th edition of *Webster's*. The role of the RN in the 1990s is evolving at a rapid pace. This evolution is due to changes in national health care policy, nursing shortages in some geographic areas, third party reimbursement, and changing RN demographics. The RN has the opportunity to successfully meet the challenge of evolution by shifting paradigms and utilizing all resources appropriately. "Nurse innovation is the key to transformation of the healthcare organization and the healthcare system" (Manion 1993, 41).

In 1991 MVH initiated a complete analysis of patient care delivery systems and roles of care providers. Committee structure and process, role analysis, plus the development and implementation of the educational program for RNs and LPNs will be described in this chapter.

Committee Structure

The mission of the Roles Subcommittee was to redefine roles and to revise the job descriptions of bedside care providers (RN, LPN, and NA)

at MVH. The care delivery system had been designed by a task force of nurses and other health care providers. The Roles Committee was to operationalize the values of this new system. The goal was to achieve the ultimate in quality and cost-effectiveness within a patient and family-centered care delivery system. This feat was to be accomplished within the framework of partners in practice and primary nursing philosophies.

Insight, new ideas, creativity, and commitment to the PACE 2000 concept were essential to success. The Roles Committee consisted of 32 persons who demonstrated these attributes. The diverse backgrounds within the group facilitated analysis of problems and possible solutions from many angles. Nurses were represented from all levels of management, education, and a broad spectrum of clinical areas. Managers and staff from the departments of nutrition and environmental services were represented. Other participants include respiratory therapists, unit clerks, engineers from management systems, and physicians (Table 6.1). The Roles Committee met weekly for three months and then every other week for two months.

Process

The initial challenges were to (1) become a team with open, constructive lines of communication; (2) dare members to dream and pave the way for a paradigm shift; (3) familiarize everyone on the committee with the current care delivery system, job descriptions, and problems; and (4) define the goals of the new patient and family-centered care delivery system.

Interaction among the group was encouraged, as were new ideas and open communication. Members were urged to talk to their peers between meetings and to bring back comments, ideas, and rumors. It was recognized that rumor control would be essential to a positive environment for change. Communication outside the committee was handled aggressively through open meetings with the senior vice president of hospital operations responsible for the division of nursing, PACE 2000 information meetings, unit and department staff meetings, and the circulation of committee meeting minutes.

Initial meetings focused on getting to know one another and gaining insight into different departments within the hospital. Each member listed five ideas for positive changes and dreams for the new system.

Once the group became familiar with one another and was comfortable speaking up, the committee progressed to compiling a list of

Table 6.1

Roles Committee Composition

Department	Number
Nursing	
NAs (maternity, CICU, neuro)	3
LPNs (NICU, medical-surgical)	2
RNs (medical-surgical, ortho, renal, labor and delivery, neuro)	6
shift managers (NICU, CICU, ICU)	3
nurse managers (Neuro)	1
director of nursing	1
PACE 2000 project leaders	2
Environmental Services	
housekeepers	4
day supervisor	1
director	1
Nutrition Services	
galley supervisor	1
manager	1
Hospital Operations	
management systems engineers	2
Miscellaneous Departments	
respiratory therapists	1
HUC (unit clerk medical–surgical)	1
medical staff physicians	2
	32

63 patient needs and tasks performed in the acute care environment (Appendix 6.A). The list was analyzed item by item asking, Does this task need to be done at all? Is it a ritual? Is there a better way to provide for this need? Are we duplicating work? By far the most crucial question was, Who is the most appropriate person to perform this task or to fulfill this need?

This exercise was the cornerstone in the role development process. Many hours were spent searching for the best answer. Group members interviewed employees and searched regulatory standards, state licensing laws, literature reviews, medical bylaws, and meeting minutes from previous years. The group gained valuable insights into the complex interactions within the patient care system. These questions stimulated many lively discussions that shook hospital tradition and nursing practice to the core. The group remained focused on the patient/family-centered care model that was being developed.

The list was long and tedious. The process of evaluating the list was accelerated by asking, Is this a function that only an RN can perform? Is this a need that only an RN can meet? Answers were validated by asking, why? Great emphasis was placed on preserving and enhancing the RN's professional responsibilities and accountabilities in areas of assessment, planning and coordination of care, education and mentoring, supervision and delegation, interaction with physicians, and evaluation of patient outcomes (Appendix 6.A).

Role Analysis

The Roles Subcommittee examined the scope of nursing practice through complete analysis of the Ohio Nurse Practice Act and national standards. The goal was to maximize the ability of the RN to utilize the nursing process with every patient care contact while promoting quality and clinical efficiency.

The division of nursing has a strong heritage of providing excellent care for the consumers of MVH. Recognition from patients, families, and physicians through marketing surveys historically validated positive responses regarding care delivery.

Prior to initiation of PACE 2000, RNs also validated satisfaction through low RN vacancy rates and responses to administrative research surveys. During October 1991, a survey was sent to each RN in the division of nursing to capture a typical day of an RN. This instrument had been utilized in various institutions nationally. The survey assessed nurses' time in minutes of care given per shift. Key activities included patient care, ancillary, education, communication, clerical/support, and unit support. This tool also assessed the RNs' opinions about delivery of care at the institution. Thirty-three percent of the division of nursing ($N = 538$) responded and valuable information was obtained to provide a foundation for future opportunities.

In summary, the majority of RNs were either satisfied or very satisfied with delivery of nursing care. The work environment of RNs was also assessed by time spent communicating, documenting, educating, delivering direct patient care, and performing nonnurse functions. The RNs reported spending 64 percent of their time providing direct patient care while almost 22 percent was spent participating in indirect care activities, and 15 percent of their time was spent communicating.

Direct patient care was defined as activities that require utilization of the nursing process and professional licensure as an RN. Ancillary activities were indirect nonprofessional aspects of care delivery such as running errands, answering the telephone, delivering food trays, obtaining medication from pharmacy, escorting patients, general cleaning, transporting patients, and running for supplies. A clear opportunity presented itself to decrease the amount of time RNs spent on ancillary or indirect activities, time that could be redirected to the delivery of professional nursing care.

Demographic analysis of the division of nursing was completed to determine the complexity of the RN work force within the institution comparing information to national trends. The average age of the RN was 42.5 years compared with the average age nationally of 41 years (Curran 1992). RNs worked at MVH on the average of 8 years and 4 months and worked an average of 5 years and 4 months on a particular patient care unit. The Roles Subcommittee determined the RN staff of MVH to be highly satisfied and highly skilled as determined by retention and experience on specialized patient care units.

Educational levels of the RNs in the work force in 1991 included a highly educated staff with nearly half having either a bachelor's of science or a master's degree in nursing. The institution promotes continuing education through tuition reimbursement and flexible scheduling options so that educational levels continue to change as each quarter or semester passes.

LPNs were a very small but valuable resource within the institution during this time. Seventeen LPNs were employed on inpatient units in the institution.

Approximately 58 percent of RNs worked full time, 28 percent worked part time, while 20 percent of the RN staff worked support (per diem, PRN Pool). Support RN staff at MVH are defined as those employees who commit to work a minimum number of hours annually without compensation of paid time off benefits. The support staff serve as an internal pool of resources for the division of nursing.

The permanent and support RN staff have a strong tradition of providing excellent theory-based patient care. This level of care is maintained and enhanced by retaining a motivated nursing staff who constantly create their own challenges and strive for improvement. The environment to promote professional practice is also facilitated by the collaborative relationship with the Wright State University–Miami Valley School of Nursing. The collaborative agreement between the university and hospital has provided many opportunities for RNs to gain knowledge over a continuum and strive for new potentials in professional practice. This has resulted in a culture that promotes and fosters professional practice and is the basic premise from which the care delivery system was designed.

Through brainstorming and discussion, three major deficits were recognized by an ad hoc task force in the existing primary care delivery system:

1. Registered nurses spent much of their time performing nonnursing activities.
2. The current abilities of NAs were not utilized appropriately.
3. Patient care was fragmented when meeting basic care needs.

The role analysis and clinical leadership vision led to the creation of the PACE 2000 philosophy statement (Appendix 6.B). This statement was reviewed with partnerships prior to PACE 2000 implementation by the shift manager or nurse manager. Units that emphasized the philosophy statement participated in development of partners and signed the statement achieved easier transition into the new care delivery system.

RN Educational Program Development

PACE 2000 implementation managers communicated information between every subcommittee during the development phase. This communication was extremely important between the Roles and Education Subcommittees because one committee could not remain stagnant while the other was developing job descriptions. The Analyst Committee served as a formal communication forum to keep everyone on track with goals, deadlines, and missions. The six-month plan to develop the roles and education seemed unreasonable at times but resulted in constant momentum toward completion of job descriptions and the necessary education.

The Education and Roles Subcommittee recognized that the role of the RN would involve several key aspects that were new in many respects to the RN at MVH. The key aspects requiring immediate reeducation included responsibilities of delegating, mentoring, evaluating, and supervising. RNs' ability to delegate had been affected by the fifteen-year history of primary nursing in the institution. Delegation and the need for refined conflict management skills became the focal points for education development for the RN staff. A subgroup of the Education Subcommittee was given the charge to develop the curriculum for the RN, focusing on developing the RN's ability to work with and through others in a partnership system. The partnerships would consist of many different relationships including dyads (RN/PCT) and triads (RN/LPN/PCT or RN/RN/PCT).

Assertive communication skills were essential for the RN. The RN Education Subgroup decided to create an education series that included philosophy of patient-centered care, risk management issues, and delegation/conflict management skill development. Each of the educational components will be described in this section.

Philosophy of Patient-Centered Care

A review of patient care delivery methods in relationship to primary nursing, case management, partners in practice, institutional demographics, national health care trends, and paradigm shifts were described in this class. A detailed review of roles/job descriptions also occurred to familiarize the RN employee with the new care delivery system. Employees were encouraged to share unit-specific strategies or ideas for applying the principles of the PACE 2000 philosophy to their specific work groups. To maintain consistency of the information being presented, the PACE 2000 program managers and Education Subcommittee chairperson served as sole instructors for this topic.

Risk Management

This content was established to give the RN employee opportunities to explore and discuss potential issues or concerns that may result from working directly with a PCT or LPN partner in care delivery. The hospital general counsel was supportive in developing a curriculum for this section based on review of PACE 2000 job descriptions and philosophy statements. The three R's of risk management were also reviewed and included rapport, recording, and reporting. The hospital attorney's expertise proved invaluable for this topic.

Delegation/Conflict Management

The CNO, Analyst Committee, and HRD representative on the RN Education subgroup suggested engaging an external consultant to develop the delegation and conflict management package for RN education. Requests for proposals were sent to four consultants with demonstrated experience in teaching communication skills, delegation, and conflict management. After reviewing the proposals and interviewing the candidates, a consultant was chosen. The choice was based on previous experience teaching to a wide variety of professionals, including employees not in the health care environment.

The consultant worked closely with an HRD staff member who also had expertise in the area of teaching delegation and conflict management skills. The consultant was given guidelines and a defined time commitment initially to keep costs to a minimum. An HRD employee served as a resource when the delegation/conflict management package was developed (Exhibit 6.1 and 6.2).

Upon completion of the delegation/conflict management package, 18 RNs in a variety of positions in the institution were given the opportunity to become delegation/conflict management trainers. This program was established to reduce consultant costs and provide future resources for the RN education program.

The delegation/conflict management educational series were based on principles of active class participation, role playing, and lively atmospheres. Delegation and conflict scenarios were developed by the PACE 2000 program managers, Analyst Committee, and RN Education Subgroup to use during the role playing sessions (Appendix 6.C). Unique scenarios were developed for speciality units to add more meaning to the process.

Implementation of RN Educational Program

The CNO, directors of nursing, and Analyst Committee approved the RN education series and devised financial support to give every RN

Exhibit 6.1

Objectives for Delegation

- Define delegation.
- Recognize problems caused by lack of delegation.
- Identify the benefits of effective delegation.
- Assess your attitude toward delegation and your level of expertise.
- Plan and execute a step-by-step process for delegation.
- Apply a situational model of delegation.
- Assertively communicate the tasks being delegated.
- Recognize and resolve problems regarding unsatisfactory performance.
- Recognize employees for positive results.
- Apply delegation skills to work situations.

Exhibit 6.2

Objectives for Conflict Resolution

- Understand the nature of conflict.
- Recognize your preferred style of handling conflicts.
- Identify the major causes of conflict.
- Learn and apply communication skills and strategies for conflict resolution.
- Apply a situational approach to conflict resolution.
- Resolve conflicts between employees and team members.
- Apply conflict resolution strategies to work situations.

at MVH the opportunity to attend the series. The PACE 2000 program managers established class schedules and sign-up sheets. Attendance was based on PACE 2000 cluster implementation dates. The goal was to have the RN attend the series one to two months before implementation of the new care delivery system. The intent was to give the RN employee ample opportunity to practice delegation, mentoring, supervisory, and evaluation skills with their new partners prior to official implementation of the care delivery system.

Prior to implementation of the RN education series, a formal four-hour presentation of the delegation/conflict management modules was offered to the shift managers, nurse managers, nurse educators, clinical nurse specialists, and directors of nursing. The goals of this presentation were to provide a preview of information to be shared with RN staff, give the group opportunities to practice and apply delegation/conflict management skills within their own day-to-day operations, and increase awareness of educator and manager roles during the care delivery transition process. This approach seemed successful, because as situations occurred on the patient care units, the managers/educators used the principles from the class to assist with problem solving.

The RN education series began in late summer of 1992 and timing of the programs was coordinated with the first PCT and service associate educational series. The nurse managers and Analyst Committee stressed the importance of establishing class sizes that would facilitate day-to-day operations but maximize efficiency of resources. Class size limits were established with a maximum of 25 students and a minimum of six. The original class was designed with 16 hours of content (Table 6.2) and revised after the first quarter of classes based on instructor and participant feedback. The revised class was reduced to 12 hours of content and offered until January of 1993 (Table 6.3). Four hours of delegation training were deleted due to the repetitive nature of the context.

At that time, based on course evaluations and the continued desire to refine our process, the course was reduced to eight hours (Table 6.4). Both conflict management and delegation were further reduced to a total of five- and one-half hours. The risk management session was taught by a hospital attorney for the first 12 sessions. The RN questions were consistent, and at this point, the RN Education Subgroup determined a need to develop a video to review this topic to conserve time and resources. Through coordination with the MVH audiovisual and production team, the hospital attorney, and PACE 2000 program managers, a 29-minute video was produced dealing with the risk management objectives.

Currently, the PACE 2000 RN class is eight hours and is offered to new employees through the MVH Center of Nursing Excellence. The

Table 6.2

RN Education Plans—Cluster 1
16-hour class

Day One		Day Two	
Time Frame	Topic	Time Frame	Topic
7:30–10:00 am	Review framework of PACE 2000	8:30–11:30 am	Delegation training
		11:30–12:15	Lunch
	Role review		
		12:15–5:00 pm	Conflict management training
	Job description review		
10:00–10:15	Break		Evaluation
10:15–11:15	Legal implications		
11:15–12:00	Lunch		
12:00–4:00 pm	Delegation training		

PACE 2000 program managers, education subcommittee chairperson, and delegation/conflict management trainers have participated in the education of 990 RNs through 80 classes since August 1992.

LPN Educational Program Development

The education of the LPN was developed in response to a needs assessment completed by LPN employees during the job description revision. A working group of five LPNs led by the Roles Committee cochairperson analyzed and revised the LPN job description. Important components of change were facilitated by the new care delivery system and the desire to foster the LPNs' maximum utilization according to the Ohio LPN Practice Act.

The LPN job description revision also included an addendum that identified areas of RN/LPN role confusion and organized activities into columns of *May* and *Shall Not*. These areas included physician orders; documentation; intravenous fluids administration and management; medication handling and administration; and care of wounds, lines, tubes,

Table 6.3

RN Education Plans—Cluster 2
12-hour class

Day One Time Frame	Topic	Day Two Time Frame	Topic
7:30–10:00 am	PACE 2000 overview	8:30–11:30 am	Delegation training
	Job description review	11:30–12:15	Lunch
10:00–10:15	Break	12:15–5:00 pm	Conflict management training
10:15–11:15	Legal implications		Evaluation
11:15–11:30	Evaluation		

and drains. Due to the limited number of LPNs in the care delivery system, it was vital to keep the LPNs informed and involved with the changes in care delivery and development of formal partnerships. The Roles Subcommittee chairpersons and the PACE 2000 program managers personally communicate with LPNs on different patient care units to ask opinions and seek information. The LPN education series was based on their stated needs and the PACE 2000 Roles Subcommittee assessment.

The education plan included review of the PACE 2000 care delivery system, review of revised and new job descriptions, legal implications of the new care delivery system, computer update, transcribing medication orders, and a session featuring refinement of skills to receive delegation and manage conflict (Table 6.5). Each of the educational components will be described in more detail in this section.

PACE 2000 Review

A review of the goals, foundations, and philosophies of PACE 2000 was addressed in this session. A detailed review of the LPN job description and relationships to the RN, PCT, and new service associate role were discussed with ample time for questions and answers. The description of partnership expectations was defined in relationship to their role and relationship with the RN and PCT. To maintain consistency of information

Table 6.4

RN Education Plans—Clusters 3–6
8-hour class

Time Frame	Topic
8:30–9:00 am	Completion of "work characteristics instrument"
9:00–10:00	PACE 2000 overview
	Job description analysis
10:00–10:30	Risk management video
10:30–10:45	Break
10:45–12:30	Delegation training
12:30–1:00 pm	Lunch
1:00–5:00	Conflict management training

being presented, the Education Subcommittee chairperson served as the sole instructor for this topic.

Legal Implications

This section was established to inform LPNs of their responsibilities in relationship to the Ohio LPN Practice Act. This session focused on the three R's of risk management: establishing rapport, appropriate recording, and review of reporting mechanisms. The hospital general counsel video for risk management was utilized as a portion of the curriculum.

Documentation

This section was included to provide a review of appropriate documentation strategies for the LPN in the new care delivery system. The LPNs were merged with the PCTs for this section to help facilitate their understanding of the PCT's role in documentation. This session was based on active participation with documentation scenarios provided to give real-life charting examples. This session was reviewed by an experienced

Table 6.5
LPN Education Plan

Thursday	Topic	Friday	Topic
8:00–10:15 am	PACE 2000 overview	8:00–11:00 am	Computer update
	Role review		Lab-work retrieval
	Job description review		Medication/order entry
10:15–10:30	Break		Nursing Kardex/care-plan review
10:30–11:15	Legal implications	11:00–11:45	Lunch
11:15–12:00	Lunch	11:45–3:30	Communication
12:00–4:30 pm	Documentation		

nurse educator with extensive knowledge of roles and responsibilities of the RN coordinating the health care team.

Computer Update and Medication Administration Record

This session was established in direct response to needs identified by LPN employees. In the early 1980s, a computerized system for nursing information and laboratory work retrieval was introduced to the institution. Due to the limited number of LPNs in the system, a data information gap existed as to ability to enter the computer system and retrieve information. Each LPN was provided an entry number for a hands-on session to introduce them to the computer system. This session was repeated five months after the initial education to provide opportunity for review and update. This session was reviewed by the educator responsible for health unit coordinator education within the institution.

An overview of medication transcription was established based on feedback from the LPNs during their job description revision meetings. Practice sessions were conducted to assist the LPN in gaining knowledge about methods of physician order transcription and transcribing the orders on the medication administration record. This function is usually performed by the HUC but can be the responsibility of the RN/LPN during off shifts or in situations when the HUC is not available. The session also included review of information available in the computerized nursing information module. Methods to retrieve the information were provided in step-by-step practice sessions. This session was also reviewed by the educator for the HUCs within the institution.

Communication

The emphasis for this session was to provide and enhance skills about receiving delegation and managing conflict. In many respects, the role of the LPN was affected with the PACE 2000 care delivery system due to the establishment of partnership situations. The LPN would receive direction from the RN to establish priorities and deliver care and also work closely with PCTs if a triad relationship existed. The communication session was based on the objectives reviewed in the RN delegation and conflict management course and taught by patient care units educators within the institution.

Implementation of LPN Educational Program

The LPN education series were split into two sessions to facilitate scheduling opportunities for the nurse managers. The sessions were offered in November (1992) and January (1993), and the PACE 2000 overview was offered separately to the LPN employees to provide opportunities to ventilate concerns/issues and feel comfortable within the participant group. The LPNs expressed negative opinions about the joint LPN/PCT documentation session and the focus on receiving delegation. Effective and positive communication for the PACE 2000 program managers and Education Subcommittee chairperson became more of a challenge. Small focus groups with LPNs were held in the spring of 1992 to diffuse rumors and negativity resulting from the formalization of the PCT role and address concerns about job security.

The Ohio Board of Nursing adopted new rules of the *Role of Licensed Practical Nurses in Intravenous Therapy* (Ohio Board of Nursing 1993), which became effective 1 April 1993. This change resulted in the need to establish a 40-hour intravenous therapy course for the LPN employee. This class was established by the MVH Center of Nursing

Excellence and implemented in the fall of 1993 for LPNs who participated in IV therapy roles within their individual patient care units. This
ruling also resulted in a change in LPN practice between 1 April 1993 and
the course offering, which further created role confusion during PACE
2000 implementation.

Recommendations

In the process of developing the role and education of the RN and LPN,
many strategies used throughout the OE and PACE 2000 effort worked.
The strategies that worked and those that could have worked better are
as follows:

What worked

- Open communication where members of the committees challenged
  other members regarding the rationale to change or not change a practice issue.
- Utilization of the professional practice acts guided role development.
- Assessment of current practice and the utilization of the literature
  explored the benefits of changing practice.

What could have worked better

- Alleviating fear over losing one's job.
- Mobilizing the energies of those who resisted the change to a more
  productive role.

Summary

The implementation of the PACE 2000 educational programs for the RN
and LPN was a major endeavor. Extensive resources were committed
both to provide the courses and to enable staff to attend. The RN Education Subcommittee made every effort to adapt and revise course content
to meet the needs of the RN and institution as a whole. The commitment
to increase the RN's ability to function and thrive in the new care delivery
system was the most important goal to be achieved. Several patient care
units have requested updates of delegation and conflict management since
the original classes. These requests have been initiated by the unit-based
educator with assistance of the PACE 2000 program managers.

The original goal set by the CNO and PACE 2000 imple... team was to increase the amount of time RNs could spend deli... professional aspects of patient care, including assessing; reporting ... physiological and emotional variances to physicians; communicating with patients and significant others; and planning, directing, and educating patients, significant others, peers, and ancillary staff. The secondary goal was to reduce the amount of time the RN spent performing indirect care activities as defined earlier in this chapter.

The goals were established to have RN work distribution divided with 75 percent of time spent delivering patient care, as opposed to the current 64 percent. It was further hoped that the proportion of time spent delivering indirect care could be reduced from 22 percent to 5 percent, and RN time spent communicating could be increased from 15 percent to 20 percent.

References

Curran, C. 1992. Personal communication, 2 September.

Manion, J. 1993. "Chaos or Transformation? Managing Innovation." *Journal of Nursing Administration* 23 (5): 41–48.

Ohio Board of Nursing. 1993. "Role of Licensed Practical Nurses in Intravenous Therapy." *Rules Promulgated from the Law Regulating the Practice of Nursing: Chapter 4723, Ohio Revised Code.* 4: 1–4.

Appendix 6.A

Care Subgroup Task Force

		Professional RN Patient Care Activities	Patient Care Activities
1.	Educa... ...ng disease process and discharge ...eeds	RN	
2.	Medication administration/preparing IVs	RN/LPN	
3.	Transcribing orders correctly		HUC
4.	Personal hygiene/care		NA
5.	Feed		NA
6.	Ambulate		NA
7.	Turn and position patient		NA
8.	Transport to other depart.		NE
9.	Documenting	RN/LPN	NA
10.	Billing		NE/HUC
11.	Patient assessments	RN	
12.	Listening to patients	RN/LPN	NA/NE/HUC
13.	Treatments: Tube care, foley, dressings, suctioning, drainage catheters.	RN/LPN	NA
14.	Coordination of care with other disciplines, resources	RN	
15.	Ongoing monitoring/assessment	RN	
16.	Talk w/Families/Significant others on patient condition	RN/LPN	
17.	Drawing lab work	RN	Lab Tech/NE
18.	Communicate w/MD on pt. needs	RN	
19.	Social service and home care referrals	RN	
20.	Answer call lights		NE/HUC
21.	Make beds		Unocc: NE Occup.: NA
22.	Collect specimens	RN/LPN	NA
23.	Deliver food trays/snacks		NE
24.	Clean room		NE

Patient Care Activities	Professional RN Patient Care Activities	Patient Care Activities
25. Empty bedpans/I&O	I&O: RN/LPN	NA
26. Make phone calls for patients		NE
27. Communicate/Schedule need items for patients/Families	RN/LPN	
28. Errands: Dietary, blood bank, pharmacy, equipment, lab, etc.		NE
29. Complete admission forms		NE
30. Obtain lab results	RN/LPN	
31. Fill water pitchers		NE
32. Consent forms	RN	
33. Find physicians	RN	
34. Transport patients out of hospital		NE
35. Develop care plans	RN	
36. Assist doctor with procedures	RN/LPN	
37. EKGs		NE/Card.Tech.
38. Respiratory therapy	RN/LPN	Respiratory
39. Occupational therapy		OT
40. Physical therapy: ROM	RN/LPN	NA
41. Nutrition assessment	RN	Dietary
42. Fill out patient menu		NE
43. Mix tube feedings		NA
44. Accompany pt. to procedures		NE
45. Patient advocate	RN/LPN	NE/HUC
46. QA activities	RN/LPN	NA/NE/HUC
47. Acuity	RN	
48. Fix TV, Adjust room temp.		NE/PS&E
49. Staff for next shift	RN	
50. Weigh patients		NA/NE
51. Shift report	RN	NA
52. Control of time cards		Staff. Sec.
53. Universal precautions	RN/LPN	NA/NE
54. Equipment/Devices On/Off pt.	RN/LPN	NA

Patient Care Activities	Professional RN Patient Care Activities	Patient Care Activities
55. Order supplies		NE/HUC
56. Central services charges		NE/HUC
57. Oversee auxiliary care	RN	
58. Admission assessment	RN/LPN	NA: V/S and Rm. Orient.
59. Discharge summary	RN	
60. Meal delivery		NE
61. Set up for meals		NA
62. Monitor pt. for procedures	RN/LPN	
63. Care of invasive equipment	RN/Physician	

NA = Nurse Assistant; HUC = Health Unit Coordinator; NE = Nurse Extender (PCT); OT = Occupational Therapist; PS&E = Plant Services and Engineering (Maintenance Department).

Appendix 6.B

PACE 2000 Philosophy

The purpose of this document is to share the philosophy and premise of PACE 2000. Positive Actions for Care Excellence, PACE 2000, is the name that represents the patient-centered care approach at MVH. A component of this new model is the relationship or partnership between an RN and PCT/LPN. This partnership will allow for development of consistency, collegiality, mutual respect, and empathy for the patient and each other.

Date: _____

Partners: RN _____   PCT/LPN _____

Inservice Preparation for Partnerships

RN: Inservice Title/Date _____

_____

_____

_____

PCT/LPN: Inservice Title/Date _____

_____

_____

_____

The partnership relationship includes but may not be limited to the following:

We understand it is preferable to work the same shift, fair-share of holidays and the majority of our work schedule together (excluding earned holidays and vacation time).

It is understood that when illness or personal time occurs within the partnership, the remaining partner will be paired with another partner or partnership.

The partnership will give care to one group of patients sharing the work and the responsibilities and function as members of the unit team, anticipating needs of other partnerships.

It is understood the RN has the authority to define the primary practice partner's role and activities, within the framework of Miami Valley Hospital job descriptions, division of nursing policies and procedures, and nursing practice standards.

It is understood that the RN has the obligation to educate, mentor, and develop the primary practice partner. Both partners are responsible for participation in the evaluation process.

We both recognize our obligation to maintain a healthy interpersonal relationship between us and with the other members of the unit staff.

We have read and understand that the relationship is entered with complete commitment of both parties. Termination of the relationship due to interpersonal problems will be the last resort. Termination of the relationship due to employment termination, job transfer, personal reasons, etc., will be accepted in writing with a minimum notice of two weeks. The remaining partner can then exercise the option to form a new partnership at the earliest opportunity.

Signed _____

_____

Shift Manager Signature _____

Appendix 6.C

Conflict Situations

Conflict Situation I

Debbie has been 20–25 minutes late for work six times within the last three months. She is very apologetic and works diligently once she arrives. She has even offered to work through lunch or stay after hours to make up for the lost time. She told you that she really needs her job because her husband is out of work.

You have been Debbie's manager on the surgical floor for six months. Her prior records indicate that she arrived for work on time. You have decided to talk with Debbie because you need for her to arrive on time. Working lunch hours or late will not meet the needs of the unit.

Conflict Situation II

Joe is a patient care technician. He seems to get his work accomplished and is pleasant and courteous with the patients. When he is out of the department on a task, however, he takes an unusually long time to return. You often have difficulty locating him when you need him. On several occasions he has been found in the snack room talking to other employees. Joe explains his absence by saying that delays in other departments hold him up and by insisting that the time he is spending in the snack room is his break time. You have talked to Joe twice about this problem and asked that he let you know when he will be taking a break or when he is prevented from returning to the department within a reasonable amount of time. You have decided to talk with him a third time about the problem.

Conflict Situation III

Fran is a member of your staff. Over the past six months, she has consistently complained to you that she is assigned more work than the other PCTs. You do not agree with Fran's assessment of the work distribution. The two of you have discussed the problem several times but have been unable to resolve the differences.

For the past month Fran has been moving slowly in carrying out her assignments (often keeping other team members waiting for supplies, information, etc.), has been complaining to coworkers about the hospital and you, and has answered two patients in a rude, abrupt manner. You have decided to talk to Fran about all of the above comments.

7

The Role and Education of the Patient Care Technician

Claire Blust Rodehaver, Nancy L. Breidenbach, Christine L. Tipton, and Linda S. Welin

A single thread takes on new meaning when it is interwoven with other diverse threads. Distinct and vibrant on its own, it becomes an essential part of something much greater than itself.

—Kaiser Permanente 1991

This chapter will outline the steps and the strategies utilized to develop and implement the curriculum (generic and unit-specific focuses) for the PCT. For the purpose of clarification, the term *patient care technician*, or *PCT*, will be used in this chapter to describe the expanded nurse extender role. The term *nursing assistant (NA)* will be used to denote the nurse extender role prior to the implementation of the partnership in practice model. The existing NAs were asked to select the title for the expanded role within the patient centered care delivery system. This was an agenda item at several of their regular monthly meetings. The title of PCT was chosen by a majority vote.

The many issues and ideas analyzed within this subcommittee will be shared, as well as the concurrent evolution of the role of the PCT, which resulted in the new PCT job description. The PCT job description summarizes the PCT role as an individual who enhances the nature and quality of patient care through a relationship with an RN. The PCT assists the RN by performing assigned tasks that facilitate direct care and the nursing process.

The material presented in this chapter was accomplished within approximately five months. The process is generally described chronologically, although work often occurred concurrently through the use of task forces within the Education Subcommittee.

Committee Structure

The Education Subcommittee comprises 34 members. It includes representatives from all levels of the division of nursing (primary nurse Is, primary nurse IIs, unit educators, CNSs, NAs, shift managers, nurse managers, and directors of nursing) and from all specialities (medical-surgical, critical care, perinatal, nursing education, and nursing research). Faculty from two universities, physicians, librarians, and HRD personnel also are represented within this committee. A conscious effort was made to choose individuals from diverse positions and varied clinical areas so that the sharing of ideas would result in the development of the best PCT educational program. Diverse representation was needed to empower the committee to mobilize its resources and enable change to occur throughout the institution in constructive and realistic ways.

Committee Processes

The committee integrated several concepts into the process of completing its goals. Empowerment, change, and communication were three of the most important concepts. The effect of enabling the members to make decisions and to act resulted in the members feeling capable and committed. This empowerment developed a sense of ownership and a commitment to successful implementation of the committee's outcomes.

The Education Subcommittee met weekly for five months, then bimonthly for three months. The Education Subcommittee continues to meet monthly for two hours to monitor and evaluate the success of the PCT education. The PCT curriculum continues to be modified and updated based on feedback from the student participants (PCT), the speakers/faculty, the RN partners, the unit educators, and the unit management team.

The charter of the Education Subcommittee was to develop, monitor, evaluate, and revise a core curriculum to meet the standards required by the patient care model for both professional and nonprofessional staff.

Step 1: Visioning for Nursing Practice

Utilizing the principles inherent in the concepts of shared governance and empowerment, the first step in the process was the education subcommittee chairperson facilitating a brainstorming session about educational issues and challenges in the current system. The Education Subcommittee, along with the PACE 2000 Implementation Team envisioned where nursing practice would or could be in five years and analyzed what nursing practice currently is. The role of the nurse extender (PCT) evolved based on the definition of what nursing practice is and the committee's future vision of nursing practice.

Step 2: Preparing for the Role

Knowing that the organization was implementing the philosophy of partners in professional practice, a concept of patient centered care, the Education Subcommittee next brainstormed issues, roadblocks, and challenges to meet the educational needs of the PCT. The overriding question became, "How do we get the PCTs ready for partnerships?" Brainstorming sessions were followed by meetings that analyzed and evaluated the potential issues of the PCT education.

Step 3: Identifying Task Forces

At this point the education subcommittee divided into four task forces to concentrate on specific issues and concepts. The first task force focused on the pre-employment screening issues, such as qualifications for the PCT role. The second task force was responsible for developing the generic PCT curriculum. The third task force concentrated efforts on the unit-specific or department-specific educational needs of the PCT. The fourth task force addressed the continuing education needs or the skill proficiency needs of the PCT. The majority of work was accomplished by these smaller task forces within the education subcommittee. Outcomes of the task forces were as follows:

- Developing and outlining ideas
- Surveying the NA group itself

- Surveying the unit-based educators
- Developing the curriculum for generic PCT education
- Developing skills checklists
- Compiling a comprehensive listing of additional unit or department-specific educational needs
- Outlining, planning, and implementing continuing education for the PCTs.

The subcommittee took on new meaning as diverse members actively participated in decision making about not only their own roles, but also their own environment. The members were truly empowered when the group accepted responsibility for directing the destiny of nursing practice at the institution. One could not have painted a more vibrant picture of empowerment.

Step 4: Developing Roles

The role of the PCT in the new patient care delivery system became clearer once the Education Subcommittee defined the boundaries of nursing practice in the partners in professional practice model. Defining RN/PCT boundaries was difficult because the institution had practiced under the philosophy of primary nursing with an RN skill mix approaching 98 percent for 20 years. The scope of RN practice was extensively reviewed and defined in the organization prior to the formation of the Education Subcommittee. Once the scope of RN practice within the Ohio Nurse Practice Act was clarified for the Education Subcommittee, the role of the PCT began to evolve.

The Education Subcommittee started with an analysis of the previously used two-tiered NA system. The institution had NA I and NA II roles. The NA I and II roles assist the RN by performing assigned patient care tasks that contribute to the delivery of patient care. The NA II role, in addition to NA I tasks, entailed the addition of more advanced therapeutic procedures such as blood glucose monitoring, urinary catheterization, and wound care.

Results of the analysis indicated that the two-tiered system was not effective and that within the new partnership concept, an expanded NA II role would be necessary. The RN would be unable to take on a larger caseload without a highly skilled nurse extender for a partner.

Another conclusion was that NAs were being underutilized. However, there were several reasons for the underutilization of NAs. First, the institution had incorporated the practice and philosophy of primary nursing in the mid-1970s. RNs were accustomed to total patient care and to not using auxiliary personnel. Each nursing unit, for the most part, had a minimal number of NAs, often only one or two. The staff had little opportunity to delegate. The delegation that did occur generally involved assigning beds and baths for one or two patients per RN. In addition to this assignment, the NAs spent much time delivering dietary trays and taking vital signs. Second, the majority of nurses had never practiced in a system other than primary nursing. For other nurses, it had been many years since they had worked on units with ancillary personnel to whom delegation was even a possibility. Third, when the two-tiered NA system was introduced, it was very confusing for the RNs to remember which NAs were level I and which were level II. Often, even after the RN discerned the appropriate level of the NA, many NA IIs did not perform the advanced skills outlined in the job description because of a lack of proficiency due to rare opportunities to perform the skill. Over two years, this cycle perpetuated itself and resulted in underutilization.

The committee's analysis of the underutilization of NAs led to the decision that one level of PCTs was needed prior to the implementation of the partners in practice concept. A one-tier system for PCTs was thought to have a number of advantages, which are as follows:

- It is easier to delegate with only one level of nurse extender.
- Role confusion would be eliminated.
- The availability of more highly skilled PCTs would allow for more efficient and effective care of the higher acuity patients.
- The number of personnel coming in contact with the patient and family would decrease.

Step 5: Pre-Entry Educational Qualifications

Once the role of the PCT began to take shape, attention was directed toward the need for and the availability of skilled and educated people to fulfill the PCT role. It was recognized that skill mix changes would necessitate more PCTs. Initial projections from the nurse managers reflected a need for a minimum of 50 additional PCTs over the first four months. Long-term projections for a two and a half–year period indicated a need for at least 200 PCTs. The committee was unsure of the internal and external availability of qualified personnel for this type of employment.

After reviewing the literature on the nurse extender role, searching for personnel with higher qualifications was thought to be ideal. There was discussion as to whether the institution should recommend an associate degree in a related field for the PCT role. What effect would the associate degree requirement have on existing NAs? Would the associate degree requirement serve as a challenge or an incentive to existing NAs? The committee realized that these questions could not be answered until further investigation of entry level options occurred.

Numerous community contacts were established and utilized over the next few weeks: searching for information, comparing the hospital to similar institutions, and determining what was available to prevent reinventing the wheel. Multiple telephone calls were made to acute and long-term care facilities investigating both entry level requirements and internal education for NAs. Community colleges and universities, in addition to companies specializing in educational materials, were contacted in search of a curriculum that would fulfill our needs. The expanded PCT role in acute care was a new concept, therefore, curricula were unavailable.

The Ohio Board of Nursing was contacted for information regarding state-tested programs, as well as for guidelines for acute care NAs. The committee discovered that NAs in long-term care facilities were required by the state to complete an approved NA course and successfully pass a state-regulated test. At this time, there were no state requirements for acute care NAs and there were no plans to develop such guidelines.

More telephone calls were made to gather information about state-tested programs offered in the region. The question was, Will the state-tested programs for long-term care facilities meet the educational needs of an acute care facility? Information sought included the following:

- What was the course content?
- Was enrollment open to the public?
- How often was the program offered?
- What was the cost of the program and did the cost include a textbook?

Until this time, the Education Subcommittee was unaware that the curriculum of all state-tested programs for long-term care was mandated and standardized as a 75-hour program. Content did not vary across programs (Table 7.1 contains the 75-hour course content). This lack of knowledge resulted in needless investigation into the content of multiple programs.

Once it was recognized that the state-tested content was the same for all long-term care programs, the group decided that these programs would not solely meet the educational needs of the PCT envisioned for the acute care setting. However, the committee thought the state-tested programs could serve as a basis from which internal PCT education could build.

After assimilating and discussing the information, a proposal was drafted outlining several options for PCT education. The proposal contained a cost analysis of each option and the manner in which internal employees and external candidates would be integrated into the system. This proposal was presented to the analyst committee with the

Table 7.1

Summary of State-Tested Curriculum by Topic Area

Topic Area	Required Class Hours
I. Overview	0.5
II. Communication & Interpersonal Skills	4.5
III. Infection Control	2.5
IV. Safety and Emergency Procedures	6.5
V. Promoting Resident Independence	1.0
VI. Promoting Resident Rights	1.0
Total Required Preclinical Hours	16.0

	Required Hours Overall
VII. Basic Nursing Skills	19.0
VIII. Personal Care Skills	22.5
IX. Mental Health & Social Service Needs	11.5
X. Basic Restorative Services	4.0
XI. Resident Rights	2.0
Total	59.0
Grand Total Required Hours	75.0

Reprinted with permission from the Ohio Department of Health. 1989. *The State of Ohio Training and Competency Evaluation Program Standards.*

recommendation that PCT partners obtain basic education (via the state-tested program/course) outside the institution. An additional four weeks of internal education would build upon this basic education and provide skill validation.

This recommendation was approved by the Analyst Committee for several reasons. First, it was impractical to find the space and equipment required for a skills laboratory and to recruit educators to teach the basic skills when such educational resources were already available in the community. Second, current employees could access the institution's existing tuition assistance benefit in order to subsidize the cost of the outside program. Finally, an external candidate would demonstrate commitment by attending a state-tested program and then returning for internal education (100 percent attendance is a requirement for successful completion of the state-tested program).

With input from the Education and Roles Subcommittees, the Analyst Committee made the decision to require external PCT candidates to have the following qualifications:

- High school diploma or general equivalency diploma (associate's degree preferred)
- CPR certification
- One of the following: completion of a state-tested program, successful completion of NA course or review course for state test, or six months acute care experience as an NA. Any of these options would ensure that employees had knowledge of some basic skills.

External candidates were directed into PCT positions by following the algorithm outlined in Figure 7.1.

With these qualifications established, the HRD requested a more in-depth evaluation of selected local state-tested programs. The HRD would utilize this information to recommend a state-tested program to external candidates, as well as internal, nonnursing personnel interested in the PCT role. Additional information sought included the following:

- Were hours flexible to accommodate day and evening shift personnel?
- What sites were used for clinical experiences?
- Was the program location accessible to public transportation?
- What percentage of students successfully completed the program?

Figure 7.1

Hire of External Candidate into PCT Role

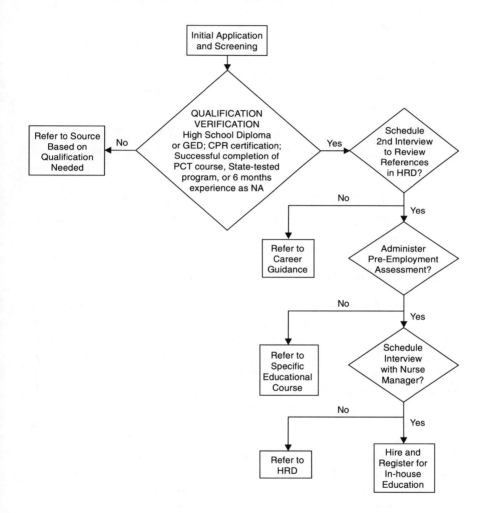

- Where did the students find employment?
- What was an average class size?

On-site visits of selected programs occurred. While all of these programs were based on the minimal 75-hour curriculum, the programs seemed to be very different depending on the level of enthusiasm of the course coordinator. Several course coordinators spent extra time and energy mentoring participants. A site comparison was presented to the Education Subcommittee. From this data, the committee chose three programs that the institution would recommend to interested personnel (Table 7.2). The pre-entry issue was beginning to be resolved. Internal personnel, outside of nursing, who were interested in pursuing the PCT role, were directed according to an algorithm developed by the Human Resources Subcommittee (Figure 7.2). A three-phase pre-employment work-up was planned as follows:

- Initially an application/CPR check was reviewed by the HRD.
- A subsequent interview was scheduled to review past experiences and references.
- After review of the references, the pre-employment assessment would be administered. If the applicant successfully passed the assessment, an interview with a nurse manager would then be scheduled.

Step 6: Pre-Employment Assessment Tool

As the role of the PCT evolved to include increased responsibility and accountability, the committee realized the need for the development of a pre-employment assessment tool for the PCT role. A tool would be given by the HRD personnel to all external candidates and nonnursing, internal personnel prior to acceptance into a PCT role. The written test would assess an applicant's interpersonal skills and ability to read, write, and perform basic mathematics related to obtaining weights and calculating intake and output. The test, serving as a screening tool, would be incorporated into the required qualifications for the PCT role.

Because part of the qualifications for outside candidates was successful completion of the pre-employment assessment, the committee's immediate concern was obtaining a tool for this purpose. The HRD personnel initially sought available pre-employment screening tools, which included topics such as reading and mathematics. Different computer programs for prescreening purposes were explored but, upon review, it was decided that they were inappropriate.

Because no applicable pre-employment screening tool was found, development of a new tool began. Development of this tool was

Table 7.2

NA Training Programs Summary

Agency	No. 1	No. 2	No. 3
Time span	2–3 weeks	2–3 weeks	2–3 weeks
Hours	Day/evenings*	Day/evenings	Day
Frequency	Q month*	Q 3 weeks	Quarterly
Cost	$240	$250	$195
Clinical hours	24	16	16
Clinical sites	1 fixed	3 fixed	Varies
Class size	8–15	Less than 24	Less than 24
Waiting list	Yes	Yes (1 month)	Varies
Curriculum additions	Yes	No	No

*Availability of class may be limited until program is expanded.

Comments:

1. Enthusiastic program coordinator. Interested in meeting flexible needs. Individual attention given.

2. Flexible hours already in place. Enthusiastic staff. No individual attention given. Independence of students encouraged.

3. Enthusiastic instructor. Individual attention given. Best-equipped skills laboratory. Complimentary feedback regarding student population.

accomplished through a collaborative effort of the HRD and the Education Subcommittee. After multiple revisions, the finished product included sections about spelling, filing, arithmetic, and customer relations. Issues at the pre-entry level were resolved with the completion of qualifications and the assessment process.

Step 7: Curriculum Development

Once the dilemma surrounding entry level requirements of both internal and external PCT candidates was resolved, the committee proceeded with development of the PCT curriculum. After reviewing the content in the state-tested program, the committee identified areas that needed more emphasis in the acute care setting.

Figure 7.2

Transfers to PCT Role from Other MVH Departments

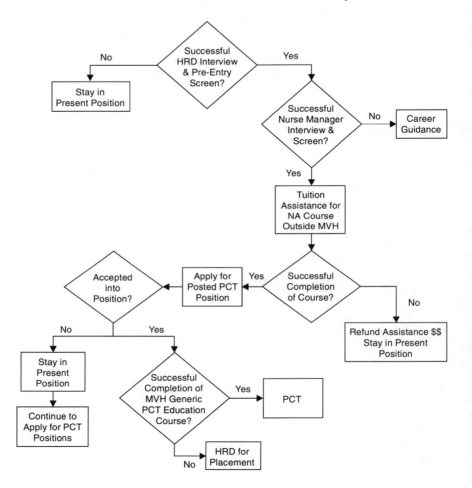

The committee began reviewing and evaluating the existing NA II course content. The NA II course was limited to two and one-half days of classroom instruction. This instruction focused solely on the attainment of a few advanced skills with minimal focus on anatomy and physiology, theory, or rationale. This deficit led the committee to consider incorporating the format of a basic review of the body systems followed by skills education and demonstration with return demonstration by the PCT.

Concurrent work with the Roles Committee occurred at this point to redefine the parameters of the PCT role. Issues related to direct patient care and therapeutic procedures needed to be clarified before curriculum development could proceed. At this time, a survey was developed and distributed to the current NA IIs for a self-assessment of skills and knowledge (Table 7.3). Information was sought related to the NA's comfort level with previously learned advanced skills. The survey elicited whether NA IIs had knowledge about each listed skill and whether they had experience performing the skills. The results of this survey helped determine which skills would be included in the generic PCT education and which skills would be reviewed at the unit or department level. The survey substantiated previous thoughts that the existing NA II course was, in fact, inadequate. Survey data provided the basis for developing the PCT generic curriculum and for redefining the parameters for the PCT job description.

Working on the curriculum before the job description was finalized created escalating anxiety for the group. The Education Subcommittee's charter was to develop a curriculum for the PCT role. However in developing the curriculum, the group was in addition unknowingly defining the role of the PCT. This created tension among the Education Subcommittee members who were aware of another committee's charter for PCT role definition (the Roles Subcommittee). This led to the realization that the role of the PCT and the curriculum were evolving simultaneously between the two subcommittees. The groups were open systems, willing to accept and evaluate many new thoughts and ideas without clinging to the past. This situation was a reflection that all of the rigid definitions of role and function had been dissolved.

Curriculum format/structure

An issue of empowerment surfaced between the education subcommittee and the Analyst Committee regarding a decision on a time frame for the course. Originally, the Education Subcommittee decided that six to eight weeks of orientation was an optimal time frame for the program (including didactic and clinical experiences). However, from a practical standpoint, the Analyst Committee thought a four- to six-week program was more feasible. The compromise became ten days of didactic content

Table 7.3

Nursing Assistants/Unit Assistants Skills Self-Evaluation

	No Knowledge	Class, No Experience	Class but Need More Experience	Class and Adequate Experience
1. Documents on patient's chart				
2. Suctions patients				
3. Performs aseptic technique				
4. Applies O_2				
5. Applies heat				
6. Applies cold				
7. Blanketrol				
8. Assesses and records chest tube drainage				
9. Catheterizes male patients				
10. Catheterizes female patients				
11. Discontinues foley				
12. Empties and rinses ostomy appliances				
13. Performs dressing changes				
14. Performs decubitus care				
15. Collects sterile specimens (e.g., urine/culture)				

and ten to twenty days of clinical experience, depending on individual need. Options at this point included the following:

- Option 1: Ten straight days of class followed by ten or twenty days of clinical time.
- Option 2: Alternating class and clinical days followed by five to fifteen days of clinical on the assigned shift.

The schedule shown in Table 7.4 was adopted. It was decided that alternative class and clinical days would provide the best environment for learning and integrating concepts into practice. Lecture content would be presented with the expectation that the PCT would perform related skills in the clinical situation the following day as opportunities were presented.

Challenge option

Next, the committee was empowered to deal with the issue of the present NA Is, NA IIs, new employees, and student nurses functioning in the PCT role. Initially, the committee considered sending all NAs to the entire ten days of didactic content. After exploring this option with the analyst team, it was decided that a challenge exam could be given to assess the present NA IIs' knowledge level and to recognize previously attained knowledge. Investigation into a modular format for the program and challenge exam occurred. The modular format might make the program more easily utilized in component parts for individuals not needing the entire course. Extensive discussion by the group about test construction and scheduling conflicts resulted in the elimination of the modular format as an option.

The most workable solution was to administer an integrated challenge exam to all present NA IIs. Student nurses who have completed at least one clinical course and are recommended by a faculty member, could also take the challenge exam. Those obtaining an overall score of at least 80 percent would not be required to attend all the classes. All new employees, all NA Is, NA IIs, and student nurses, not obtaining an 80 percent score on the challenge exam, would be enrolled in the ten-day curriculum.

Curriculum content

Although the NA IIs and student nurses who passed the challenge exam would not require the entire course content (see Exhibit 7.1 for topic outline), it was recognized that certain essential information about the new PCT role would be necessary. This information could be presented in two days of the ten-day curriculum. Content for these two days would include such topics as the PACE 2000 overview, review of roles and job descriptions (such as RN and PCT), customer relations, and communications (see starred items in Exhibit 7.1 for topics in two days of content). The two day mandatory offerings for all NA IIs would also provide an opportunity for networking.

The committee identified common themes important to the core curriculum. These included medical terminology, signs and symptoms to

Table 7.4
Patient Care Technician Program

Sunday	Monday	Tuesday	Wednesday	Thursday	Friday	Saturday
1	2 Hospital Orientation	3 Lecture	4 Lecture	5 Lecture	6 Lecture	7
8	9 Lecture	10 Clinical 7 am–3:30 pm	11 Lecture	12 Clinical 7 am–3:30 pm	13 Lecture	14
15	16 Clinical 7 am–3:30 pm	17 Lecture	18 Clinical 7 am–3:30 pm	19 Lecture	20 Post Test 7 am—10 am Clinical 10 am–3:30 pm	21
22	23 Clinical on Shift	24 Clinical on Shift	25 Clinical on Shift	26 Clinical on Shift	27 Clinical on Shift	28
29	30	31				

Exhibit 7.1

Topic Outline for Patient Care Technician Class

* PACE 2000 Overview
* Review of Roles and Job Descriptions
* Risk Management
* Customer Relations
* Patient Safety
* Spirituality
  Infection Control and Asepsis
  Nurse Extender Role in Cardiopulmonary Resuscitation
  Medical Terminology
  Suicide Precautions
  Admitting, Transferring, and Discharging
  Pre/Post Surgery Care
  Documentation
* Cost Containment
* Sexuality
* Growth and Development
* Communication

Review of Systems
  Respiratory
  Cardiovascular
  Gastrointestinal
  Geritourinary
  Musculoskeletal
  Endocrine
  Nervous
  Integumentary

* Items discussed in the two-day mandatory offering.

immediately report to the nurse, complications of immobility, patient's right to privacy, psychological implications, communication skills, proper body mechanics, and infection control principles. Speakers were asked to integrate these strands into each lecture. Curriculum development continued with the generation of objectives and proposed time frames for individual lectures.

The Education Subcommittee then contacted potential expert speakers regarding refinement of objectives and content. It was identified at this time that nurse experts at all levels of the clinical ladder should serve as the educators for the content outlined because they were actively involved in the development and evaluation of the partnership model at the unit level. Speakers' input regarding course content was solicited in a very short time frame. Numerous additions and deletions were made to both the original objectives and the content. Because of the large number of speakers involved, this process was extremely labor intensive. The topics ranged from anatomy and physiology of the pulmonary system to communication and patient relations, so no one person had all of the expertise necessary to develop or present all of the content.

After potential speakers were contacted and their input was obtained, the committee sought the speakers' commitment to teach in an ongoing curriculum. Many of the speakers also needed to commit time in the skills laboratory. The attainment of this commitment was vital because speakers served in other roles in the institution and the classes were to be ongoing, initially being offered every month. The range of time required for such a commitment was one hour to sixteen hours per month. Alternate speakers were also contacted in case of emergencies. In-depth lecture outlines were requested from the speakers to facilitate alternate speakers' presentation of the lecture.

The speakers were motivated through the realization that their commitment would impact the success of the PCT role. "Empowerment develops a feeling of ownership and is more likely to increase one's energies to produce extraordinary results" (Costello-Nickitas and Mason 1992, 53). Speakers realized that time invested up front to teach the classes and staff the skills laboratory would minimize individual instructions on the unit. This realization motivated the speakers to commit their time and energy to the program.

Step 8: Planning, Organization, and Implementation

As the committee entered the fourth month of work and converged on implementing the PCT curriculum, it began to examine the availability of short-term and long-term resources. It was recognized by everyone that the implementation, facilitation, and monitoring of the PCT classes as established could not be accomplished entirely by the committee. The group was charged with evaluating all of the options that would lead to successful implementation of the developed curriculum. The committee decided that one person needed to be responsible for implementing and monitoring the curriculum as developed. A facilitator was proposed and the following job functions were outlined for this vital role:

- Set up and coordinate on-going classes.
- Evaluate and update course content.
- Evaluate speakers.
- Serve as a contact person for PCTs.
- Identify and monitor continuing education programs for PCTs.

The Analyst Committee discussed and agreed upon the qualifications for the role. The nurse educator had to be an RN involved in the change to a new delivery system and aware of the educational needs of the PCT. A facilitator was named to fulfill the above expectations.

With the curriculum developed and speaker commitments solidified, the focus of the committee shifted to obtaining necessary space and equipment for the skills laboratory. There were several roadblocks encountered, which are as follows:

- Unavailability of space
- Location of skills laboratory
- Availability of personnel to staff the skills laboratory and check off the numbers of participants on time-consuming skills
- Obtaining equipment
- Variability of class size.

The institution's diploma nursing program closed several years ago, so there was not a skills laboratory on site. The subcommittee explored the possibility of utilizing the nursing skills laboratory at a local university but questioned the feasibility of the travel time required. The optimal solution was to have the skills laboratory located on site in a vacated four-bed recovery room. The facilitator assumed responsibility for obtaining and maintaining the equipment and for scheduling RNs in the skills laboratory to check off the PCTs on their skills. Originally class size was limited to 24 students to facilitate learning. However, due to the fourfold increase in the number of PCTs that needed to be accommodated, class sizes were increased while maintaining the 1:6 ratio of instructor to students.

Step 9: Developing Unit/Department Specific Tasks and Continuing Education

One focus of the Education Subcommittee was to compile a comprehensive list of specific tasks/skills that the new PCT would be educated to perform on a specific unit or within a specific department. In addition, the subcommittee thought it was necessary to examine ways to keep the PCTs proficient in skills. Initially, two task forces were formed to develop each of the above foci separately, but it soon became apparent that the two task forces could be blended into one.

The first agenda item for this combined task force was to survey the unit educators to generate a list of unit-specific needs. To make this list versatile, all data received from the survey were entered into a d-Base software program. This list was then organized into two separate areas: skills listed by individual units and like skills grouped together with the units also identified. In this way, units could begin identifying other units where similar skills would be taught/performed. By month two of the Education Subcommittee's existence, this list was shared by the task force at the Education Subcommittee's meeting, and determinations were made regarding skills that would be obtained by all PCTs and skills that would be addressed at the unit/department level.

As data returned from this first survey, the task force began work on the second major focus, identifying how to keep PCTs proficient in their newly acquired skills. A recognized advantage of the RN/PCT partnership is that the RN can mentor the PCT and review skills performance on a day-to-day basis. However, it would be ideal to have a list of specific skills and the means by which each unit would evaluate the PCT's skill performance. The Education Subcommittee felt a strong need to evaluate PCTs' skills on a regular basis based on the organization's history. When the institution first introduced the two levels of NAs several years ago, there was excitement about the roles. Soon after, however, RNs and NAs alike found that if the NA did not perform the skill on a regular basis, the mechanics of the skill were lacking. RNs, usually not working with the same NA for any length of time, began doing many of the skills that the NA had been educated to do. This further compounded the problem. NAs lost proficiency and pride in their recently acquired skills. RNs assumed more of the workload, leading many times to dissatisfaction and, in some instances, burnout. One way to prevent this scenario from recurring with the new PCT role in PACE

2000 was to monitor skills more closely, that is, through partnerships and annual skills validation.

At this point, the task force distributed a survey of the newly generated unit-specific skills to the unit educators and nurse managers. This second survey included the skills generated by all units, sorted by unit as well as by like skills. Educators could then review the entire list and identify skills inadvertently omitted. In addition, units with similar unit-specific skills could collaborate to develop the education required to teach the PCT these skills.

Nurse managers' input was also requested for several reasons. First, it was recognized that these unit-specific needs would be taught to the PCTs on the unit, either by the educator or RN partner. Second, annual assessment/evaluation and education of the PCT require additional resources, financially and in personnel time. With the nurse managers having the fiscal management responsibility, it was extremely important to obtain their input.

Unit educators and nurse managers were given several objectives to accomplish with the second survey, which include the following:

- Review and verify the accuracy of the specific skills listed for their unit.
- Add or delete any skills not relevant to their unit.
- Indicate the personnel now responsible for providing the education required.
- Indicate personnel they think might be involved in the future to provide the education (with the evolution of the institution's clinical ladder for the bedside nurse, RNs seeking a higher level on the ladder might elect to provide education for some specific unit skills).
- Estimate the amount of time necessary to orient the PCT to the task.
- Indicate which skills should be reviewed annually.
- Indicate the format for this review, that is, skills validation or written format.

Step 10: Developing Skill Guidelines

While awaiting the return and computerization of data from the second survey, the task force turned its attention to developing skill guidelines for the PCT for unit-specific skills. Issues surfaced regarding responsibilities for educating the PCT on unit-specific skills. Again, input was solicited from the Education Subcommittee on the development of the guidelines. As brainstorming occurred, several themes emerged, including ensuring skill proficiency and documentation of that proficiency.

The committee examined unit-specific needs in terms of volume (frequency) and risk (potential injury for patient). High-risk skills performed on a high-volume basis would require an annual written exam or skills validation. Competency statements would be part of the written exam that the PCT must pass by at least 80 percent. An example of a high-risk/high-volume skill requiring an annual written exam would be arrhythmia interpretation. This exam is given to PCTs in the intensive care and telemetry units. Skills validation would require a criterion checklist. An example of a high-risk/high-volume skill requiring a criterion checklist on the step-down intensive care unit would be tracheostomy care. The PCT must meet the unit's requirements to continue employment on that unit.

Another consideration was the category of high-risk skills performed on a low-volume basis. These are skills that PCTs perform with some risk to the patient but that are performed infrequently. Further discussion centered around the need for an annual review of high-risk/low-volume skills. An example of a high-risk skill on a low-volume basis on a medical-surgical unit would be application of a cooling blanket. At the end of the fifth month, a task force member attended the unit educators' monthly meeting to discuss direction for unit-specific education. Guidelines for the PCT's skills were also shared at this meeting. Educators were asked to identify those skills on their own units that were high risk/high volume and high risk/low volume.

Because the unit educators were ultimately responsible for overseeing the orientation of the PCTs, it is easy to see how the new unit-specific skills guidelines became the "straw that broke the camel's back." Some unit educators were unclear as to how or even why these skills guidelines were needed. Other educators were struggling with how to get the PCTs oriented on their units. Perhaps a few educators had not yet accepted the planned change. Whatever the reason for the resistance, it became clear to the Education Subcommittee that additional communication needed to occur with all levels of educators prior to the start date of PACE 2000.

To resolve this communication dilemma, the Education Subcommittee planned a two-hour meeting with all nurse educators to review the education subcommittee's progress to date and to obtain feedback on the unit-specific education. In preparing for this two-hour meeting, the committee members concluded that high-risk/low-volume skills should not be performed by the PCT. This decision was based on previous experience with NAs. If the skill is not performed frequently enough, proficiency is not maintained. At the two-hour meeting, the nurse educators agreed to delete any unit skill that was identified as high risk/low volume, unless the unit educators could provide laboratory settings to make the skill high volume for the PCT.

Step 11: Evaluating Performance

Evaluation is an integral component to the entire partnership concept. The PCT evaluation is initiated with the PCT facilitator on the first day of classroom education. Evaluation continues throughout the classes via the PCT skill checklists, written homework, and a final exam. Skills are demonstrated in the laboratory setting with return demonstration by the PCT. Attainment of each skill is documented on the skill checklists. The skill checklist serves as a communication tool between the classroom education and the clinical unit.

The responsibility of the PCT evaluation is then given to the clinical nurse educator and the RN partner. Skills are revalidated in the clinical setting by the RN partner and documented on the PCT skill checklist (for an example, see Appendix 7.A). Three formats for annual proficiency are utilized and include the following:

- Skills validation involving a laboratory setting.
- Written test.
- Performance review by the PCT's RN partner.

PCTs are responsible for completing their annual written exam(s) and/or skills validation(s) in collaboration with the unit managers and educators.

A comprehensive list of unit/department-specific skills (Table 7.5) includes the following:

- The unit on which the skill could be performed
- Specific skills
- Identification of those skills that are high-risk/high-volume
- The person responsible for educating the PCT now and in the future

Table 7.5

Unit-Specific Instructional Needs—Patient Care Technician Position

Unit	Topic	Person Responsible Now	Future	Time Estimate	Periodic Continuing Education (Y, N)	Annual Proficiency P = Perf. Review S = Skills Valid W = Written
CICU *118	Remove ace wraps, paint incision with Betadine, and place ted hose		RN	30 min.	No	P
CICU 64	Obtain open heart patient supplies from old floor		RN	30 min.	No	P
CICU *66	12 Lead EKG	PNIV	PNIII,IV	2 h.	Yes	P
CICU *41	Arrhythmia class	SRN	PNII,III,IV	26 h.	Yes	W
CICU 61	Take open heart bed to O.R.	TA	RN	10 min.	No	P
CICU 63	Stock pacer, Swan cart		RN	20 min.	No	P
CICU 62	Order supplies when stock is down on various pods		RN	15 min.	No	P
CICU 44	Set-up arterial line tubing for new A line or tubing change		RN/PNIII	30 min.	Yes	P
CICU 42	Set-up pulmonary artery or CVP line tubing for new PA or tubing change		RN/PNIII	30 min.	Yes	P
CICU 56	Connect to cardiac monitor	RN	RN	15 min.	No	P
CICU 60	Set-up open heart bed	RN	RN	30 min.	No	P

*Denotes High Risk/High Volume

- Whether the skill will require periodic continuing education
- The annual review format (one or more of the three formats described above).

Evaluating PCT performance is an on-going process through the partnerships. Nurse managers, clinical nurse educators, and the RN/PCT partners are responsible for the continuing performance review.

Recommendations

Maintaining a climate of trust, support, and confidence is crucial when faced with a dramatic change (Kozier and Erb 1988). Communication is vital to the establishment of such a climate.

Despite the extensive communication plan, information did not reach everyone. As described earlier, brainstorming sessions occurred frequently at subcommittee meetings, but finalization of plans needed approval of the Analyst Committee, which took varying amounts of time. Occasionally, follow-up subcommittee meetings resulted in further revisions of previous plans. This process allowed for input from a variety of resources, but one inherent problem was that incomplete or inaccurate information also reached personnel. The heightened anxiety from this incomplete information coincided with the anxiety felt as the institution drew closer to the projected start date for PACE 2000 on the pilot units.

It is important to realize that despite extensive and thorough communication, some level of anxiety is inherent in the process. Those not actively involved in the planning and development of change need more support and a stronger link to the committee members. The committee members had established support and trust within the group. However, transferring that support and trust to peers outside the committee was not feasible due to time constraints.

Summary

When we convert problems to goals to be met, we see that often no one person has all the resources to meet the goals, yet several nurses, working in collaboration, often have more than enough. If we think of the resources to meet goals in terms of power that can be enhanced and expanded through the power of others, we have the incentive to work together to meet mutual goals. (Boyle 1990, 199)

The Education Subcommittee began by addressing the problems of the previous care delivery system, including the issues surrounding the PCT role. Through group process, road blocks and challenges were analyzed to address the educational needs of the PCT. The group also developed and implemented resolutions to meet the needs.

Advantages and disadvantages are inherent in any group process. One of the major disadvantages was that of incomplete and untimely communication. The large number of people involved and the necessity for making decisions in a short time exacerbated the problems of miscommunication. However, the collaboration that occurred in the group allowed the committee to maximize human and environmental resources. This collaboration and empowerment enabled a monumental task to be accomplished in a very short time frame.

> We are now in an era of massive changes, which can lead to a multitude of opportunities for those who are ready. It has been said that luck is the crossroads where opportunity and preparation meet. It is the time for nurses to be lucky—to achieve power and to use it productively for improvement in the delivery of health care (Sanford 1990, 403).

References

Boyle, K. 1990. "Power in Nursing: A Collaborative Approach. In *Contemporary Leadership Behavior*, edited by E. Hein and M. Nicholson, 195–99. Glenview, IL: Scott, Foresman/Little, Brown.

Costello-Nickitas, D., and D. Mason. 1992. "Power and Politics in Health Care Organizations. In *Nursing Administration*, edited by P. Decker and E. Sullivan, 45–67. Norwalk, CT: Appleton & Lange.

Kaiser Permanente. 1991. "RN Recruitment Advertisement." *American Journal of Nursing* 91 (5): 40.

Kozier, B., and G. Erb. 1988. "The Process of Change." In *Concepts and Issues in Nursing Practice*, edited by B. Kozier and G. Erb, 451–58. New York: Addison-Wesley.

Sanford, N. 1990. "Nursing Opportunity in the World of 21st Century Technology." In *Contemporary Leadership Behavior*, edited by E. Hein and M. Nicholson: 403–11. Glenview, IL: Scott, Foresman/Little, Brown.

Appendix 7.A

Miami Valley Hospital
Patient Care Technician Skills Checklist

	Lab Check Off	Unit Validation	Comments
1. Performs post mortem care	N/A		
2. Observes suicide patients and records information on appropriate records	N/A		
3. Observes and cares for patients on escape or safety precautions	N/A		
Therapeutic Procedures			
1. Obtains and records:			
a. Temperature*			
b. Pulse-Radial*			
Pulse-Apical*			
c. Respirations*			
d. Blood Pressure*			
e. Intake and Output			
f. Bed Weights*			
2. Sets up oxygen			
3. Assists patient with performance of incentive spirometry	N/A		
4. Performs blood glucose monitoring and records data appropriately*			
5. Shaves/preps/clips hair per procedure	N/A		
6. Changes drainage bottles, records and reports drainage	N/A		
7. Inserts and removes rectal tubes	N/A		
8. Inserts and removes straight and foley urinary catheters*			
9. Performs urine dipstick tests/dextrastix	N/A		

* Indicates Individual Criterion Checklist.

S = Satisfactory, U = Unsatisfactory, N/A = Not Applicable.

8

The Role and Education
of the Service Associate

Rebecca J. Czachor and Jennifer L. Eddlemon

The service associate (SA) role is the "wind beneath the wings" of the PACE 2000 patient care model and the foundation for the success of skill-mix changes. This unique role facilitates the attainment of quality patient-centered care, cost-effectiveness, and employee satisfaction. As an entry-level position, the SA role provides an opportunity for advancement into a health care career. The development of this multifunctional unit support and hospitality-focused role by the Roles Subcommittee is described in this chapter, including development and implementation.

Evolution of the Service Associate Role

Through analysis of the patient care activities list, the RN role and PCT and LPN roles were evolving simultaneously. The PCT/LPN roles were based on the assumption that they would be working within the context of a partnership with an RN and would receive comprehensive orientation, continuing education, and supervision. Because of these assumptions, the Roles Committee became comfortable with the PCT performing more invasive and complex patient care procedures. This meant that the PCT would be assuming a greater role in direct care, resulting in less time for unit support services, nutritional, clerical, and stocking activities. A need for a third category of health care worker was recognized—someone who could provide nondirect patient care tasks.

As the Roles Committee began to explore the nature of nondirect patient care services that were required, it became clear that they fell primarily into the realms of either environmental or nutrition services. The group arbitrarily identified major task categories as host/hostessing (nutrition services) and housekeeping (environmental services) and examined the needs and alternatives of each area. Representatives from both departments presented an overview of their current systems. Problems and desired outcomes were identified during brainstorming sessions.

Hosting

Meal delivery to patients was a continuous problem. Under the existing system, trays were delivered to the galley from a central kitchen where they were heated by galley personnel and delivered to the patient by an NA. Often, the patient was not prepared to eat, the overbed table was cluttered, the patient was not positioned correctly, the patient's dentures were not in, or the patient had urgent toileting needs. Many times the NA became sidetracked meeting these needs, resulting in slow, unreliable tray delivery. This caused patient complaints of cold, poor-quality food. Menus for the next day were often lost or not completed.

Patient priorities included having fresh cold water at the bedside, an opportunity to wash their hands before a meal, and eating in a clutter-free environment. The goals were to ensure that someone was available to help complete menus, follow through on questions about meals, obtain meal items, and add that extra touch like coffee before breakfast or more butter for toast.

The idea of a host/hostess position similar to the one described by Parsons (1992) was explored by the Roles Committee. The host or hostess responsibilities would revolve around meal tray delivery, food services, answering patient lights, and talking with and greeting patients. The decision was made to pilot the role.

Although employees of the Nutrition Services Department, the host/hostess would report to the unit shift manager for direction. Salaries and hours would be charged to the division of nursing. The nutrition services department was excited about implementation of this role; they were very involved in designing the job description and recruiting volunteers from their staff for a trial position. Nutrition services had long wanted some improvement in the way meals were delivered to the patient and had made similar proposals with a position pilot in past years. However, the climate for a change had not been present. Now with all departments of the hospital involved in PACE 2000, there was no reason to delay a trial period on the 34-bed Neurosciences Unit. The position was to be piloted for three months with an evaluation after six weeks and again at three months.

Five volunteers from nutrition services were selected for the trial. Their backgrounds and previous jobs varied, but candidates who were motivated, self-directed, and had strong customer relations skills were encouraged.

The five new hosts/hostesses were given a unit orientation and education related to some of the new tasks to be performed and service standards (Table 8.1). The new role was introduced to the staff of the unit as well as physicians and other hospital personnel with whom they would come in contact through staff meetings, memos, and a poster display.

Within two or three weeks after pilot implementation, the hosts were assuming many nondirect patient care tasks (meal tray delivery and filling water pitchers) and the NAs became noticeably more available

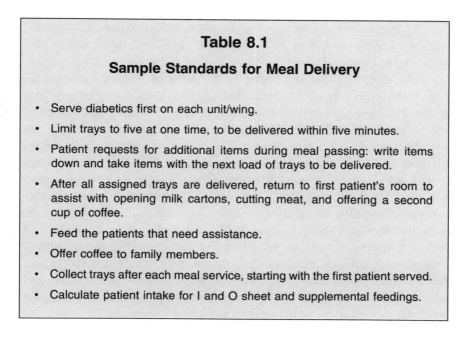

Table 8.1

Sample Standards for Meal Delivery

- Serve diabetics first on each unit/wing.
- Limit trays to five at one time, to be delivered within five minutes.
- Patient requests for additional items during meal passing: write items down and take items with the next load of trays to be delivered.
- After all assigned trays are delivered, return to first patient's room to assist with opening milk cartons, cutting meat, and offering a second cup of coffee.
- Feed the patients that need assistance.
- Offer coffee to family members.
- Collect trays after each meal service, starting with the first patient served.
- Calculate patient intake for I and O sheet and supplemental feedings.

to assist the RNs and perform direct patient-care activities. As the staff became comfortable with the new role, the skill mix was changed slightly on some shifts, increasing NA staff and decreasing an RN staff member.

Housekeeping

While the hostess trial proceeded, the Roles Committee continued to address other care delivery problems. One concern that continued to recur was the lack of cleanliness and tidiness of the units, along with a prolonged bed turnover time for admissions. The staff were frustrated that garbage cans overflowed on the off shifts and that RNs were responsible for emptying these plus doing other basic housekeeping tasks for patients.

Under the existing system, housekeepers were employed and supervised by a centralized environmental services department. Some areas were fortunate to have the same individual clean their unit on a regular basis; others were not. Poor performance was difficult to address because two diverse departments were involved, the division of nursing and the environmental services department, and their goals did not always appear to be the same. Motivation, self-direction, and pride in a particular area were not encouraged or stressed, and the job satisfaction for housekeepers seemed low. In addition, environmental services employees were adjusting to a change in management structure and were stressed.

The Roles Committee began to design a unit-based housekeeper role, identifying tasks other than cleaning that they could be involved in, for example, transport, lifting, bedmaking, restocking of supplies, first response to call lights. During the initial weeks of developing the housekeeper job description, the committee began to see overlap between the tasks of the host/hostess and the housekeeper. The concept of a multi-skilled worker, cross-trained between a host/hostess and housekeeping role, was vigorously discussed. The idea of a combined role sent tremors throughout the division of nursing and environmental and nutrition services. Rumors and anxiety abounded as the news of the possibility of such a role spread and the magnitude of the change was anticipated. Departments and individuals alike speculated as to how the role might affect them. The initial response was negative because departments and individuals felt threatened by perceived loss of familiar management structure, job security, and increased workload responsibilities.

A third job description was drafted, combining the roles of host and housekeeper, which, in fact, was later to become the role of the SA. Now three options were available for evaluation and comparison.

Option A

The first option incorporated the RN/PCT partnership roles without significant changes in the system of providing environmental and nutrition services. This option, if chosen, could allow the PCT to slide back into the NA role, and the RN would pick up NA responsibilities. This option offered the possibility of maintaining the status quo without a lasting change in the care delivery. This option would not allow implementation of the proposed system improvements.

Option B

The second option was to continue the trial of separate housekeeper and host/hostess positions. The host position would continue to have a hospitality and nutritional services focus with little environmental responsibility. Each would report to the shift manager for direction and be assigned to the same unit daily. The Nutrition Services Department would keep the employee cost center and hire, orient, and evaluate the employee. The shift manager/nurse manager would have input into the evaluation and unit-specific orientation. Nutrition Services would control staffing and scheduling.

The housekeeper position focused on unit cleanliness, bed turnover, and stocking with very little patient interaction. The reporting mechanism was envisioned to be similar to the host position with additional concerns regarding the differences in priority setting by the Division of Nursing and Environmental Services.

The trial of the host/hostess position was going well. There were many positive comments from patients, families, and physicians regarding the role. A slight change in RN/NA staffing ratios had been accomplished, and the unit clerks were noticing a decrease in patient calls. Although the host/hostess role had many advantages, it was limited. There were peaks or spurts of activity with resultant down time. An additional drawback to this option was that there would be no guarantee an oriented employee would be assigned to the unit. If the host/hostess called in sick, it was possible that nutrition services would send someone up from the dishroom or tray line.

Option B would not facilitate the goals of continuity, esprit de corps, better communication, supervision, and versatility within the role. However, this alternative seemed like a valid and safe choice for an institution undergoing so many other rapid changes.

Option C

The third option, a combined role (later the SA position) was the most radical and risky alternative. The combined housekeeping and host role would encompass aspects of nonclinical patient care, nutrition, environmental, and clerical unit support services. It was envisioned that units would require more than one SA position according to census and need.

Under the combined role, the employee's cost center would shift to the division of nursing, with the nurse manager/shift manager responsible for hiring, evaluating, orientating, and supervising. The nutrition and environmental services departments would participate in Quality Assurance/Improvement (QA/I) and orientation activities, as well as in development of policies, procedures, standards, and evaluation in their area of expertise. Staffing and scheduling would be handled by the nursing unit or nursing's staff resources department. The employee could be requested to float to a similar nursing unit from time to time, similar to an RN or PCT employee.

Nonclinical aspects of patient care performed within the combined role would be under the direction of an RN or PCT and would include such tasks as answering call lights, assisting with lifting and positioning patients, transporting, and making occupied beds with an RN or PCT. Clerical duties might include ordering supplies, entering charges into the computer, assembling charts, and running errands. A customer service philosophy would be emphasized and patient interaction encouraged.

Nutritional and hosting aspects would include preparing the patient for meals, clearing off overbed tables, meal and snack delivery, providing fresh water at bedside, stocking and rotating supplies in refrigerators, and assisting with menu completion. A large part of the job would encompass housekeeper responsibilities. Stocking, cleaning, and maintaining a tidy atmosphere in patient rooms and unit areas would be a priority.

Instituting the combined role would facilitate attainment of the goals of the PACE 2000 care system regarding cost and quality. It was anticipated that a sense of belonging brought about by integrating the employee into the unit team might result in greater pride in work, increased job satisfaction, a sense of accountability and team spirit, and increased productivity. Nurses would be in a position to prioritize the needs of patients and the unit rather than negotiating with the Environmental Services Department for services.

Valid objections and concerns from many different sources revolved around Option C (Table 8.2) The significant investment of each department and the uncertainties involved in bringing about such changes were recognized as a source of anxiety.

Table 8.2

Prominent Concerns of Service Associate Role
(Option C)

- Aesthetic perception of patient regarding the same employee mopping the bathroom, then serving their dinner tray.
- Role too fragmented; employee to drift to familiar part of job and neglect total responsibilities.
- The fit of employee on the unit from a public relations standpoint (literacy, grooming, interpersonal skills).
- Too much for one person; unit would not be given enough help. Unrealistic expectations.
- No one will apply.
- Nurse manager/shift manager may not welcome increased responsibilities.
- Role will adversely affect patient safety.
- Compliance with hospital and regulatory standards.
- Cost-effectiveness; increase in cost of management and training; increase in number of employees.
- Worker not self-directed, may require inordinate amount of supervision from the RN staff.
- Hospital culture not ready for such change; timing not right.
- Shift in cost centers; overall financial impact.
- Potential loss of positions in environmental and nutrition services departments.
- Daily staffing, human resources, and development issues.

A Decision

The pros and cons of separate versus combined job descriptions were presented to the PACE 2000 Steering Committee and the Analyst Committee for input and discussion. Meetings were held between the hospital vice presidents, department directors, and the cochairs of the Roles Subcommittee to discuss possibilities.

It was decided that the combined role was just too exciting and the possibilities (if a trial was a success), too good to pass up. The combined role (Option C) was approved for a trial with the following recommendations:

- Individuals performing the combined role would be called SAs.
- The SA would receive formal orientation and basic life-support training.
- The SA would be expected to dress in the same manner as other members of their nursing unit and to maintain a professional appearance.
- The SA would be clearly identified with a hospital identification badge and a bright yellow name tag.
- A profile of the unit (including such factors as the patient population, daily census, and acuity), would be evaluated to ensure that enough SAs were staffed for a reasonable workload.
- The SA would receive wages on a pay grade above the Environmental Services role, as value was placed on patient interaction and interpersonal skills.
- The SA would possess the minimum qualifications of a high school diploma (or equivalent) and receive standardized pre-employment screening for communication and interpersonal skills by the HRD.

Role Implementation

Orientation

The next major task was to design an orientation course that would share the philosophy of patient and family-centered care and prepare the SAs for their new roles. It was to be fast-paced, interesting, and concise with opportunity for skills practice. The newly acquired skills and information would be validated by return demonstration or explanation, utilizing a checklist format. Reading assignments and written exams were to be avoided. There were no SA role models currently within the system to act as preceptors.

Utilizing the talents and expertise of a multidisciplinary team, a curriculum was developed that spans six days, including both didactic and practical teaching methods (Table 8.3). It is important for SAs to understand the background or history of their role, as well as the goals of the new care model and the roles of the other care providers with whom they work. A brief introduction to clarify the SA role occurs at the beginning of orientation.

Patient relations, interpersonal skills, team work, conflict management, and the service philosophy are taught in a joint presentation to the SA and PCT orientees using role playing, a play, and videos. Confidentiality, telephone standards, and customer relation skills are presented by the consumer relations department.

It is mandatory for the SA to have a basic understanding of the concepts of infection control and universal precautions, along with germ theory, host defenses, and chain of infection. This portion is taught by infection control nurse clinicians.

A large part of the orientation is taught by environmental services, covering such topics as waste management, basic cleaning, preparing and diluting chemicals, safety on the job, hazardous materials, and recycling within the hospital. The SA learns to add special touches to a clean room to give it a welcoming ambiance, such as one would find in a fine hotel, during a special learning session called *the final touch*.

The nutrition services department presents information on tray preparation and presentation, food handling, types of diets and restrictions the SA may encounter (e.g., low sodium, diabetic snack). In this class, SAs learn how to record intake from patient trays, complete menus, and obtain nourishments when the galley is closed.

Because of the lifting, pushing, bending, pulling, and reaching a SA will do while on the job, a physical therapist was recruited to instruct the SAs in proper body mechanics. This class also provides the opportunity to demonstrate wheelchair and cart transport safety.

One of the areas SAs are most apprehensive about is their interaction with patients. SAs are taught how to position, ambulate, and assist with making occupied beds. Role playing is used to discuss how to answer a call light. They are taught what hospital emergencies they may

Table 8.3

Service Associate Orientation

Day 1	Place	Topic	Method
8:00–10:00		Intro to orientation Patient care model PACE 2000, teamwork Why start this role?	Discussion
10:00–10:15		Break	
10:15–11:45	Merge with PCTs for this session.	Intro to health care Patient perspective of care Communication tech.	Lecture Demonstration Role playing
		Lunch	
1215–1:45	Merge with PCTS.	Confidentiality Patient Bill of Rights	Video
1:45–2:00		Break	
2:00–4:30		Clinical preceptorship assignment with experienced SA	Direct observation
Day 2	**Place**	**Topic**	**Method**
8:00–1:30	Per assignment	Clinical preceptorship assignment with experienced SA	Direct observation
1:30–1:45		Break	
1:45–4:30		Chain of infection Disinfectant Clean technique Universal precautions Disease specific isolation Precautions OSHA/JCAHO Who? What? Where? When? Why? Basic host defenses Basic hygiene and sanitation Evaluation	Lecture Demonstration Overhead Video Game, quiz Audience Participation Case studies Group Discussion

Continued

Table 8.3 Continued

Day 3	Place	Topic	Method
8:00–11:00		Environmental servs. • Waste management • Recycling • Cleaning of rooms • MSDS stress • Safety • Chemicals and dilution • Clean room demo (includes break)	Lecture Demonstration Role playing Video Audience
11:00–11:30		Lunch	
11:30–12:15	3SW	Final touch demo	
a. 12:15–1:45 b. 1:45–3:15	3SW 3SW	Final touch practice Final touch practice	

a. 12:15–1:45
 	
b. 1:45–3:15
	Comp. room
	
	Comp. room
		Computer class and
		  Alphabet soup
		Computer class and
		  Alphabet soup
			Demonstration
			Lecture/video

3:15–3:30		Break	
3:30–4:30		Conflict management Receiving delegation Body language	
Day 4	**Place**	**Topic**	**Method**
8:00–10:30		Hostessing Nutrition services	Lecture Demonstration Role playing Audience participation
10:30–10:45		Break	
10:45–12:45	Skills lab	Body mechanics	Demonstration Slide show
12:45–1:30		Lunch	
1:30–4:30	Skills lab	Assisting with Pt Care and safety Reinforcement/review of SA role	Lecture Demonstration

Continued

Table 8.3 Continued			
Day 5	**Place**	**Topic**	**Method**
Based on preceptor schedule	Per assigned preceptor unit	Clinical preceptorship assignment with environmental SA	Direct observation and practice
Day 6			
1st day of unit orientation			

encounter and how they are to respond. The SAs are given scenarios (e.g., What do you do if you find a patient smoking in bed?) to help them recognize appropriate actions.

Finally, the SA needs information regarding the communication systems within the hospital, that is, how to use the intercom, beeper and paging systems, the pneumatic tubes, telephones, and computers. A unit clerk presents a session geared to these learning needs.

The SAs need orientation specific to their unit and patient population. The SA in the labor and delivery area encounters very different patients and unit needs than a SA on a step-down telemetry unit. The unit implementation teams and educators from each area developed handouts, including information on types of patients and the services of each unit, a unit map, and explanation of roles specific to the unit assigned.

Human Resources Issues

After the orientation process was in place, the next issues addressed related to human resources and implementation issues. Cochairs of the Roles Committee and nurse managers of units ready to implement the new care delivery system joined the Human Resources Committee to address these issues.

Because SAs would be replacing housekeepers, a plan was developed for handling current employees. The plan assessed the needs of environmental services, the hosts who had been involved in the trial, and current division of nursing NAs who did not wish to become PCTs. A flowchart to guide the filling of positions was developed (Figure 8.1).

Figure 8.1

Posting of SA Positions

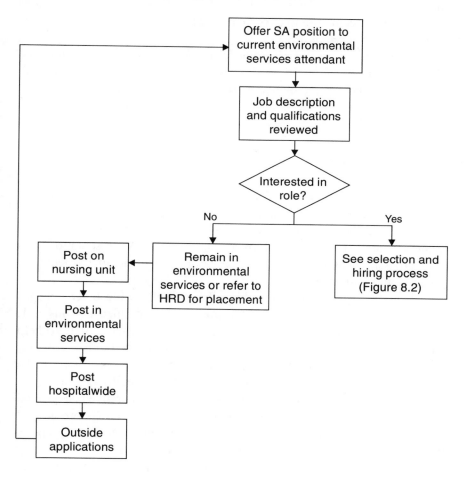

It was decided that if a unit had a regular housekeeper(s), house-keepers would have first choice for the SA positions available on their unit if they met the qualifications. The position would then be posted on the unit for other unit personnel to apply (unit NAs or hosts). Next positions would be posted hospitalwide, and then open to outside applicants (Figure 8.1).

It is important that the SA possesses reading and writing skills. The HRD utilizes a pre-employment screening tool to screen current employees wishing to assume SA roles. Basic knowledge related to reading, math, and customer service are also assessed. If a current employee does not pass the screening, an action plan is developed to help them achieve their goal of becoming a SA.

Nurse managers were provided guidelines for interviewing and hiring candidates (Figure 8.2). A dress code for the SA was approved. On the unit where personnel wear scrub suits, the SAs also wear scrub suits. On other units, the SAs wear white knit short-sleeved shirts and dark blue pants.

Communications

Communication between the Roles Committee, Analyst Committee, and PACE 2000 Steering Committee was ongoing, but it was necessary to make sure the unit nurse managers understood the role, as well as managers and supervisors all over the hospital. A presentation was planned with detailed information regarding the role, the orientation process, and human resources issues.

Units ready to implement this role, as well as the other changes underway (i.e., new RN/PCT partnership) were identified as Cluster 1. Education and handouts were developed for the Cluster 1 units to help them prepare for the changes. Each unit was encouraged to involve their unit nursing council or to develop an implementation task force in the education of all staff and planning. Members of the Roles Committee volunteered to go to unit meetings to discuss concerns or give background information on the changes. Monthly informational meetings brought all the units implementing the new care delivery system together, and reports from all the committees were offered during these sessions.

The underlying concerns at all these meetings related to the SA role. There were many questions about how successful the role would be: Would it make up for the RN/PCT skill-mix changes that were planned? Would the patients accept the role? Would anyone want to perform the role? Until the role was pilot tested for a time, the answers would be unclear. The uncertainties were unsettling for some. However, the Roles Committee really believed in the SA concept and their intuition was that the plan would succeed.

Figure 8.2

Flowchart of SA Selection and Hiring Process

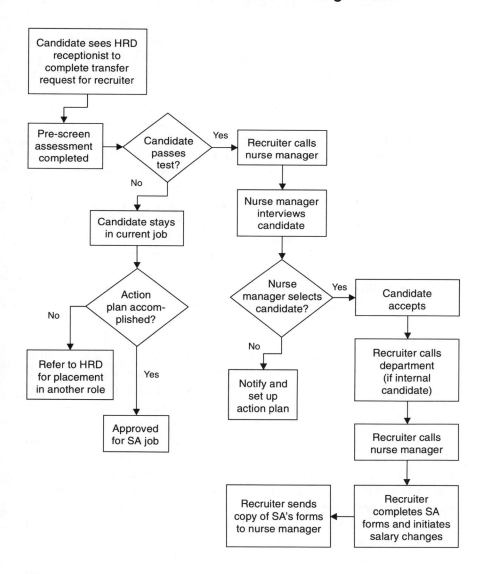

Trialing the Concept

The Neuroscience Unit was chosen as the trial unit because they had trialed the host role and had made some skill-mix changes. They also had a very strong unit council and participatory management environment.

The RNs and PCTs signed up for the preparatory classes designed by the Education Committee to cover the new SA job descriptions, delegation, and role conflict. The first group attended classes during the months of June and July 1992.

The unit was close to the target skill mix identified during the OE process with RNs and needed only to hire a few additional PCTs. Many of the RN/PCT partnerships were being formed and were already scheduled to work together. The entire staff was well informed about the role of the SA. The unit implementation team had developed a unit orientation for the SA personnel. The hours the SAs should work were also decided, that is, 6:30 a.m.–3:30 p.m., 3:00–11:00 p.m., and 10:30 p.m.–7:00 a.m.

The first SA class was held 11 August 1992. Eight people from varying backgrounds were employed for the SA role on the neurosciences unit. Four positions, three full-time and one part-time, were filled by environmental services department employees; one full-time and one part-time position were filled by nutrition services employees (one was a previous trial hostess); two part-time positions were filled from outside the hospital. Part-time positions were difficult to fill from within the hospital, and this was to become a challenge for units in the future.

The classes went smoothly. The new SAs were very excited, a little nervous, and apprehensive about their new roles. They were welcomed onto the unit and received unit orientation from the educator, staff nurses, PCTs, unit clerks, and manager. Because they were the first SAs, they developed their routine themselves while operationalizing the role.

Within a week, there were noticeable positive changes: the unit and patient rooms appeared noticeably cleaner and more tidy, corridors were kept clear, and food was delivered more promptly. Patients were voicing satisfaction with the extra touches, such as a warm wash cloth prior to meals and refreshment rounds. Other units (i.e., ICU and Emergency and Trauma Center) did not have to wait as long for beds to be turned around after a patient was discharged.

The nurses on the unit noted that equipment was cleaned and returned to storage appropriately, stock levels were maintained, and rooms for admissions contained all the necessary equipment (i.e., suction equipment, airway, and admission pack). The number of patient call lights declined, which meant patient needs were being met before patients had to ask. There was also more help available for lifting patients and for transfers to other units. The unit clerks experienced the benefits of having Central Service records maintained daily, coverage at the desk for lunch and meetings, and a decrease in call lights.

A month following their orientation, the SAs met with members of the unit implementation team to fine-tune the role and discuss any problems. (These focus groups, as well as staff meetings, have continued.) The meetings have identified a number of concerns/problems or educational needs that the unit has been able to handle. The unit also offers feedback to other units as they implement SAs. Communication, teamwork, and integration into the division of nursing continue to be the areas of fundamental importance to the success of the role and the PACE 2000 changes.

Progress and Evaluation

The orientation process for SA orientation has been modified based on feedback from SA evaluations and observations by the education department. The original SAs worked alone during their clinical orientation, with no experienced SA available to show them the ropes. New SAs now have the benefit of spending two days with a seasoned SA in the role during orientation and then have two days to practice.

Day 1 was reorganized, the SA and PCT groups were merged for customer relations, patient rights, and teamwork class content to make efficient use of instructors' time and conserve costs. Day 3 was changed slightly based on SA feedback that smaller class size during Final Touch Practice was more beneficial.

Because the SA role is so new and much of the information unfamiliar, nurse managers and unit educators are encouraged to attend the environmental and nonclinical patient care portions of orientation. This helped solve the problem of the SAs being taught one way in class and then meeting different expectations once on the unit.

The Roles Committee disbanded in September 1992, upon completion of their objectives. The evaluation of the SA role was then assumed by the Analyst Committee. The cochairs of the Roles Committee have begun the process of transferring the education program for SAs to the Division of Nursing's Center for nursing excellence (education and training department). In six months, 75 SAs were trained for eight units. Units have from one to three SAs per shift depending on workload.

Guest speakers for the SA program are asked to continue their commitment in the future. Potential speakers (including outstanding SAs) are encouraged and developed to expand the pool of available resources.

Purchasing and storage of environmental supplies is an area that will need to be investigated in the future. Other issues to be clarified include the respective responsibilities of environmental services and nursing units for budgeting of cleaning agents, paper towels, and toilet paper; also dry cleaning of curtains and drapes, as well as managing the replacement of housekeeping costs and utensils. The possibility of a hospitality service department, where SA personnel are managed from a central department and contracted to work on particular units, has also been discussed.

A particular area of concern for nursing management has been the inclusion of ancillary staff in nursing department budgets and hours per patient day (HPD) reports. For this reason, financial reports separate RN, PCT, and unit clerk hours from SA hours. Also the increased fiscal component to the units as census fluctuates increases stress on the unit budgets. Another consideration is the possible increase in management time related to working with an increased number of nonprofessional staff.

A process for evaluation of the critical aspects of the SA role, as well as its impact on MVH, was developed by the Analyst Committee and is ongoing. The effect of the SA role on facets of RN job satisfaction is also being examined. The process includes a comparative interpretation of a nursing satisfaction survey, the nurse work characteristics excitement tool (discussed in Chapter 12) and a questionnaire regarding new roles for both PCTs and SAs, distributed at intervals prior to and during the implementation process.

In March 1993, twelve shift managers/nurse managers on units implementing the SA role were surveyed with a questionnaire. The return rate was 100 percent. The survey asked if they believed the SA was integrated into the patient care team. Seventy-five percent responded "yes," 25 percent indicated "somewhat," and zero percent said "no." Eighty-four percent said that supplies were more readily available at the bedside, and 16 percent said sometimes. All respondents indicated increased satisfaction in aspects of care now performed by SAs compared to before implementation of the role. A Likert scale was used with 5 representing strong agreement and 1 representing strong disagreement.

Comments solicited on the survey indicated merit for the role, but a need for greater understanding, utilization, and integration into the units over time.

Shift managers and nurse managers were asked to indicate the amount of time the SA spends performing different activities. Of special interest were the differences in utilization of SAs according to unit-specific needs. It was noted that on the obstetric units, the bulk of the SA's time was spent stocking supplies and setting up special procedure trays. Medical-surgical units utilized their SAs mostly for environmental and nutritional aspects. Flexibility and versatility of this role is what makes it work.

The SAs are also being surveyed periodically. In March 1993, five SAs completed a questionnaire revealing that while they enjoyed the direct patient care and contact aspects, less of their time was spent in these activities. Environmental aspects consumed the largest part of their time, followed by nutritional aspects, stocking/supplies, and patient care. Job satisfaction was apparent in their comments on the survey and in their response to questions. SAs believed they were important and were making a difference. All indicated they enjoy being on the patient care team.

Unit-specific and hospitalwide patient satisfaction surveys indicate an upward trend in satisfaction with care, although high marks were received in this area prior to implementation of PACE 2000. The nutrition services department has developed SA performance standards and monitors tray delivery and food handling. Patients were surveyed by the nutrition services department in October 1992, just a few weeks after the initiation of the SA role on one unit. The responses of 79 patients surveyed at random on units without SAs were compared with 40 patients surveyed on the first unit with SAs. There was no difference in menu selection or food preparation between these areas. However, the surveys showed a trend of more positive feelings about food services on the unit with SAs (Table 8.4).

Environmental services also developed standards for SA performance. Periodic spot checks are completed by the environmental services supervisor in conjunction with the shift/nurse managers to monitor unit/patient room cleanliness (Appendix 8.A). A periodic room cleaning checklist (Appendix 8.B) was also developed to monitor frequency of more in-depth cleaning activities by environmental services. This list is kept in a discreet area of the patient's room. The SA notifies

Table 8.4

Service Associate Comparison Evaluation
from Inpatient Surveys—October 1992

	October 1992 Random Survey (70 Patients)	October 1992 4W/SW (40 Patients)	4W/SW
Overall	4.2	4.4	+ .2
Temperature	4.2	4.4	+ .2
Taste	3.9	4.1	+ .2
Attractive	4.4	4.6	+ .2
Menu choices	4.1	4.5	+ .4
Received all items	4.5	4.7	+ .2
Timeliness	4.5	4.5	—

Scale of 1–5 (5 being the highest)

Conclusions

- Surveys show a trend of more positive feelings about food service.

- Priorities related to tray passing seem to vary by area and by individuals. When it is a problem, it seems to relate to tray stands not being cleared and ready for trays. Also a concern is return of dirty trays.

- Areas that seem to do best consider the Patient Food Service Assistant as a member of the team.

- Some problems (Nutrition Services) initially related to time of tray service to 4W/SW due to Patient Food Service Assistant serving 4NW first. Temporarily resolved (except for two instances) by using team leaders and supervisors to start. Investigating a long-term solution (Nutrition Services).

Recommendations

- Continue to provide direction/reinforcement to the SA on their role/responsibilities.

- Develop a long-term solution (4W/SW) to resolve issues related to time tray service begins (Nutrition Services).

- Provide opportunities for Patient Food Service Assistant to interact with patient care team.

environmental services when the room is empty and when heavy cleaning activities are needed. This facilitates completion of more intensive activities when patients are not in the room, thus decreasing health hazards and inconvenience to patient while allowing the room to be thoroughly cleaned at regular intervals.

SA turnover rates are being monitored as well as advancement into the PCT or other roles. Within a six-month period, four SAs have become PCTs.

Recommendations and Practical Suggestions

In retrospect, there are a few things that would have been done differently. There would be a focus on the leadership of the unit, making sure they understand the role, job description, and rationale for the basic concept of the role. There would be a greater effort to have the unit council and unit leadership embrace the role in its pure form. There was a tendency of units to alter the role, to increase or decrease functions. This has led to role confusion, inefficiency, and difficulties in skill mix changes.

Nurse Managers were placed in an awkward position of having to hire employees into the SA role from other departments who were not an appropriate fit for the unit. This put increased burden on the shift manager to deal with work ethic and performance issues.

We believe there would be greater benefit and greater skill-mix changes made if all units could have a trial period. Nurse Managers and unit councils could be encouraged to be adventurous or daring with their initial projections.

Finally the Role Subcommittee may have disbanded too early. It could have taken a more active role in all unit implementation and ongoing evaluation. Perhaps units could have presented their unit-specific implementation plans to the Role Subcommittee for feedback and troubleshooting strategies.

Summary

Despite the risk involved in the implementation of the SA role, the role has been very successful. The SA role has enabled skill mix changes to occur, contributed to increased patient/family satisfaction with the environment and meals, and decreased delays related to bed turnaround time. The SA role also provides an avenue for many career opportunities within the health care industry.

It remains to be seen whether the needs of all nursing units are met by this new type of personnel. An ongoing review of the role and its utilization by the units is vital to maximize optimal staff functioning and delivery of patient care. With high competition and service orientation, it may ultimately be the SA who makes the biggest difference to the survival and success of a hospital.

Florence Nightingale observed in her *Notes on Nursing* (1918, 8):

> For the first time, it was brought to my attention of those caring for the sick that their responsibilities covered not only the administration of medicines and the application of poultices, but the proper use of fresh air, light, warmth, cleanliness, quiet, and the proper selections and administration of diet.

The concept of the SA role has married cost-effectiveness and quality by freeing the RN and PCT to again focus on the basic care needs while continuing to meet physiological patient needs.

References

Nightingale, F. 1918. *Notes on Nursing: What It Is and What It Is Not.* (Original work published 1860.) New York: Appleton.

Parsons, H. 1992. "Southern Hospitality." *Food Management* 3: 116–24.

Appendix 8.A

Service Associate Room Cleaning Evaluation

Unit _____   Nurse Manager _____

Room Number _____   Evaluator _____

Date _____   Time _____

Check Points	S	U	Comments
Restroom			
Soap dispenser			
Paper towel dispenser			
Toilet paper dispenser			
Faucets			
Sink			
Toilet			
Hand rails			
Counter			
Mirror			
Shower curtain			
Shower stall			
Bathtub			
Urinal Rack			
Window(s)			
Inside of window			
Window frame			
Window covering			
Storage Units			
Outside of closets			
Inside of closets			
Outside of drawers			
Inside of drawers			
Appliances			
Clock			
Lamp(s)			
Television			
Television arm			

Check Points	S	U	Comments
Microwave			
Stereo			
Furniture			
Bed			
Chairs			
Bedside table			
Bed table			
Table(s)			
Desk			
Sofa			
Other			
Radiator			
Telephone			
Head wall unit			
Bed bumper guard			
IV holder			
Blood pressure monitor			
Baseboards			
Walls			
Floor			
Cubicles			
Call lights			

S = Satisfactory, U = Unsatisfactory.

White copy: Evaluator

Yellow copy: Nurse/Shift manager

Pink copy: Environmental services director

Gold copy: PACE 2000 project leaders

Appendix 8.B

Service Associate Periodic Room
Cleaning Checklist/Sign-Off Sheet

Room Number _____

Task		**Date**	**Sign**	**Date**	**Sign**
Baseboards:	Scrubbed main part of room				
Carpet:	Shampooed				
Ceiling:	Washed				
Cubicles:	Replaced with clean set				
Doors:	Washed entire surface				
Drapes:	Replaced with clean set				
Floor:	Buffed Side A				
	Buffed Side B				
	Buffed entire room				
	Stripped and waxed				
	Shower scrubbed				
Lamp Shades:	Damp wiped/vacuumed				
Light Fixtures:	Cleaned				
Furniture:	Cleaned				
Vents:	Vacuumed				
Walls:	Washed				

This form is to be posted on the back of each patient-room door.

9

The Process of Changing Documentation

Robin G. Bashore, Mary E. Benson-Landau, and John K. Wiley

Failure to distinguish between facts and politics can doom an important change to failure.

—Costello-Nikitas and Mason 1992

This chapter describes the process of revising patient documentation at MVH. Discussion includes Documentation Subcommittee structure and processes, environmental analysis, development of the plan, identification of related issues, evaluation of the project's success, and results.

Documentation Subcommittee Structure and Processes

Getting Started

The Documentation Subcommittee was a subgroup of the Patient Care Model Committee. The subcommittee's goal was to evaluate, revise, and monitor the documentation system to ensure effectiveness and efficiency. The nurse leaders of the Documentation Subcommittee had a broader agenda—to revolutionize patient documentation. The subcommittee set out to examine all possibilities.

Subcommittee Structure

The Documentation Subcommittee was cochaired by two nurses identified by administration; one with a critical care and staff development background, the other, a perinatal background. Additionally, one physician (a neurosurgeon) served in a consultant role with the cochairs and as a liaison to other physicians.

Documentation issues were divided functionally into those affecting perinatal patients only, those affecting main hospital patients only, and issues affecting both groups. The group handling problems not associated with perinatal soon became known as the *Main House* Group, while the perinatal group was referred to as the *Berry* Group, which is the name of the perinatal facility (Figure 9.1).

Each committee and subcommittee's membership was composed of a cross-section of hospital staff, including physicians, staff nurses, nurse educators, clinical specialists, social workers, unit secretaries, and management system engineers. Managers were asked to make recommendations for membership to the committee. Four weeks into the process, a representative from a local business forms corporation was added. Twenty-three members in the Main House Group and ten persons on the Berry Group were involved in the project for about two years.

Figure 9.1

Relationship of Documentation Groups to Larger Model

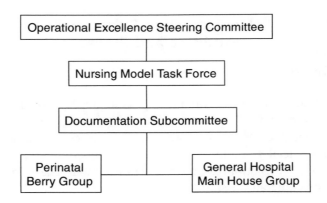

Committee Processes

OE suggestion boxes were placed throughout the hospital. The boxes yielded great numbers of suggestions, including complaints, ideas, and comments. An OE analyst routed a list of relevant suggestions to each of the cochairs on a regular basis. As each suggestion was reviewed by the subcommittee, it was quickly evident that the issues focused around common themes: nursing notes, automation, laboratory reporting, forms, process problems, care plans, and miscellaneous.

The Main House and Berry Groups met separately and jointly each week. The groups discussed the feasibility of suggestions and brain-stormed solutions.

Simultaneously, the groups also tried to identify every document that was used in the patient record. Each form's data, redundancy, use, and value was identified. After group discussion and screening, the most promising OE suggestions were assigned to individual members for investigation and financial analysis. Group members were also required to identify the customers (users) of the form or data in question, estimate the impact on customers if a change in a form was made, and project the risks associated with revisions. After developing this information, individuals reported back to the group. Each group recommended or rejected a suggestion. The chair then reported the decision back to an analyst and provided supporting data. The OE analyst assumed responsibility for responding to each original submitter of an OE suggestion and explaining the group's decision.

The best suggestions, which progressed through investigation and group review, were taken to both the OE analyst and steering committees for presentation by one of the cochairs. If approved by both committees, the group began planning for changes (Table 9.1).

Environmental Analysis

The literature shows that considerable thought has been given to ways to capture patient care information (Campbell and Dowd 1993; Rosenthal 1992; Knapp-Spooner and Brett 1992; Fondemiller 1991; Lucaterto et al. 1991; Thomas 1992). At MVH, multiple issues emerged:

1. Data were often duplicated many places within the same chart.
2. Expensive proprietary prenatal and inpatient forms were being used in obstetrics.

Table 9.1

Documentation Process Landmarks

1991
November: First meetings
December: Main House and Perinatal Committees linked

1992
January: Problems investigated
                                   Literature reviewed
                                   Timeline developed
                                   Time studies began
                                   Customers identified
                                   Proposal developed
                                   Financial impact estimated
                                   Evaluation criteria formulated
                                   External advisor added

February: Prototypes developed
                                   Coalition building began

March/April: Samples circulated
                                   Directions for use drafted
                                   Implementation plan developed
                                   Customer strategies identified

June: Multidisciplinary approvals obtained
                                   Communication plan implemented
                                   Computerized charting gained momentum
                                   Link created to Case Management group

July/August: Staggered implementation began

October: Link created to computer charting group
                                   Problems arise with trending data
                                   Audits reveal improved documentation

November: Opinion surveys circulated
                                   Meeting to solve trending problems

1993
February: Trend analysis sheet trialed

July: Follow-up surveys conducted

August: Time studies and audits repeated

September: Electronic charting proposed

3. Low levels of compliance and satisfaction were evident with the present computerized patient care planning system.

4. Individual units had pursued independent solutions to their documentation problems, resulting in a variety of systems and forms.

5. The patient's chart had become fragmented, with parts of it being kept at different locations.

6. A majority of nurses believed more writing meant higher quality charting.

7. There was widespread misunderstanding of documentation principles and liability.

8. Physicians generally did not read or value the nursing record, except vital signs and intake/output charts.

9. Trending data over time was difficult.

10. Neither nursing nor other disciplines were satisfied with the quality of patient information.

11. The current automated admit/discharge/transfer system was neither time-efficient nor cost-effective. Order entry, although computerized, could take as many as 19 separate steps.

12. Unit secretaries' time was used trying to trace illegible physician signatures.

13. The existing system wasted large amounts of paper.

14. Commercially available technology was not being utilized institutionally to support documentation.

15. Finally, and perhaps a driving force for many of the preceding problems, documentation often did not occur at the point of care.

Time studies were conducted by the Main House and Berry Groups to measure current documentation demands. Results indicated that medical-surgical nurses spent an average of 71 minutes per shift documenting, or 18 minutes per nurse per patient. For critical care nurses, the average time was 27 minutes per patient. The average documentation time was 32.5 minutes in maternity per nurse per mother and baby couplet, and 33 minutes per patient for an initial prenatal visit.

Analysis of the existing environment concluded with a retrospective review of how preceding changes in the patient record had been received. The graphic record, used for vital signs and intake/output housewide, had previously been revised. The new version met with great physician resistance and was abandoned within one day. Similarly, there was an attempt to replace the standard proprietary perinatal admission assessment form. The form contained colored fields, which made information easy to find. The proposed revision initially did not include color because of cost. After trying for two years to get the form accepted, addition of a color bar at the bottom edge finally led to the form's adoption.

Practitioners at MVH had historically resisted documentation changes that changed their practice. In the current situation, however, several critical differences were present. First, physicians were involved in the proposed changes at every level, from conceptualization to implementation. Second, physicians who were respected as formal or informal leaders served in leadership roles. Third, the institution made a visible commitment to the changes. Fourth, physicians saw changes as probably leading to easier access to data. Fifth and most significantly, the system of health care in America was poised for change. It was evident to all health care providers, and especially physicians, that a change in how hospitals do things was inevitable.

MVH's decision to be proactive rather than reactive with respect to shrinking health care dollars empowered the committees to a degree unheard of in previous endeavors. With that support in place, the groups proceeded to identify and prioritize changes needed.

Development of the Plan

The committee began to realize the processes involved were multifaceted and complex. In the time frame demanded by OE, some changes were idealistic and impossible to complete. Eventually, a three-stage proposal was developed, outlining the implementation of flow sheets, adoption of charting by exception, and implementation of computerized bedside charting (Exhibit 9.1).

Stage 1: Flow Sheets

The highest priority was given to the problem of fragmented patient information. Separate sheets in different locations contained intake/output, vital signs, parenteral fluids, admission assessment data, and nurses' notes. The goal was to consolidate information and reduce nursing documentation time by 25 percent through the use of comprehensive flow sheets.

Exhibit 9.1

Documentation Proposal

Three-Stage Solution

Stage 1
Streamline nursing documentation across similar areas by creating simplified flow sheets and reducing redundancy. This will be pursued in mother/baby nursing, medical-surgical, and critical care. Target date: 1 June 1992.

Stage 2
Move as an institution to CBE. This system consists of flow sheets with clearly defined norms, references to standards of nursing care, and charting at the bedside. In CBE, the nurse is required to record only deviations from the norm, rather than duplicating normal or unremarkable data time after time (Burke and Murphy 1988). Target date: March 1993.

Stage 3
After CBE on paper is solidified, move to documentation via bedside terminals. Advantages include decreased overtime, reduction in documentation time, fewer transcription errors, increased QA/QI compliance, decreased lost charges, and decreased forms expense (Fournier 1992; Thomas 1992). Target date: 1995–1996.

The Main House Group drafted a generic flow sheet that combined intake and output, vital signs, parenteral fluids, assessment data and nurses' notes. The Berry Group used a similar template, but substituted parameters of antepartum, intrapartum, postpartum or newborn assessment. A trifold form was developed to capture information common to all nursing areas in the hospital. Telemetry, critical care, and advanced care/neuro units, however, were each creating different layouts for the same information. The physician representative provided valuable input into content and layout for the form that would best facilitate physician usage. Each time the drafts were updated, they were presented to the Patient Care Model Committee, which included interdisciplinary users. Portions of the latest versions are included in Appendixes 9.A–9.E.

Recycled paper was considered as a positive environmental effort but rejected due to a 10 percent increase in the cost of forms. However, all flow sheets were constructed using recyclable papers and inks.

The subcommittee continued to design, revise, and obtain feedback about the forms while concurrently pursuing buy-off from multiple users. Before ideas moved forward, they were reviewed by the consumer groups who would be most affected by the change (Table 9.2). Consent was obtained before work proceeded. By obtaining buy-off in this manner, it was hoped to instill a sense of ownership of the changes within the affected groups. Many excellent ideas for improving the forms were also obtained during the buy-off process. The hospital had a large and diverse group of physicians who would be affected by the documentation changes. The task force chairs were asked to ensure that physicians understood the components and impact of the documentation changes by intensifying the one-on-one buy-off interactions.

Task force members from the Main House and Berry Groups worked diligently to seek physician support. Appointments were made to meet with physicians in their offices, or on the nursing units, to go over samples of the new forms. The intent of these one-on-one sessions was not to educate the physicians in the use of the forms, but to make them aware that a major change was about to occur.

The organization's cultural indicators (image, status, symbols, rituals, sacred cows, environment, communication, management, and generally any accepted way of behaving) were clearly being challenged by proposed changes (Comstock and Moff 1991). The potential for difficulties was high. It was understood that staff would have a tendency to resist documentation changes when they correctly sensed their cultural assumptions were being threatened (Conger and Kanungo 1988).

Table 9.2

Customers to Consider in Implementation

- Nursing staff
- Physician staff
- Administration
- Information systems
- Unit secretaries
- Risk management
- Utilization review
- Finance
- Medical records

The committee believed that before communicating the changes to others, it needed to identify the impact of these changes on the organization. Cultural adjustments would need to be considered and conveyed to the organization. Potential strengths of the proposed documentation changes included the following:

- More visibility of trends since nurses and physicians would get a snapshot of the patient's status from viewing the flow sheet
- More complete charting and fewer denied charges from third party payers
- Provision of a bridge to the electronic patient record
- A potential to decrease liability by including cues for charting

Vulnerabilities of the changes included several areas, which are as follows:

- Users would require a period of adjustment
- Practice patterns of both physicians and nurses would be affected
- Key patient information would be on the flow sheet at the bedside instead of a nursing station

Several of the nursing areas were using forms specific to their patient populations. The proposed documentation changes required these areas to obtain a design that would serve the whole, not an easy task when all believe their own information is the most important. Some areas on the form required specificity for the medical-surgical, critical care, advanced care, and obstetrical units.

The communication plan for nurses focused on informing, involving, and updating the nursing staff about each draft of the form. Samples were circulated on the units, and the unit-based subcommittee members would report feedback to the full subcommittee. Progress on the new flow sheets was reported in the hospital's newsletters. Strategies and guidelines for use of the flow sheets were developed in each nursing unit. The educational time frame for each unit was planned in relation to the implementation date of their form.

Before the forms were distributed for hospitalwide feedback, the cochairs sought approval from several key hospital committees. These included the OE Steering Committee (composed of physician and administration leaders), the Medical Records Committee, the Medical Staff Executive Committee, and the Hospital Policy Committee (composed of the CEO, CFO, COO, and CNO). After approval from these committees, the project proceeded.

The physician communication plan included attendance of sub-committee members at each department/section meeting. Not only was feedback solicited, but physicians were informed of the strengths and vulnerabilities of the documentation changes. One-on-one meetings with key physicians were held to clarify concerns. Finally, a massive mailing of the sample forms to frequent admitters was planned just prior to the go-live dates. Documentation committee members wore neon-colored buttons, so that all users would know whom to contact for assistance about the new forms.

There was communication of the changes to other departments (e.g., Nutrition Services and Pastoral Care Services), although not as aggressively as with the physicians and nurses. The involvement of the forms representative influenced the support of the changes by purchasing, storeroom, and medical records, enabling the process to move forward more smoothly.

Although the OE process ended after six months, the Documentation Subcommittee continued working to meet the short implementation timeline. The subcommittee chairs met with the Hospital Policy Committee to obtain final approval for the implementation timeline (Table 9.1).

Massive changes in the organization had been occurring almost immediately with the inception of the OE process. No area had been unaffected. Procedural and material changes had occurred, but more important, human resources had been affected in many departments in one way or another.

The Hospital Policy Committee requested the task force chairs slow down implementation of the forms to allow the organization time to assimilate the changes. In general, even though change may be intended to achieve better ways of doing or managing situations, it *always* requires a transformation of the existing status. The acknowledgement of what used to be must be honored. Individuals need time to validate that a change or loss has occurred. Organizations that dishonor this transformation process risk jeopardizing the benefits to be gained by the change (Schein 1990).

Operationalizing: Going live

Initially the plan was to start using the new flow sheets on the same day in all the nursing units. After considering the nature of the consumers involved in the change, it was decided to alter the timing of the proposed changes to fit the culture of each work group.

A staggered implementation plan was designed to allow nurses and physicians an opportunity to adjust to the changes in the presentation and usage of each area's flow sheet. Nurses were provided with inservice education about documentation on their unit-specific flow sheet two weeks prior to their go-live date. Flow sheets for other units were reviewed to show similarities and differences. Learning boards containing all the new flow sheets were created for physician lounges and nursing units.

Paper is used as a major tool for communication in American society. The new flow sheets represented a disruption in the standard paper process of communication for the organization. Inservice programs had been designed to inform the staff about how to use the forms. However, until a process has been mastered, individuals usually experience disorientation and powerlessness (Conger and Kanungo 1988).

Reactions to the change: Physicians

Nurse managers were asked to increase their staffing during the first week of implementation to allow unit-based group members to be available to answer questions. During the first 48 hours of usage, a subcommittee member or the nurse manager tried to greet each physician who came to the unit, complete rounds with her/him, and assist each in finding information about their patients on the new flowsheets.

Feedback from physicians about this particular strategy was positive. They did not have to spend as much time searching for information about their patients. In addition, the presence of the nurse made patient rounds a collaborative effort.

On one occasion, a cochair was approached by a physician department chair who related receiving multiple complaints and who demanded immediate restoration to the old format. Conversation with the physician revealed the problem was not the flow sheets themselves, but nurses' inability to leave them at the bedside. The physicians were having to locate the patient's nurse to find each flow sheet. A solution was negotiated in which the cochair agreed to post a subcommittee member on the units for several days to ensure chart availability, and the physicians agreed to continue to support the change.

There were glitches. In the Main House, two key concerns arose with physicians. The first concern was the layout of information and language. All along, the challenge for the subcommittee had been to create forms that would clearly reflect not only the generic needs, but the population-specific needs of each nursing unit. The language and layouts used were driven by the unit's nursing needs. Physicians, however, were reporting frustration when they followed their patients in different areas because the major areas had somewhat different flow sheets. A change in layout to present information in a more uniform way was an easily negotiated item.

The absence of the graphic record sheet was the second concern. The previously used graphic record had contained the cumulative intake and output of the patient per shift, as well as a 24-hour total. Temperature, pulse, and respiration were recorded on this five-day sheet. This information was still available as raw data on the new flowsheets, but it was no longer collected, transferred to a document that showed trends, and available at the desk. This was a dramatic inconvenience for the physicians. If their practice pattern was to see the patient and go back to the chart to write orders or progress notes, physicians did not have this information, because the data remained at bedside.

Although the perinatal forms had enough space to trend vital signs and intake/output for the patient's entire stay, the main hospital sheets did not. The average length of stay is longer in the Main House and physicians had to compile the data from several flow sheets to view trends.

In response to these concerns, a focus group was formed with the physician committee member and vice president of hospital operations as facilitators. The goal of the meeting was to develop ways in which the form revisions could be adapted to be more user-friendly for physicians, yet keep the underlying concept of bedside charting. From discussion at the focus session, the following themes emerged:

- Physicians were upset at the change that flow sheets at the beside created.
- It did take longer for a physician to make rounds until they learned the new system.
- Vital signs and intake/output were valuable clinical information the physician needs to trend quickly and easily.
- Some physicians were now looking at what nurses recorded for the very first time.
- Several physicians were clearly frustrated and stated that they just wanted things to go back the way they were. They expressed dissatisfaction with change in general.

The issue of trending data, on the surface a seemingly innocuous concern, was actually weighted with other issues for both physicians and nurses. Physician control, real or perceived by the nursing staff, and who is perceived as being really important to the hospital were among several covert issues. If a win-win situation was to be achieved, all of the issues needed to be placed on the table to allow everyone to be clear about the implications of any decision made.

A strategy was developed by the Main House Group that would address the physicians' concerns about the graphic record and maintain the goal of reducing duplication of data. The forms representative designed a new trend analysis sheet that would display information for four days: temperature, pulse, respiration, and 24-hour intake and output for each patient. The information could be placed on the trend analysis sheet in one of two ways. It could be transcribed from the flow sheet onto the trend analysis sheet or transferred by using a specially designed sticker. The sticker would be placed with the original flow sheet, then after the information was written on it, the sticker was transferred onto the trend analysis sheet in the patient's chart.

The subcommittee decided to trial both methods in the Main House. The Telemetry Unit trialed the sticker. The remaining units in the Main House recopied the information by hand. The sticker method was expensive in terms of forms cost and consumed an additional 30 minutes per day of staff time to transfer. Recopying, while low in forms cost, consumed 45–60 minutes per shift in staff time. After the trials, the focus group reconvened and approved use of the sticker format housewide.

Reactions to the change: Nurses

Nurses quickly identified that they were documenting more efficiently. They expressed enthusiasm in having more time to focus on their patients.

The expanded role of the PCT and emphasis on PCT documentation contributed to confusion regarding who was allowed to chart what information. Updates were provided by both education and documentation committees. As people who had never charted before moved into roles where charting was required, education was provided on how to chart, where to record information, and what data should or should not be recorded.

There was resistance from staff nurses on several fronts. Initially, labor and delivery nurses objected to the recording of recovery room information on the postpartum flow sheet—a form labor nurses perceived as belonging to postpartum. This was overcome by pointing out that they were actually writing less but in a different location. Also, nurses were reminded of the clinical value of having recovery period data serve as the baseline for all subsequent patient information after delivery.

In the early days of use, misunderstanding arose about how to properly complete forms, despite extensive inservice programs and learning activities. Memoranda in newspaper format were drafted to correct misinformation and were posted in strategic areas. Task force chairs randomly met with staff to review charting, suggest timesaving tips, and reinforce appropriate use of the new forms. A portion of every staff meeting was devoted to discussing and troubleshooting the new documentation.

Many nurses who were new to a flow sheet format still chose to duplicate the information in longhand notes. They perceived an absence of narrative charting as exposure to liability. An attorney from the risk management department agreed to provide forums where issues and concerns could be addressed. These sessions diminished the problem somewhat, although some nurses who were educated to record everything longhand persisted with unneeded duplication. Ongoing inservices and staff meetings have addressed the difference between important and unimportant data, and more nurses are changing.

Initial plans called for the newborn chart to remain with the infant regardless of the baby's location (nursery or mother's room). This proved to be troublesome for pediatricians and staff, however, and the decision was made to return the newborn flow sheet to the nursery so as not to sabotage all the other changes. Keeping the infant chart with the infant may be reinstituted in the future.

Several weeks into the changes, satisfaction surveys were performed. Although the sample was self-selected and the tool was created by the cochairs, several important findings were evident. The majority of respondents reported they made fewer longhand entries, spent less time charting, found shift reports less lengthy, made fewer errors, and had more time to devote to patient care. However, most respondents were uncomfortable writing less and found it difficult to change their charting. This survey was repeated in July for comparison (Table 9.3).

Time savings

Time studies on four units evaluated whether the desired 25 percent reduction in documentation time has been achieved. Time spent charting in the postpartum areas has been reduced by 17 minutes per mother/baby

Table 9.3

Comparison of Documentation Opinion Survey Results in Percentages between Two Groups at Two Different Times

	Perinatal Response in Agreement		Medical-Surgical/ Critical Care in Agreement	
	7th week (%)	12th month (%)	12th week (%)	12th month (%)
I made fewer longhand entries.	87	92	84	92
I spend less time charting.	78	84	89	77
I have more time for patient care.	69	70	59	73
I am uncomfortable writing less.	57	38	36	11
I record more important information.	75	92	53	89
Clinical trends are easier to identify.	54	77	46	75
Report takes less time.	11	31	25	50
I make fewer errors.	81	54	65	65
Patient documentation is more complete.	66	69	46	80
It was hard to change my charting behavior.	65	77	40	33
	$N = 33$	$N = 13$	$N = 119$	$N = 42$

couplet per shift per nurse, a decrease of 48 percent. Documentation time during prenatal intake interviews has been cut by nine minutes per patient, or 32 percent. Medical-surgical charting time has been reduced by three minutes per patient per nurse per shift, or 17 percent. Critical care area charting time has been reduced by 13 minutes per patient per shift, or 52 percent.

Stage 2: Charting by Exception

Consultants listened to Documentation Subcommittee brainstorming sessions and presented concepts that had been successful elsewhere. Charting by exception (CBE) was one such concept that seemed a natural predecessor to case management and a method to reduce actual documentation time (Burke and Murphy 1988). The subcommittee chairs began to investigate organizations that had implemented CBE.

The underlying philosophy of CBE is charting only significant findings or exceptions to norms. Advantages include identification of clinical changes, trending of patient status, and highlighting of abnormal data. In addition, standards of nursing practice eliminate the need to document routine care. Redundant transcription and duplication of charting would be eliminated. The disadvantage of CBE is the presence of less supporting data in the patient record. As CBE was reviewed, the hospital's legal counsel and risk management office were contacted to ensure appropriateness regarding regulatory agencies and local, state, and federal laws.

The chairs contacted a CBE author and nine institutions that were identified as users of the CBE concept. It was believed possible to move to case management by developing care maps using the principles of CBE to document care delivered. The establishment of standards of care and protocols for each case type then allows the nurse to chart assessment findings that are abnormal on the flow sheet or variances on a care map. The care map might also replace the present unsatisfactory method of care plan documentation.

Discussions with various sources identified only one institution that was merging the concepts of CBE and care maps. The project managers at that facility strongly recommended against introducing both CBE and case management simultaneously.

Other factors influenced the progress of CBE at MVH. One was the identification of a relationship between CBE and the Case Management Documentation Subcommittee's goals. The two Documentation Subcommittee chairs were asked to join the case management group to evaluate the possibility of articulating CBE into whatever format the case management group developed (see Chapter 13 on Case Management).

Little information was available on the JCAHO's position regarding CBE. It was apparent that considerable time would be needed to develop CBE at MVH. These factors prompted the Documentation Subcommittee to table the CBE concept.

Stage 3: Computerization

The two documentation group chairs believed at the beginning of the project that rapid implementation of bedside computers would be the first step in solving the institution's documentation problems. A large number of the suggestions received during the OE process had been requests for computerization of patient documentation. However, review of the literature, site visits, networking, and workshops convinced the group not to move directly to computerization. The focus was changed to scaling down, consolidation, and fine-tuning of the paper-based patient record as a prelude to computerization.

The long-range strategic plan recently released by the hospital's information systems (IS) department projected consideration of an electronic medical record in 1996. External forces, a possible federal mandate of an electronic medical record, and the overwhelming number of OE suggestions requesting computerization dictated revision of the strategic plan of IS. A meeting to discuss patient care information management needs was convened by the senior vice president of hospital operations. As a result of this meeting, a patient care information needs assessment has been moved up significantly.

The outgrowth of the computerization concept was the establishment of the Point of Care Information Task Force. This task force is composed of IS staff, physicians, nurses, and other interdisciplinary staff. To date, this committee has completed a timeline for investigating and implementing bedside terminals throughout the institution. An assessment of the current environment of documentation and computerization has been completed, and all paper sources used directly or indirectly to document care have been compiled (over 700 different forms). In addition, a survey of what features users would like in a computerized system was recently completed.

Vendors are under review and site visits are being planned. Task force members continue to review the literature and attend workshops to remain current about changes in patient information management. A proposal is being formulated for the upcoming fiscal year that will include a project manager.

Identification of Related Issues

Care Plans

Formerly, after the nurse had constructed a care plan, it was laser printed automatically on the back of the nursing progress notes each midnight. This system was unsatisfactory for nurses for several reasons: some staff were resistant to computers, insufficient numbers of terminals were available, and the system used only a nursing diagnosis format. Staff compliance with care planning was unacceptable. The objective was to develop a method of patient care planning that was practical, useful, and acceptable by regulatory agencies. Alternatives to the existing system were not quickly identifiable. Therefore, the nursing diagnosis-driven method was continued.

Compliance with patient care planning was influenced by the institution of flowsheets. Care plans had been automatically printed each one on the back of nursing progress notes. Since the new trifold flowsheets could not be loaded into the laser printer, nurses had to be reminded to generate individual care plans on plain white paper as needed. Nurse managers and task force members reemphasized the need for the staff to document plans of care. Currently, the Quality Improvement Committee has been assigned responsibility to identify strategies to improve compliance.

Elimination of Proprietary Forms

Generic intrapartum, postpartum, and newborn flowsheets were approved and implemented. Generic replacements were developed for proprietary obstetrical and discharge summary forms and were approved by physicians of the department. These changes reduced proprietary form costs by 50 percent. Generic prenatal forms were not approved, however. The department believed that unless all the hospitals in the area converted to use of the new forms, confusion would occur from one institution to another.

The director of purchasing and the cochair with perinatal background had been networking to share the new generic forms with area institutions. As news of the quality and cost-effectiveness of the forms has spread, regional hospitals have gradually adopted them. National marketing of the obstetrical forms is being planned. If national marketing is successful, the obstetrical physician groups will be approached again to approve change over to exclusive use of generic prenatal forms in their offices. Hopefully, the obstacle of different forms in different institutions will no longer exist.

Nursing Admission Assessment

Revision of the Nursing Admission Assessment tool was needed but delayed in order to reach agreement on a controversial segment. The chemical dependency unit had been campaigning for two years to include a brief alcohol abuse screening tool in the assessment. The assessment tool was tabled while chemical dependency staff and physicians met with medical and surgical departments to seek approval of the alcohol-related questions. The Main House and Perinatal patient history and nursing assessment forms were eventually approved to include the alcohol questionnaire.

The Main House admission assessment has been designed as a bifold with the first three pages of information to be completed by the patient or significant other and the last by staff. Implementation took place in October 1993. A pilot of the perinatal assessment first draft began 1 September 1993.

Legibility of Physician Signatures

Another objective was to identify physician signatures on orders and eliminate legibility problems. Physician signature legibility was explored through a time study. Findings showed that up to 23 minutes had been used by personnel to identify just one physician's signature. A name stamp for each physician was considered a possible solution. The cost of manufacturing a stamp for every physician defeated this idea. As yet, no suitable solution has been found.

Evaluation

Medical information services (medical records) had supported the efforts of the Documentation Subcommittee throughout the change process for several reasons. First, reducing the bulk of the patient record would help medical information services decrease work load and storage. The department was moving toward an electronic medical record and saw consolidation into flow sheets as a necessary step in that direction. However, the initial trial versions of flow sheets were met with less than overwhelming response. Flaws that the committee members had not picked up became evident after the chart was bound. For example, initial versions did not have each side labeled A and B, so it was difficult to tell which side of the flow sheet had been used first. The paper selected was too lightweight and folds tore during handling. Addressograph boxes were not placed properly, and nonstandard abbreviations were sometimes used. Worst of all, one form was excessively long, and once bound in medical records, the pages could not be opened. Medical information services identified each of these problems and helped the committees devise solutions.

Nutrition services, while supporting integration of all disciplines on one form, expressed concern with the changes in documentation. Space for special supplements and enteral feedings was insufficient. The problem was solved by the inclusion of several blank spaces that could be designated for nutritional supplements.

Utilization management supported integration of multiple chart forms into one, but was wary of the bedside charting concept. This is understandable, considering that patient information can be gathered more quickly if all the data is at the nurses station and near the telephone— a vital tool for utilization review nurses. Moving the most significant data to the bedside meant reviewers had to retrieve and return each patient's clipboard, which slowed their work. Utilization management has remained supportive nonetheless. Concurrent review is more difficult; however, retrospective review has been enhanced.

Financial Impact

For detailed financial data regarding the impact of OE, see Chapter 11. Although the portion of overall time savings directly attributable to charting changes are not delineated, overall hours per patient day were significantly lower for four out of the last six months of 1992.

Compliance with Standards

The institution regularly monitors housewide compliance with the JCAHO standards. Several months after the trial of new forms began, monitoring demonstrated significant improvement in compliance. Care planning, however, remained unacceptably poor. Many claimed that the new documentation system had created the care plan problem, but review of prior audits demonstrated similar results. The documentation leaders believed the care planning compliance problem was no worse than before, only more visible. The chairs then became members of the Case Management Documentation Subcommittee, so efforts of both could focus on alternatives to the present method of planning patient care. To date, ongoing monitoring has shown mixed results with few clear trends. Documentation of interventions has improved, but care plans remain a problem.

During the hospital's JCAHO survey visit in November 1993, the chart audit results yielded a 99.4 percent compliance. In addition to JCAHO criteria, problem areas of documentation in the perinatal areas were audited. Results were mixed—improvement was noted in the recording of patient teaching, nursing interventions, patient response to intervention, and maternal rubella immunity status and blood type. Poorer performance was noted, however, in charting intravenous line changes and monitoring parameters during epidural labor analgesia. The codes for descriptors and flow sheet structure have been modified slightly, and staff have been reeducated about how to use the form.

The Process Itself

The events described in this chapter were more simultaneous than sequential. Multiple events, such as investigation of computerization, seeking administrative buy off, and financial analysis occurred simultaneously over a five-month period. The committee initially believed that solutions had to be in place by the end of the official OE initiative. It was several months before the cochairs realized that plans only needed to be in place, not operational. More time to allow the change to be accepted might have been an advantage. Conversely, the excitement and momentum generated by other OE projects may have enhanced the successful implementation of documentation changes.

Perhaps as an outgrowth of coordinating all the changes in patient documentation, departments began routing all forms complaints and issues to the documentation groups. After discussion with the Analyst and Nursing Model Committees, it was decided that only patient documentation issues were within the scope of the documentation groups. The committees then began to focus only on documentation ideas that would enhance patient care and redirect all others. Soon afterward, a standing hospital committee was formed to review all forms requests and address related problems.

It is important to note that OE had six months in which ideas were to be generated, researched, and prototype solutions developed. It became clear that the hospital's print shop would be unable to support the rapid turnaround necessary. The institution's contracted forms supplier allowed the hospital full-time use of one of their consultants. The consultant proved so beneficial to the documentation change process that she was subsequently provided with office space within the hospital.

The subcommittee members were meeting on a weekly basis with the contracted forms supplier to make revisions to the forms. Revisions occurred within two weeks of implementation. The average development time during OE for a form was eight to twelve weeks. In comparison, our contracted supplier informed us that the average time is normally 12 to 18 months. Samples of the most recent flow sheets are provided in Appendixes 9.A–9.E.

Lessons Learned

The cultural aspects of change and power were not fully appreciated by either the Main House or Perinatal Groups. Physician focus groups from the beginning of the project might have helped identify potential pitfalls and develop more support. Vocal physicians should be pulled into the process very early; they are influential even if they hold no formal position.

As forms are revised, color is gradually being eliminated for easier microfilming, to reduce cost, and to prepare for computerization. Some physicians have had problems with this change, as the colors enabled quick identification of sections in the chart.

The committee also learned that both physicians and hospital boards like hard data. Such groups do not want extensive explanation or theory, but merely a quick rundown with the costs, risk, and impact.

Even though physicians heard the new flow sheets explained at department/section meetings, received a copy with explanatory notes in the mail, and were reminded in newsletters of the change, most failed to realize how the change would affect their practice. Rounds did take longer in the beginning, and several acted as though they had not heard of the flow sheets.

A major factor influencing physician acceptance is the ability to trend patient data. Physicians see a large number of patients in a short time and need to be able to identify significant changes quickly.

Physicians are not alone in resisting change. Regardless if the change was to their advantage, some staff hated the revised forms because they were a change, any change. Nurses repeatedly stated how hard it was to leave the clipboard at the bedside and to write less but more important information. One nurse, when asked why she had written in the narrative the same data she had recorded in the flow sheet columns, responded, "I just felt like I had to write something!" Indeed, many schools of nursing educate their students to chart in ineffective ways, and old habits are hard to break.

Many nurses seemed to relate the length of their charting to their degree of nursing expertise (e.g., "if you write more, you're a better nurse"). For some, writing is a part of task-oriented practice.

Some nurses continue to keep all their patients' flow sheets together and go to the station to chart, not realizing others need access to the data as well. Most hospitals are designed to facilitate the performance of care at one place and the recording of that care at another, but as technologies mature, future facilities will need to be designed to record data at the point of care delivery.

A multitude of other nursing issues are visible now that were not evident before. Many nurses need to have a so-called cheat sheet to take report, record notes, and so forth. This sheet, although not a part of the permanent record, serves communication and organizational functions. Nurses who have multiple patients cannot give it up unless a suitable replacement is found. The committees were not able to develop such a tool.

One discovery during implementation of the new flow sheets was that some nurses were not well informed about unit policies and procedures regarding charting. Opportunities then arose to not only educate staff regarding the new forms, but to enhance practice as well.

Comment boxes in nursing lounges and locker areas were not used and have been discontinued. Nurses tended to page the cochairs or send the questions through the management structure.

As with nurses, physicians tended not to use the comment boxes placed throughout the hospital. Only a few physicians expressed opinions to medical staff leadership. Most addressed their concerns to members of the Documentation Subcommittee and openly shared both positive and negative feedback.

The committees failed to realize the key role that unit clerks would play in the documentation changes. When inservice schedules were posted, most unit clerks believed the sessions were for nurses only and did not attend. Since the unit clerk is the person most often approached with chart questions, problems arose when they were not knowledgeable about the flow sheets. Future projects of this nature should identify the unit clerk as a key customer.

Individual units adapted uniquely to the forms changes. In retrospect, each unit is culturally quite different from one another. Those units in which patient acuity was high, patient diagnoses were similar, and nurse-patient ratios were low, adapted readily. However, nurses on these areas valued psychosocial data and family participation much less. Conversely, nurses on units with more varying diagnoses and larger patient loads adapted more slowly. Varying methods of introducing the changes to each area may have been more beneficial.

Finally, offering a neutral option on the Likert scale, used to assess user satisfaction, was a mistake. A large portion of respondents selected that option. Future tools will utilize a forced-choice format without a neutral indicator.

Results

The Documentation Subcommittee worked to condense the patient record and streamline the process of documentation. The perinatal areas moved from a total of 34 nursing forms to 17. Telemetry reduced nursing documentation from six sheets to one (later two with the added trend analysis sheet). A medical-surgical nurse now charts on two sheets rather than four, while critical care nurses chart on two instead of nine. These changes were completed in an eight-month period.

Nurses on all units report higher satisfaction with each revision, and final revisions are underway. Future time studies and quality assurance activities will evaluate the degree of success with time savings and improved compliance with documentation standards. The next steps entail moving to case management and later, introduction of bedside terminals. The committees' initial goals were to revise the patient documentation process and free nurses to perform nursing. The groups believe success has been achieved.

Summary

In this chapter implementation of a process to reduce the cost of documentation and at the same time make it more efficient was described. The problems and solutions are outlined, and overall nursing documentation time has been significantly reduced.

References

Burke, L. J., and J. Murphy. 1988. *Charting by Exception: A Cost Effective, Quality Approach.* Albany, NY: Delmar Publishers.

Campbell, J. T., and T. T. Dowd. 1993. "Capturing Scarce Resources: Documentation and Communication." *Nursing Economics* 11, (2): 103–6.

Comstock, L. G., and T. E. Moff. 1991. "Cost-Effective, Time-Efficient Charting." *Nursing Management* 22: 44–48.

Conger, J. A., and R. N. Kanungo. 1988. "The Empowerment Process." *Journal of Management Review* 13 (3): 471–82.

Costello-Nikitas, D. M., and D. J. Mason. 1992. "Power and Politics in Healthcare Organizations." In *Nursing Administration: A Micro–Macro Approach for Effective Nurse Executives*, edited by P. J. Decker and E. J. Sullivan, 45–67. Norwalk, CT: Appleton & Lange.

Fondemiller, S. 1991. "The New Look in Nursing Documentation." *American Journal of Nursing* 9: 65–76.

Knapp-Spooner, C., and J. Brett. 1992. "Less Is More: A Medical/Surgical Flow Sheet." *RN* 55 (3): 36–39.

Lucaterto, M., D. M. Petras, L. A. Drew, and I. Zbuckvich. 1991. "Documentation: A Focus for Cost Savings." *Journal of Nursing Administration* 21 (3): 32–36.

Rosenthal, K. A. 1992. "ICU-CCU Flowsheet." *Critical Care Nurse* 12 (8): 58–62.

Schein, E. H. 1990. "Organizational Culture." *American Psychologist* 45 (2): 109–19.

Thomas, J. M. 1992. "Minimize Paperwork, Maximize Patient Care." *Computers in Healthcare* 3: 33–35.

Appendix 9.A   Portion of Medical-Surgical Nursing Assessment and Intervention Record

Note: All materials in the appendixes are reprinted with permission of the Reynolds and Reynolds Company, Copyright 1992.

DATE / TIME			Score	Night						Day						Eve				
GLASGOW COMA SCALE	**BEST EYE OPENING RESPONSE**	Spontaneously	4																	
		Open to Verbal Command	3																	
		To Pain	2																	
		No Response	1																	
	BEST VERBAL RESPONSE	Oriented & Converse	5																	
		Disoriented & Converse	4																	
		Inappropriate Words	3																	
		Incomprehensible Sounds	2																	
		No Response	1																	
	BEST MOTOR RESPONSE	Obeys Verbal Command	6																	
		Localize Painful Stimulus	5																	
		Flexion–Withdraw	4																	
		Abnormal Flexion (decorticate rigidity)	3																	
		Extension (decerebrate rigidity)	2																	
		No Response	1																	

Coma Score Total Points																				
Feet Push E = Equal W = Weak F = Flacid	R																			
	L																			
Feet Pull E = Equal W = Weak F = Flacid	R																			
	L																			
Hands Grasp E = Equal W = Weak F = Flacid	R																			
	L																			
Pupil ® Size/Reaction																				
Pupil Ⓛ Size/Reaction																				

Pupil Scale (mm)   + = Reacts   − = No Reaction

● 2 ● 3 ● 4 ● 5 ● 6 ● 7 ● 8 ● 9

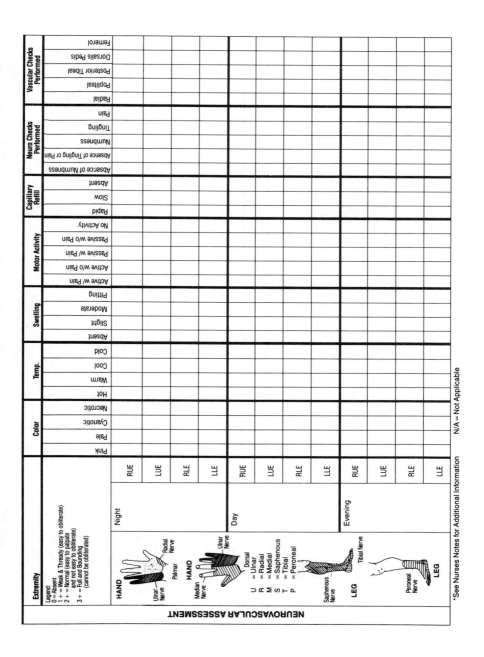

NEUROVASCULAR ASSESSMENT

Extremity		Color				Temp.				Swelling				Motor Activity					Capillary Refill			Neuro Checks Performed					Vascular Checks Performed				
		Pink	Pale	Cyanotic	Necrotic	Hot	Warm	Cool	Cold	Absent	Slight	Moderate	Pitting	Active w/ Pain	Active w/o Pain	Passive w/ Pain	Passive w/o Pain	No Activity	Rapid	Slow	Absent	Absence of Numbness	Absence of Tingling or Pain	Numbness	Tingling	Pain	Radial	Popliteal	Posterior Tibeal	Dorsalis Pedis	Femeral

Legend:
0 = Absent
1+ = Weak & Thready (easy to obliterate)
2+ = Normal (easy to palpate and not easy to obliterate)
3+ = Full and Bounding (cannot be obliterated)

Night — RUE, LUE, RLE, LLE
Day — RUE, LUE, RLE, LLE
Evening — RUE, LUE, RLE, LLE

HAND
Radial Nerve
Palmar
Ulnar Nerve

HAND
Ulnar Nerve
Median Nerve

Dorsal
U = Ulnar
R = Radial
M = Medial
S = Saphenous
T = Tibial
P = Peroneal

LEG
Tibial Nerve
Saphenous Nerve

LEG
Peroneal Nerve

*See Nurses Notes for Additional Information   N/A = Not Applicable

Appendix 9.B   Portion of Telemetry Unit Flow Sheet

	11-7	7-3	3-11
Level of consciousness: AO = Alert & orient x 3			
L = Lethargic D = Disoriented U = Unresponsive			
Mucous membranes:			
P = Pink C = Cyanotic D = Dusky PA = Pale			
Respirations: U = Unlabored L = Labored			
S = Shallow SOB = Short of breath			
DOE = Dyspnea on exertion			
Cough: N = Nonproductive P = Productive			
Breathsounds: Clr = Clear — RUL			
C = Crackles			
R = Rhonchi — RML			
W = Wheeze			
Ins = Inspiratory			
Exp = Expiratory — RLL			
Dim = Diminished			
Ø = Absent			
T = Tubular — LUL			
P = Posterior			
— LLL			
A = Anterior			
Chest Tubes:			
Location:			
Suction: _____ cm WS = Waterseal			
N = No Leak A = Air Leak CP = Clamp			
Pulse Oximeter			
Oxygen Ls _____ %			
NC = Nasal cannula M = Mask H = Humidified			
Incentive Spirometer _____ cc			
I = Independent A = *Assist Frequency			

RESPIRATORY SYSTEM

CARDIOVASCULAR SYSTEM

HT's

TTX #

TELE-METRY

Heart Sounds & Telemetry:
M = Murmur
I = Irregular
G = Gallop
Rb = Rub
C = Click
R = Regular
D = Distant
S = Strong

Aortic valve   Pulmonic valve   Tricuspid valve   Mitral valve

EDEMA: P = Pitting   NP = Nonpitting
P + 1 = Slight   P + 2 = Moderate   P + 3 = Marked

Capillary refill: B = Brisk   S = Sluggish

Pulses: 0.3
0 = Absent
1 + = weak and thready (easy to obliterate)
2 + = normal (easy to palpate and not easy to obliterate)
3 + = full and bounding (cannot be obliterated)

	R	L	R	L	R	L
Radial			ℜ ℒ		ℜ ℒ	
Brachial			ℜ ℒ		ℜ ℒ	
Posterior Tibial			ℜ ℒ		ℜ ℒ	
Dorsalis Pedis			ℜ ℒ		ℜ ℒ	

GI SYSTEM

Abdomen: R = Round   F = Flat   S = Soft
Fi = Firm   T = Tender   D = Distended

Bowel Activity: N = Normal   A = Absent
FL = Flatulant   L = Laxative/Stool softener
BM = Bowel movement   HO = Hypoactive
HE = Hyperactive

Meal intake = NPO   100%   75%   50%   25%
Diet

NG □   G-Tube □   J-Tube □   Suction □   Gravity □
Tube Placement Checked   Yes   No   Y N   cc   Y N   cc   Y N   cc
Residual Amount in cc

Feed/Assist: I = Independent   S = Setup
C = Complete   NS = Nsrg supervision

ELIMINATION

Urine: Clr = Clear   C = Cloudy   Y = Yellow   A = Amber
P = Pink   T = Tea   CH = Cherry   BR-CH = Bright Cherry
Pe = Peach   B = Burgundy   O = Odor
CBI = Continuous Bladder Irrigation

Output: BR = Bathroom   BP = Bedpan
F = Foley   FC = Foleycare   S = Specipan
BSC = Bedside Commode   U = Urinal   I = Incontinent
EUD = External urinary device   IC = Incontinence Care

*SEE NURSES NOTES FOR ADDITIONAL INFORMATION   N/A = Not Applicable

Appendix 9.C   Portion of Antepartum/Intrapartum Flow Sheet

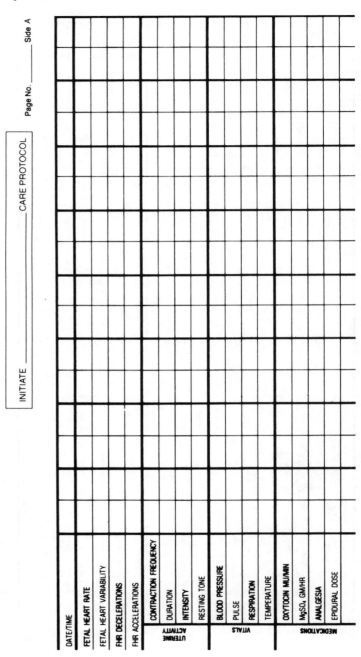

INITIATE _____ CARE PROTOCOL

Page No. _____ Side A

DATE/TIME																					
FETAL HEART RATE																					
FETAL HEART VARIABILITY																					
FHR DECELERATIONS																					
FHR ACCELERATIONS																					
UTERINE ACTIVITY — CONTRACTION FREQUENCY																					
DURATION																					
INTENSITY																					
RESTING TONE																					
VITALS — BLOOD PRESSURE																					
PULSE																					
RESPIRATION																					
TEMPERATURE																					
MEDICATIONS — OXYTOCIN MU/MIN																					
MgSO₄ GM/HR																					
ANALGESIA																					
EPIDURAL DOSE																					

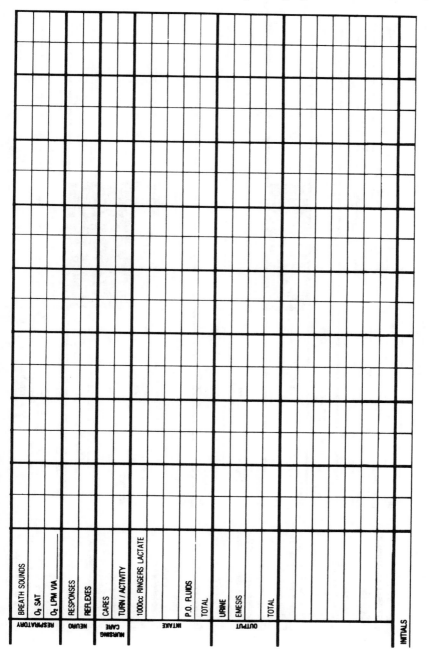

Appendix 9.D   Portion of Obstetric Nursing Care Flow Sheet (Postpartum)

Date: ___ Time: ___   Initiate: ___   Date: ___   Shift: TRANSFER   Time: ___

Blood Pressure								
Pulse								
Respirations								

LUNGS
Breath Sounds — CLR = Clear   W = Wheezing   CR = Crackles   R = Rattles

BREASTS
Nipples/Areola — I = Intact   R = Reddened   CR = Cracked   BL = Bleeding
Tension — S = Soft   E = Engorged   F = Firm

ABDOMEN
Soft/Firm
Tenderness — NT = Nontender   M = Moderate   S = Severe
Bowel Sounds — A = Absent   HE = Hyperactive   HO = Hypoactive   N = Normal

UTERUS
Tension — F = Firm   B = Boggy
Level of Fundus — L = Left   M = Midline   R = Right
Tenderness — NT = Nontender   M = Moderate   S = Severe

WOUND
Appearance/Dressing
Type of Drainage
Staples/Steri Strips

PERINEUM   Epis type _____   Laceration _____
I = Ice Pack   S = Surgigator   Z = Sitz
Appearance — R = Reddened   EC = Ecchymosis   A = Approximated   E = Edema   D = Drainage

IMMEDIATE P.P.
MATERNAL EMOTIONAL RESPONSE

☐ Doesn't look at baby
☐ Unresponsive to S.O., nurse, visitor
☐ Tenses face and arms
☐ Doesn't talk about baby
☐ Turns or pushes baby away
☐ Turns away from S.O. & nurse
☐ Doesn't touch baby
☐ Answers in monosyllables
☐ Seeks considerable support for own discomfort
☐ Complains of difficult labor & birth
☐ Voices unhappiness over sex of baby
☐ Requests that baby be taken to nursery
☐ Calls baby "it"
☐ Sleepy, not drug induced
☐ Asks S.O. or nurse if baby is all right
☐ Smiles at baby
☐ Looks, reaches out to baby
☐ Positive eye contact with S.O.
☐ Talks about baby
☐ Calls baby by affectionate terms
☐ Calls baby by name
☐ Comments on beauty of baby and realistic defects

☐ Undresses baby
☐ Hugs, touches baby
☐ Kisses baby
☐ Holds S.O. hand
☐ Breastfeeds baby

Hemorrhoids

LOCHIA
Amount	H = Heavy	SM = Small
	M = Moderate	S = Scant
Color	R = Rubra	S = Serosa
Odor		

URINARY
Foley /Voiding
Appearance   C = Clear   CL = Cloudy

SKIN
| Description | W = Warm | D = Dry |
| | Di = Diaphoretic | |

Rashes/Lesions/Itching

Edema

Homan's Sign

SELF/BABY CARE SKILL
I = Performs Independently   SELF
D = Needs Assistance   BABY
N = Does not participate in care

Date/Shift	Signature/Title	Initials	Date/Shift	Signature/Title	Initials	Date/Shift	Signature/Title	Initials

Appendix 9.E   Portion of Newborn Assessment Record

Miami Valley Hospital
Newborn Assessment Record

Initiate _____ Protocol _____

BIRTHDATE	Birth Time	am pm	Admit Time	am pm

MATERNAL COMPLICATIONS
Maternal Drug Use

Premature Labor	Maternal Diabetes	PROM

Elevated Temp   Other

Dr. Notified	Date		Time	am pm	By

FETAL COMPLICATIONS
Resuscitation   Laryngoscopy   Meconium Staining

Congenital Anomalies   Abnormal Presentation   Nuchal Cord

Gestational Age by TN Exam   _____ weeks   SGA   AGA   LGA

Date:		
Time:		
Initials:		

ACTIVITY
- Sleeping
- Crying
- Tremors
- Quiet Alert
- Active Alert

CARDIO
- Color Pink
- Acrocyanosis
- Circumoral Cyanosis (CC)/Central (C)
- Murmur

RESP-IR
- Full/Equal/Bilateral
- Chest Symmetrical
- Tachypnea

HEAD
- Molding
- Caput (C) / Cephalhematoma (T)
- Sutures WNL
- Bruising (B) / Petechiae (P)
- Scalp Lesion
- Fontanels WNL

EYES
- Clear (C) / Drainage (D)
- Scleral Jaundice
- Ears: Reacts to Sound
- Nose: Narés Patent
- Mouth: Palate Intact

ABDOMEN
- Soft (S) / Tense (T)
- Nondistended (N) / Distended (D)
- Bowel sounds   +   –
- 3 Vessel Cord   Y   N

RESPIRATORY	
Retractions	
Expiratory Grunt	
Nasal Flaring	

REFLEXES	
Equal and Bilateral	
Moro	
Grasping	
Sucking	
Rooting	

Cry: Lusty (L) / Weak (W) / Shrill (S)

SKIN	
Clear (C) / Rash (R)	
Meconium Stain	
Jaundiced	
Mottled	
Vernix (V) / Dry (D) / Peeling (P)	
Birthmark	

FACE	
Symmetrical	
Bruising (B) / Petechiae (P)	
Forcep Marks	

CORD	
Cord Clamp On / Off	
Moist (M) / Dry (D)	
Drainage	

GENITALS	
Patent Anus	
Male: Testes descended	
Circ. Site N/A WNL	
Female: Normal Appearance	

MUSCULOSKELETAL	
Tone: Flaccid (F) / Average (A)	
Hyper (H)	
Full ROM	
Palmar Surface WNL	
Clavicle Intact	
Symmetrical Movement	
Full Hip Rotation	
Spine Intact	
Polydactyly	
Clubfoot	
Other	

Comments: 8FR NG L / R narus and position checked per auscultation. Aspirated and returned / discarded;

R1732 (1/93)

10

Enablers to Change in the Patient-Care Model

Sally Clements, Debra K. Fearing,
Keith A. Lakes, and Victoria A. Studebaker

This chapter will describe the structure, processes, and ideas used in three enabling subgroups: pharmacy, respiratory services, and clinical laboratory. Enabling is defined as a time-saving function that allows more efficiency in delivering patient care while decreasing time spent in nondirect care functions. Reallocating tasks to the most appropriate individual results in keeping direct caregivers at the bedside to meet patient needs. Enablers need to be in place prior to the implementation of a patient care delivery system.

Structure

The major enabler functions and activities occurred during the six-month OE Project at MVH. Each of the three departments participated in a related OE task force. Pharmacy collaborated with the Medication Administration Task Force, respiratory care services contributed to the Patient Care Model Task Force, and the clinical laboratory worked with the Laboratory Task Force.

Processes

Each department's representative participated in task force processes of brainstorming, assessing, analyzing, evaluating, and recommending. "Bright ideas" submitted by hospital employees were a major contributing factor for changes within the system. Every idea or concept was assigned an identification number for tracking. Task force members reviewed each idea and discussed the feasibility and impact on patient care. Many of the suggestions only shifted inefficiencies from one department to another or simplified a process for one department while complicating it for another. The task forces created a list of key issues on which to focus. Additional analysis included

1. Rough estimates of materials/supplies to be saved
2. Rough estimates of labor saved
3. Estimated ease of implementation
4. Projected time frame for implementation.

Members used investigative methods that included time studies, tally sheets, and input from resource staff within the hospital. After the information was collected, the task force discussed the idea again and assigned a risk notation. The notation of risk was high, medium, or low depending on the impact to all customers (patients, physicians, nurses, and other departments). Targeted savings were determined and reported by labor or nonlabor dollars.

During the OE process, ideas relating to medication administration, the respiratory department, and clinical laboratory were analyzed by the appropriate task forces. All recommendations were forwarded to the Analyst and Steering Committees for input and then to the Hospital Policy Committee for decisions about implementation. Implementation of the approved ideas from each task force involving enablers was recognized as instrumental to the success of the new patient care delivery model. Implementation of those accepted ideas was rolled into the framework of PACE 2000. All three groups continue to provide input into the PACE 2000 Steering Committee, and pharmacy remains active on the Medication Administration Subcommittee of PACE 2000.

The following sections describe specific enabling ideas evaluated by each of the three groups: pharmacy, respiratory services, and clinical laboratory. There is a brief introduction about each of the areas.

Pharmacy

The pharmacy services department consists of a main pharmacy and four decentralized satellite areas, including surgery and home health care. Thirty-two pharmacists and 30 technicians provide services throughout the organization. The pharmacy processes 44,000 new or changed orders per month, 103,000 cassette line orders per month, and 25,000 IV medications per month. Representatives from pharmacy services were active participants and leaders on the OE Medication Administration (MA) Subcommittee. This section includes a discussion of the purpose of the MA Subcommittee, committee membership, and ideas considered for implementation.

Purpose

The mission of the MA Subcommittee was to streamline the entire medication process in the hospital, from prescribing the medication to patient outcome, while enhancing accuracy and efficiency. Initially, two subgroups were formed to address medication administration in the medical-surgical population and the maternity-neonatal population. Early in the process, similar problems were identified in both groups with similar resolutions, thus the two groups were combined.

Membership

Membership consisted of nurses, pharmacists, physicians, health unit coordinators (unit clerks), pharmacy technicians, management system engineers, And the assigned consultant analyst. The committee was cochaired by an emergency department shift manager and an assistant director of pharmacy services. The combined efforts of these two departments had a very positive outcome. Addressed were patient care concerns, nursing effort to obtain and administer medication, and frustrations from nursing, pharmacy, and the medical staff, along with product requirements and effectiveness.

Ideas Considered

The subcommittee suggested and discussed 68 different ideas, and maintained an average of 12 active ideas (discussion at meetings and data collection). Many of the ideas were beyond the scope of the task force and

:ively pursued but were referred to other appropriate groups.
concepts included syringe pump, recycling distribution bags,
.......emation of new orders, and improvement of pharmacy communication. Other major ideas discussed were medication distribution and
documentation.

Syringe pump

Another task force during the OE process submitted the concept of
minimizing the use of minibags and instead, using syringes and a syringe pump for delivery of intermittent IV products. The MA Task
Force quantitated the potential nursing labor savings. The Bard syringe
pump was the product recommended and subsequently approved from
the other task force, so the MA Task Force did not investigate any other
pump. The Bard syringe pump system eliminated the need for minibags
for intermittent medication delivery. After the purchase of 200 syringe
pumps and the manufacturing equipment necessary in the pharmacy,
the estimated three-year product savings was $219,000. The syringe
pump also saves nursing set-up time. The MA Task Force quantified
the nursing time saved with the conversion to syringe pumps. It was
also recognized that patients are less likely to have fluid overload with
the smaller amount of diluents used in the syringe system, and the
medication delivery time is more accurate. The estimated annual labor
savings from this idea was 1.5 minutes saved per dose with the syringe
pump, or $87,000.

Recycling distribution bags

The task force also addressed recycling pharmacy plastic distribution
bags. A patient's unit-dose medications are distributed to the nursing
unit in a plastic zipperlike bag with one patient's medications per bag.
These bags could be recycled without compromising patient care. Re-
alistically the task force did not think 100 percent recycling could be
achieved. However, the task force believed that at least 50 percent of
the bags could be recycled. Fifty percent of the annual purchase cost
was submitted as a potential savings, or $2,000. However, one year
after implementation of this idea, soiled plastic bags were being placed
in the container for recycling. Pharmacy and infection control recommended discontinuing recycling due to potential compromise of employee safety.

Implementation of new orders

Physicians perceived that there were unnecessary delays in implementing new medication orders due to the confusion of chart placement on the nursing units. Signage in the nursing unit for immediate or routine orders was suggested to expedite the delivery of patient care. The MA committee spent much time discussing potential solutions to this issue. However, due to task force time constraints, no resolution occurred. At the conclusion of the MA Task Force, this idea and the suggested solutions were forwarded to another hospital committee for further investigation and implementation.

Improvement of nursing-pharmacy communication

Nurses believed that they spent undue time attempting to contact a pharmacist. The existing decentralized pharmacy system caused confusion because pharmacists could either be in the satellite pharmacy, or out on the nursing units. The MA Task Force recommended phone mail and pagers for the pharmacists. With the implementation of these communication devices, a nurse could easily reach a pharmacist and obtain needed medication or information.

The pharmacists thought that the phone mail, however, has created new communication problems. They believed the majority of messages left on the phone mail were inadequate, and they must return the call to the nurse to complete the transaction. This forced a second interruption for the nurse. The phone mail is not widely used. The voice pagers, however, alert a pharmacist immediately. Generally when the nurse phones the pharmacy satellite, a pharmacy technician answers the phone and then pages the pharmacist. Nurses seldom page the pharmacist directly. The advantage of the pagers is that the pharmacy technicians can immediately contact the pharmacists, and patient care needs can be met in a more expeditious manner.

Medication distribution and documentation

Bar-coding. The processes for distributing, documenting, and administering medication were evaluated. Problems were identified in controlled substance documentation, the process of documenting patient medication administration, and the timeliness of medication delivery to the patient. The concept of bar-coding was discussed. The central services department stocks products by using bar-coding. Could bar-coding assist pharmacy with medication dispensing, nursing with documentation, and simplify medication administration? A bar-coding consulting company specializing in hospital use presented such a proposal to the group. At the time, the consulting company was only trialing a robotic arm for use in pharmacy unit-dose cartfill. The nursing interface was only conceptual. The bar-coding company had not addressed the nursing role of documentation and administration using pen-lights and bar-coding. Because this company did not offer both a pharmacy and nursing use of bar-coding, the idea was dismissed. The task force was only aware of one company experimenting in bar-coding. This technology was still only in alpha site testing. (Other sites were involved with the pharmacy robotic arm cartfill.) A total system involving pharmacy dispensing, nursing administration, and patient identification is still not available. Another automatic medication dispensing system has recently begun marketing bar-coding for pharmacy dispensing and nursing administration, but does not involve bar-coding on the patient's identification band. The technology we were looking for during our OE experience is still not available.

Automated dispensing machine. The presentation on bar-coding led to discussions on what technology could provide the institution. Automated dispensing systems for medications were investigated. Members of the task force visited an area hospital with such technology. The consulting institution had two different automated systems. One system dispensed individual doses (one tablet, one syringe) but held a limited amount of doses. Pharmacy refilled the machine with one syringe per pocket, or one tablet per pocket. This system was utilized in the hospital when the pharmacy was closed. Pharmacy refilled the machine daily. The second system demonstrated was the Pyxis MedStation. Pyxis allowed larger quantities of medication to be stocked in each pocket. Therefore, pharmacy spent less time refilling the machine.

The task force did not think the individual unit-dose automated system was appropriate. The limited amount of medication and the lack of flexibility in the system did not meet MVH's needs. The Pyxis Med-Station, however, could be adapted to the needs of a nursing unit and could be changed when a nursing unit's needs changed or when packaging of a medication changed. This system appeared more adaptable to organizational needs.

The task force began collecting data to critically analyze the purchase of automated equipment. The majority of data collected pertained to nursing time related to handling controlled substances (i.e., the end of shift narcotic counts, location of the narcotic keys, and discrepancy resolution).

After investigation of product availability, the Pyxis MedStation was selected because this product best met nursing and pharmacy needs. The diversity of patient needs (from emergency room to medical-surgical unit to labor and delivery to surgery) were met with the flexibility of this system. The advantages of Pyxis included

1. Better inventory control
2. Greater charge capture
3. Reduced nursing time spent in obtaining medication
4. Automated narcotic documentation
5. Deletion of end of shift narcotic count
6. Elimination of manual inventory.

Individual Pyxis MedStations communicate via phone lines to a pharmacy console (PC computer), usually located in the pharmacy. The pharmacy console is connected to the hospital's admission/discharge/transfer information. These communication links provide the MedStations with current patient names and current medication inventory.

The expense of the system for a hospital of this size was significant. The task force began time studies and data collection to provide a rationale for the expense. It was determined that under the manual system, the time spent accessing was approximately two minutes per dose. Manufacturer's documentation suggested 15 seconds to access the same dose through automation. The task force utilized 30 seconds in the labor calculations. Data collection from each nursing unit included documentation for the average number of narcotic doses per 24 hours. The time estimated to access controlled substances in the manual system versus an automated system was calculated. The difference between the manual and automated system was used as labor savings. The task force estimated 208,794 controlled substances administered per year or 6,969 nursing hours annually to access controlled substances by a manual system. Accessing 208,794 doses in an automated system would require only 1,740 nursing hours.

Another medication distribution issue was the amount of time required to accomplish the end-of-shift narcotic inventory (narcotic count).

Results from the end-of-shift inventory investigation indicated that critical care nursing units and the emergency room had as many as 8 inventories per 24 hours. The variety of nursing schedules (i.e., shifts of 8, 10, and 12 hours) forced multiple inventories through the day. With an automated system the end-of-shift narcotic count could be deleted. This time saving was studied and multiplied to approximate a year's worth of labor savings. The annual savings were calculated to be 16,997 hours to complete end-of-shift narcotic count discrepancies. The end-of-shift narcotic count was timed, dated, and signed by two nurses. The controlled substance withdrawal entry immediately following the end-of-shift narcotic count was occasionally timed before the inventory. Upon investigation, it was found that nurses counting the controlled substances occasionally found a discrepancy but did not report it. The nurses located the missing dose and documented the dose on the line immediately after the inventory. The time that dose was administered was before the inventory. Time studies indicated a narcotic discrepancy required an average of two nurses 15 minutes each to resolve a discrepancy in the count. The task force obtained data from three months and counted narcotic discrepancies. It was speculated that more discrepancies occurred. Only the discrepancies that were documented were utilized. While the automated system would not alleviate all narcotic discrepancies, the record as to who last accessed the medication would be recorded, therefore, less time would be necessary to track the discrepancy. The resultant nursing labor savings, documentation time, end-of-shift narcotic counts, and discrepancy resolution were calculated for each nursing unit.

Lost medication charges in the intensive care units and the emergency room were addressed. These units were the only nursing units in the hospital that had significant station stock (i.e., large quantities and expensive medications). Due to the existing manual system, lost charges were a routine occurrence. The task force tracked a year's records of lost charges (i.e., medications that should have been charged to a patient and were documented as given to a patient, but were not charged by pharmacy). These lost charges also were utilized in cost justification for the automated medication station. Installing the Pyxis MedStations in all units at MVH would result in the recovery of $400,000 of lost charges. The dollar value of lost charges reduced by the contractual adjustment percentage resulted in an incremental revenue gain of $142,000.

After presentation and approval of the initial proposal, Hospital Administration agreed to trial Pyxis MedStations on several units. Because of the diversity of the hospital, several units were selected as trial sites: the emergency room, a labor/delivery/recovery/postpartum unit, the medical and surgical ICU, the cardiovascular ICU, and high narcotic use medical-surgical units (oncology and orthopedics). A total of eight medication stations and three auxiliary stations were installed for the trial.

The Pyxis units normally communicate via dedicated analog telephone lines. New digital telephones (Rolm System) were recently installed in the hospital. Pyxis had never installed MedStations in an institution utilizing digital phone lines. The information systems department was determined to make Pyxis communications occur over digital Rolm telephones. Simply stated, information travels over digital phone lines much faster than information traveling over analog phone lines. The Pyxis equipment was not designed for the rapid information transfer over digital phone lines. The pharmacy console and the individual MedStations were not communicating. After much cooperation between the information systems department and Pyxis engineers, the Pyxis units now communicate over digital phone lines.

The hospital internal auditor and a management systems engineer assisted with data collection and projections to determine acquisition options. The finance department determined that the most cost-effective method of acquiring equipment was to purchase rather than lease. The hospital has agreed to maintain a service contract to ensure maintenance of the units.

The Finance Committee of the hospital's Board of Trustees approved the purchase of the 25 MedStations and seven Auxiliary units to be installed in three phases (Phase 1 was the trial units). The additional phases were spread over two quarters.

All the units received the Pyxis MedStations within 12 months, and all nursing and pharmacy personnel have been instructed. A survey completed after the trial units documented that nurses thought the equipment was user friendly and was an enabler. They were particularly happy with the deletion of end-of-shift narcotic counts.

Pharmacy did not gain any labor savings with Pyxis installation. Manual billing and ordering each narcotic and station stock patient charges are now replaced with refilling Pyxis units.

The final cost and savings for the Pyxis implementation project were:

> Pyxis Equipment Purchased, $705,000
>
> Construction, Phone Equipment and Labor, 15,945

Annual Nursing Labor, 480,000

Annual Medication Charges Recovered, 94,000

The hospital internal auditor calculated the amount of lost charges per unit, the collection percentage, and the potential patient charges that Pyxis could recover.

The implementation of the Pyxis system has provided an opportunity for nurses to spend more time in patient care. The time studies, documentation, presentations, and implementation were a multidisciplinary team effort. The newly created relationships and communications have strengthened the organization.

The use of Pyxis in the hospital has created many opportunities for nursing and pharmacy conveniences. Nursing pagers, unit-dose cart and epidural keys are now stored, accounted for, and dispensed by the MedStation. The camera in the labor/delivery nursing unit is also tracked by the MedStation. The pharmacy and nursing units are continuing to brainstorm and trial labor saving ideas and convenience concepts with this technology.

Future Directions

Several ideas were communicated to other committees in the hospital, while other ideas were not feasible (lack of physical space and qualified personnel). A task force will address the current standardized medication administration times. The concensus was that the current schedule was not the most efficient for the new patient care delivery model.

Standardizing certain IV medication concentrations (e.g., lidocaine, dopamine, dobutamine, etc.) was also addressed. The process for determining the concentration and the procedures with the nursing staff, the medical staff, and pharmacy is still being pursued.

Recommendations

- *Group Leader Preparedness.* The group leaders could have been better prepared. A more thorough understanding of the expected outcome of the OE process, the consultant's role, and the expected role of team members would have provided a better direction for the team initially.
- *Group Dynamics.* The group consisted of many diverse team members. The leaders were not as capable in group dynamics as they might have been. Some meetings were not as productive as they might have been.

Agendas, minutes, action plans, time lines were all used; however, the goal was frightening to some team members (loss of work, loss of control, etc.). All team members were expected to fulfill their routine jobs, the OE meetings, and committee tasks (such as information and statistic gathering and time studies). Not all team members realized the intensive work required when they volunteered to participate on the committee.

• *New Technology.* A literature search revealed very little information published on new technology or the potential of becoming alpha or beta research sites for experimental technology. Thorough research regarding all current and future technology was difficult to accomplish. There was little information available on bar-coding and automated dispensing machines. Personnel within the hospital alerted the committee to the availability of the companies. The committee made contacts with these manufacturers for presentations.

Respiratory Services

Respiratory care services had two goals through the process of OE and the development of the new patient care model. The first goal was to identify areas where the department could demonstrate cost savings by changing a process, procedure, equipment, or supply. The second goal was to identify those areas of patient care where professional respiratory therapists could use their knowledge, training, and skills to enhance patient care as a part of the team approach to the patient-focused model, PACE 2000. This section includes ideas considered and future directions.

Ideas Considered

Numerous ideas were considered and evaluated. The discussion includes ideas about unit-focused respiratory therapists, low flow oxygen, incentive spirometry, arterial blood gas sampling/specimens, and resuscitation bags.

Unit-focused respiratory therapists

The department of respiratory care services is a centralized department of about 65 therapists who provide respiratory care to all nursing units within the hospital. Historically, the staffing patterns for the department rotated therapists to different nursing units on a biweekly basis. A therapist would be assigned all aspects of respiratory care on a nursing unit for two weeks, then would be rotated to a different assignment for the next two weeks. This rotation would last about two months, when the therapist would again be assigned to the original unit. The advantage of this system was that every therapist was familiar with each area and able to work any assigned area whenever necessary. The disadvantage of this system was that the nursing staff on a given unit never knew which therapist was working with them nor the strengths of that therapist. The close working relationship vital to an effective health care team did not develop because each therapist spent such a short time working in each unit.

Although this assignment system had been used for many years, two factors led the department to consider a change. First, before the OE process began, the respiratory care department surveyed the therapists regarding the strengths and weaknesses of the department. A large percentage of the staff indicated the rotation of assignments made it difficult to get to know the nursing staff with whom they worked on a daily basis. The assignment system also made it difficult for therapists to establish a therapeutic relationship with their patients. Second, as a part of the patient care model of the OE process, nurse managers had indicated their staff strongly believed that the skills of each individual respiratory therapist could best be utilized if the nurses and the patients were better acquainted with them. For these two reasons, the respiratory care services department adopted a focused therapist staffing model. Therapists were asked to identify three nursing units in order of preference, where they would want to work. Interestingly, 90 percent of the staff was eventually assigned to the unit they ranked highest, and 95 percent were assigned to their first or second choice.

Therapists are now assigned to the same area every scheduled shift. The staff nurses know who the therapists are and have developed a strong working relationship with each of them. Patients now receive their respiratory care from a small group of therapists, often having the same therapist on a shift for at least five days in a week. Three direct results of this change, as identified by an employee attitude survey conducted for the department in the fall of 1992, have been greater therapist satisfaction, better working relationships and team building with the staff nurses, and fewer patient complaints involving respiratory care services.

Low flow oxygen

The set up of low flow oxygen (oxygen by nasal cannula) had always been performed by respiratory care services. When an order was received by a nurse on a unit, or a need for oxygen was perceived by the nurse, a call was placed to the respiratory therapist on call. This therapist was responsible for a variety of things, including covering the Emergency and Trauma Center (ETC), initiation of new treatments, respiratory emergencies throughout the hospital, and initial oxygen setups. Since many of the therapist's responsibilities cannot be delayed, oftentimes the initiation of low flow oxygen was the lowest priority. This resulted in the nurse placing a second call. If the therapist could not get the oxygen set up promptly, a third call might be made to the main department. The main department would locate another therapist who could set up the oxygen. Regardless, the therapist would also have to locate a flow meter prior to setting up the oxygen at the patient's bedside. The results of this process were frustration for the nurse for the delay in getting oxygen set up, substantial time wasted by the nurse with several phone calls and pages, frustration for the therapist on the main beeper because they could not respond promptly for a needed therapy, delay in a patient receiving needed oxygen, and family dissatisfaction at the length of time their family member waited to receive oxygen.

To address these concerns, respiratory care services purchased 400 new oxygen flow meters. A flow meter was then placed in the oxygen outlet at every patient bed. They were attached to the wall by a small chain. Central services began stocking nasal cannulas on their supply cart on each nursing unit. When low flow oxygen was needed, a cannula was obtained from the central services' cart on the unit and set up by the nurse very quickly, with no time wasted. The order for oxygen was entered in the computer to respiratory care services by the health unit coordinator, and the respiratory therapist initiated the paperwork necessary for documentation and billing at the first opportunity. This system alleviated each of the problems of the previous method. The multiple calls to respiratory care services were completely eliminated, frustration and time wasted by the nurse and therapist were reduced, patient and family satisfaction were increased, and most important, patients received oxygen in an expeditious manner.

Incentive spirometry

Respiratory care services had been responsible for the initiation of incentive spirometry therapy. Since it is regarded primarily as a prophylactic therapy, it was often put at the bottom of the busy respiratory therapist's work list. This often resulted in similar frustrations as described in the previous section on oxygen therapy. Nurses spent substantial time calling the respiratory therapists to obtain the incentive spirometer. In addition, there were delays between ordering and receiving the therapy. This delay could result in the onset of pulmonary problems, such as postoperative atelectasis, possibly leading to an increased length and cost of hospital stay.

To address these concerns, incentive spirometers were stocked on the central services' cart on each nursing unit. In addition, RNs, LPNs, and PCTs were trained to effectively initiate and administer incentive spirometry. This eliminated a source of frustration for both the nursing staff and the respiratory care services staff and allowed incentive spirometry to be initiated promptly and monitored closely.

Arterial blood gas sampling/specimens

Historically, respiratory care services has not been involved in performing arterial punctures. In the critical care areas, the staff nurses were primarily responsible for this procedure. Training the respiratory therapists who are focused in the critical care areas provided an additional group of professionals who could provide this service. In the medical-surgical areas, the laboratory would be called or notified, and therapists would respond when available. The blood sample would be drawn and returned to the laboratory for processing. Now the therapist who is responsible for the area is available to draw the sample. This has expedited the drawing and processing of the arterial sample.

Resuscitation bags

Because disposable resuscitation bags have been readily available, the hospital has used them as the primary method of manual ventilation. The disposable bag performance closely approximates the nondisposable resuscitation bag, and use of the disposable bag eliminated the need for processing the used bags. However, the cost of the disposable bag varied from $15 to $20 each. These bags were charged to the patient. The change to nondisposable resuscitation bags required the purchase of an additional 150 resuscitation bags. This was a substantial capital outlay, but at the normal utilization of resuscitation bags, that outlay should be compensated for in one year.

Future Directions

The department of respiratory care services continues to identify areas where costs can be reduced. The two main areas are supplies and time utilization. Another idea was the use of heated wire circuits on adult ventilators. Committees within the department will be organized to evaluate and implement additional bright ideas that were approved by the OE Steering Committee.

Recommendations

It is important that all role changes involving respiratory care be carefully checked for compatibility with all applicable licensing laws in the state. Respiratory therapists are licensed in most states and many of their responsibilities cannot be delegated to nonlicensed personnel.

Clinical Laboratory

MVH's laboratory services are provided by a joint venture, for-profit laboratory owned by the parent corporation of the hospital. The laboratory participated in the hospital's improvement efforts, specifically in identifying enablers, even though savings in laboratory employees' labor costs and supply costs were not included in the overall hospital cost-reduction targets. The focus of examining laboratory processes with relation to nursing processes was to identify potential overall improvements.

Most laboratory issues were dealt with by the Customer Service Subcommittee of the Ancillary Task Force. Staff from the laboratory, as well as from nursing, finance, information systems development, and the HUC Group made up the membership roster.

Ideas Considered

The key issues, their analyses and resolutions are presented as follows: consolidating draws, patient location, arterial or central lines, and computer process.

Consolidating draws

Laboratory orders for a single patient were not coordinated at any point; patients were being stuck multiple times a day when laboratory draws could be consolidated. Different physicians seeing a single patient often wrote overlapping or duplicate orders.

To determine the magnitude of duplicate or unnecessary patient venipunctures, a computer-generated list of all patients having multiple laboratory testing done during one 24-hour period was printed. From the list, two to six patients were randomly selected from each nursing unit in the main building and their charts reviewed. Laboratory test requests from the computer-generated list were checked against physician written laboratory orders. Timing and test prioritization (STAT, ASAP, Now, and Today) were compared. Of the 38 patients audited, six patients had opportunities for consolidating draws. The HUCs, in most of the other cases, were already assigning a common specific time for daily or routine test orders for their unit so that the bulk of draws would be done at the same time, even though they had been instructed to enter orders exactly as the physicians wrote them. To improve the process, HUCs were officially encouraged and empowered to consolidate draw times as orders were entered.

Patient location

Patients were frequently unavailable for laboratory draws due to conflicts with other diagnostic tests or therapeutic procedures. As a result, specimen collection was delayed and much time was wasted tracking patients and rescheduling. Patient location changes for procedures such as medical imaging exams, therapy, cardiac catheterizations, and surgery are not tracked in the hospital computer system. Ancillary departments have no way of discerning patients' exact locations at a given time by computer.

Addressing this problem within the hospital information systems was beyond the scope of this committee and has been referred to an ongoing committee. A week-long study was conducted to evaluate the problem. Phlebotomists documented that 3–5 percent of the time patients were not available for laboratory draws. When specimens could not be collected, 62 percent of the time conflict with another procedure was the documented reason. Phlebotomists estimated that an equal number of patients were not readily available for laboratory draws but were quickly located on the unit.

Most nursing units have manual systems in place for documenting patients' locations when they are out of the room. An effort was made to standardize those systems across units. Phlebotomists began using forms for documenting unsuccessful attempts to locate patients. The slips are left at the nursing station with instructions to call the laboratory when the patient returns. The slips have reduced the number of subsequent telephone calls between the laboratory and the nursing units to check on patient return.

Arterial or central lines

Phlebotomists had no way of knowing which patients had arterial or central lines from which blood specimens were to be obtained. At each bedside, phlebotomists were responsible to check for the presence of lines before performing venipunctures. Many times, they needed the assistance of the nursing staff to make the determination. Phlebotomists would then provide collection tubes and wait for the nurses to collect the blood and label the specimens. Nurses, on the other hand, often had their work flow disrupted when a phlebotomist arrived at an inconvenient time. To streamline this process, the existing laboratory order entry software was adapted to include a field to indicate whether the specimen was to be drawn from a central line. A list of patients with lines was supplied by nursing to the HUCs shortly before laboratory order entry time. The information prints on each laboratory requisition. Nurses were educated how to properly fill the blood collection tubes. When a line draw is indicated on a laboratory test order, phlebotomists assemble the correct collection equipment, the requisitions and labels, and a plastic bag and send them by pneumatic tube to the nursing station. The nurse draws, labels, and returns the samples to the laboratory by pneumatic tube. This improves phlebotomy efficiency by eliminating time spent at the bedside of patients who do not require venipuncture and on the units looking for the appropriate nurse. Nurses can collect blood samples at times most convenient to them. Working relationships between the two groups have improved. The phlebotomists served in a teaching/advisory role for once, which was a great morale booster. Nursing also used this opportunity to begin using Luer adapters to draw blood from lines directly into the collection tubes, eliminating the potential for needle-stick injury in the blood collection process.

Computer process

The computer process for ordering laboratory tests and documenting collection time and receipt in the laboratory had some inefficiencies. The information systems development representative on the committee was very knowledgeable about the system and made several laboratory nursing enhancements, which are as follows:

1. A screen was developed for frequently used comments that could be selected quickly for order clarification such as check for blood in laboratory and draw from left arm only, etc. In the past, these comments required multiple key strokes.

2. Six keystrokes were eliminated when entering the date and time of specimen collection by having the date default to current date. With about 2,000 collection dates per day entered, this was a significant time saver.

3. Collection lists for timed and routine laboratory test orders print in the laboratory every hour on the half hour. Orders with a priority of STAT or STAT Collect print at the time of order. A problem was encountered when test orders were placed after the collection list printed (i.e., an order for a 2:00 p.m. test placed at 1:35 p.m. would not print in time to be collected at 2:00 p.m.). The test ordering software was enhanced so that when a timed order is placed for a test to be collected in the hour preceding the desired collection time, a message is displayed on the order screen: collection list has printed; order STAT Collect. The order then prints immediately in the laboratory rather than being stored until the next collection list prints.

4. Lists of test priorities, which had been part of the computer system standard laboratory package, were reviewed and changed to meet the institution's needs. For example, the priority *Pre-Op* was available for use, but tests ordered as Pre-Op were handled by the system as routine orders. This priority was eliminated so that system users did not mistakenly believe that Pre-Op orders would be completed before scheduled surgery times.

5. A data base for tests requiring special handling by nursing (e.g., 24-hour urine tests, etc.) was created. Special handling notes will be generated on the printer of the nursing unit when the test is ordered. This project is still in progress.

A similar laboratory task force dealt with laboratory process issues in the perinatal area. This group's purpose was not to reduce inefficiencies in the general laboratory process, but to focus on issues unique to the new maternity facility. Obstetricians and pediatricians had feared that service levels from ancillary areas would decrease once perinatal services moved into a new facility farther from the main hospital. After the move, the laboratory had conducted numerous turnaround time studies documenting that response time and transport time had not suffered due to the extra distance between the areas. Yet, the perception of the physicians was not changed. One of the most common suggestions for improvement from physicians was to move laboratory services close to the birthing center and the neonatal ICU. The task force wanted to define specifically what physicians wanted changed or improved.

One of the members of the task force, a member of the hospital's marketing department, designed a questionnaire to collect information from physician users of laboratory services in the perinatal building. Written surveys were distributed to some physicians; other practitioners were interviewed by telephone. Of the ten physicians who responded, six were obstetricians and four were pediatricians or neonatalogists. Each of the ten physicians had different expectations and a diverse wish list. Combined results could identify no major recurrent issues.

Plans for an extensive satellite laboratory in the perinatal building were developed. However, space for the facility could not be designated. A laboratory consultant was brought in to survey the situation and talk to physicians to develop an alternative approach. The ultimate resolution was to locate a small space near the neonatal ICU to house a few pieces of laboratory equipment to perform a limited menu of critical tests. A new medical technologist position was created to perform testing and serve as a liaison between the main laboratory and the laboratory's users in the perinatal building. The exposure and proximity of the laboratory has immensely improved relationships and perceived service levels. Physicians no longer voice concerns about the distance to the main laboratory. Regular communication ensures that any minor problems are investigated and resolved quickly.

Future Directions

Some of the more complicated ideas brought forth during the process continue to be developed and perfected. Many of the ideas submitted cannot be implemented with the current hospital computer system. These have been stored until the time that a new computer system is considered.

Nursing and the laboratory are now much more aware of all steps involved in the laboratory process. The success of the enablers has paved the way for more improvements. Everyone is aware that current protocols need to be continually challenged.

Recommendations

- The ideas considered as opportunities for improvement were selected by committee members from their perspectives as links in the chain of the overall laboratory process. In retrospect, if the process had been thoroughly studied from start to finish, the broader perspective may have been more helpful in identifying inefficiencies and duplicate efforts.
- Studying best practices from other institutions may have helped generate ideas that would work for MVH.
- Instead of polling individual physicians for their ideas, facilitated discussions with groups of physicians to determine real needs would have yielded better results.
- Researching data communication technology for the immediate future would have given a better perspective on how to perform some steps in the laboratory process in five or so years. This would have enabled MVH to prioritize improvement efforts to better prepare systems for future technological advances.

Summary

Many ideas approved by the task forces are awaiting implementation. The limited time line made it impossible to enact all of the ideas. These ancillary departments continue to operationalize these ideas.

The enablers implemented streamlined care not only for the departments involved, but also for the nursing staff. The implementation of the ideas mentioned were so critical to the success of the new delivery system that units did not begin trials of the partnership concept until the enablers were in place. The original time line was modified by three months to allow for these changes. The analysis of numerous ideas and the implementation of ideas shared in this chapter were instrumental to the success of the new patient-centered care delivery system.

Part IV

Evaluation of Model

Part IV, Evaluation of Model, addresses the financial impact and evaluation of the model by different stakeholders. Chapter 11 focuses on financial monitoring of the model. The authors discuss the financial analysts' structure and process in assessing, planning, and implementing the new patient care delivery model that included a change in skill mix. They share tips on what worked and what did not work with recommendations. This chapter includes tables with financial formulas, examples of worksheets, FTE summaries, variance reports, and tracking graphs. Chapter 12 explains the evaluation plan and the seven indicators that are evaluated: patient satisfaction, patient outcomes, employee satisfaction, physician satisfaction, community response, cost-effectiveness, and clinical efficiency. Examples and interpretations are provided for each indicator. Appendices for the chapter include the SA survey, the PCT evaluation, and the RN evaluation format.

11

Financial Impact

Maribeth Richwalsky, Candace Skidmore,
and Arlon Zabel

Financial monitoring is an end result of approximately 18 months of identifying and implementing cost reduction activities on each of the inpatient nursing units within the division of nursing. When OE was initiated, it was designed as encompassing three phases: Phase I was to be initial data analysis for MVH at the cost-center level examining three years of patient days, discharges, and full-time equivalent (FTE) data. This phase also included examining hospitals similar to MVH for the same type of information. Phase II was to bring interdepartmental groups of individuals together in a task-force setting to examine ways to cut costs and extensively investigate, quantify, and present to upper management those that were feasible. Finally, the purpose of Phase III was to systematically implement ideas to achieve a more favorable cost position in the competitive marketplace.

The entire process was developed on a rapid timeline, which proved to be quite stressful to the organization, but in the long run was probably beneficial. The timeline kept the entire organization focused on this one goal and forced every team working on ideas to place this as their top work priority. The process spanned the entire hospital, although this chapter will only focus on its impact within the division of nursing.

This chapter outlines how a series of ideas impacting the care of patients moved from suggestions through quantification to implementation and 18 months later are being continually evaluated for their financial impact on the organization and their effectiveness in the primary goal of the OE program—cost reduction. Phase 1 is divided into a discussion about the Analyst Committee and the analyst process, followed by a description of Phases 2 and 3. Monthly monitoring is then discussed, concluding with cost of implementation and recommendations.

Phase 1: Analyst Committee

The Analyst Committee was formed during Phase 1 of OE. It consisted of a team from the consulting group and an internal hospital team. The consultants supplied two directors, a full time project manager, and three analysts to the Analyst Committee. The institution appointed a vice president as the team leader, a director as the lead analyst, and six analysts for the committee. The division of nursing identified the program manager of the air ambulance service and the business manager of the division of nursing as analysts on the team. They worked closely with the senior management engineer from management systems. What follows is a description of the Analyst Committee and process as experienced by the latter three individuals.

The reason the analysts were brought together was to complete extensive data review to determine cost reduction opportunities based on internal information as well as information from local, regional, and national competitors. This detailed analysis was done early on in the project with only two of the eventual analysts involved along with the outside consulting group. Data were retrieved from various financial and productivity systems within the hospital as well as from cost reports from a number of hospitals around the country. Detailed analysis within the division of nursing focused on two key indicators: skill mix and worked HPDs. For both skill mix and HPD reductions, internal and external data were analyzed, and the possibility of achieving benchmark levels was explored at great length. Internal goals for skill mix consisted of driving units to their lowest RN percentage based on actual performance of like units (i.e., if all critical care units could function at the level of the unit with the lowest RN percentage, what would the cost savings equate to?). For savings related to HPD reductions, several years of internal data were examined to determine best demonstrated practice once again. Then, hospitals across the nation that had been chosen as most like MVH both programmatically and demographically, were analyzed for their skill mix and HPD achievements within the inpatient care setting. All these data elements were reviewed side by side with current data to determine potential areas of opportunity for cost reduction.

Through weekly meetings and detailed assignments, the Analyst Committee reviewed the work plan for Phase 1 and began to compare cost data from the various competitors. The nursing representatives on the team were assigned use of a tool developed by the consultants to detail current operational expense at various census levels. Much of this information was gathered by interviews then entered manually into the program, which proved quite time consuming.

In retrospect, the nursing analysts would have profited from being assigned the cost comparison analysis, because it would have increased their confidence that the high initial targets were attainable. The nursing analysts doubted that the proposed expense-reduction targets were attainable and conveyed their private estimate to senior management in an effort to make the target realistic. The steering committee did take the various cost reduction opportunities and weigh them to determine a final target, which was a stretch, but still attainable, based on the institution's reputation for quality care. The final target was within 5 percent of the analysts' private estimation.

The detailed analyses from the division of nursing was presented to the OE Steering Committee for discussion. Eventual finalization of a cost reduction target was driven in the end primarily from savings in skill mix, although HPD savings in the RN category were offset by HPD increases in the NA's role expansion.

The Analyst Committee worked under certain ground rules that contributed to the success of the process. Members' roles as analysts were clearly defined as facilitators of the process and supporters of the various task forces and their leaders. As such, analysts were not free to present their own ideas for cost reductions, but could submit these in written form via a process that allowed for anonymity while the ideas were assessed. Analysts were also cautioned to resolve all concerns about the process or targets within the Analyst Committee or appropriate task force rather than outside the group. This enabled issues to be addressed at the proper level and did not contribute to the general anxiety that employees at various levels in the organization felt about the process. Analysts also had to work confidentially with a variety of individuals on sensitive proposals while providing detailed analysis within the operational framework.

In Phase 2, the analyst role evolved into one of questioning the assumptions underlying each idea presented in order to quantify them without overlooking or duplicating any ideas. The consultants asked if additional steps could be taken to reduce cost such as reducing the number of staff delivering care or changing the mix of the staff. The managers frequently focused on the staff assignment, census, and patient intensity in order to maintain the quality of care delivered. The director's job was to mesh the perspectives into a plan that was operationally feasible. The analysts interacted with all of the previously mentioned roles in helping to design the plan, quantify it, and present it to the OE Steering Committee.

Phase 1: Analysts' Process

The initial process began with the analysts from the nursing areas working on a spread sheet Nursing Cost Calculator (NCC) tool supplied by the consultants. The tool was intended to calculate operational costs, HPDs, and nonproductive time on all inpatient nursing units. The concept was that virtually any staffing pattern could be entered into the tool, and the overall costs could be measured against a current or proposed staffing pattern.

The NCC tool required baseline information from every unit. This proved to be quite time consuming for the analysts because the information was obtained via interviews with nurse managers, management systems data collection and analysis, and unit budgets. Baseline information needed on every unit included average daily census as well as maximum and minimum census recorded over a 12-month period; average salaries of all categories of employees; differential analysis of employees; shift and weekend differentials; percent of overtime being experienced on the unit; staffing pattern for the maximum to the minimum census on each shift; time spent in orientation and education; fixed overhead costs for clinical specialists, etc.; paid time off and sick time for each category of employee; and total FTEs for each category of employee. One of the most complex issues centered around the institution's use of alternative staffing plans. These plans involved various shifts and differentials and necessitated a great deal of analysis to determine an average RN hourly salary.

Once current information was input for a specific unit, the NCC tool produced the operational costs and HPDs. This was compared with the current budget and actual financial performance on that unit to validate the results of the NCC tool (see Table 11.1 for an example from one unit).

Table 11.1

Nursing Cost Calculator Input

Unit Information:

Nursing unit: BURN/6810
Number of beds: 8
Average census: 6.00   103.15%
                         1.17
Average occupancy: 75%
Base period cost: $662,234

Personnel Information:

Benefit %:   20.00%
Hours worked/shift: 8
Hours per FTE: 2083
Days worked/FTE: 260.375

		Day ($)	Eve Dif	Night Dif	Weekend Dif
1. Nurse manager	NM	21.66	$0.00	$0.00	$0.00
2. Primary I & II	RN	18.56	$0.00	$0.00	$0.00
3. Primary III	III	0.00	$0.00	$0.00	$0.00
4. Primary IV	IV	0.00	$0.00	$0.00	$0.00
5. Nurse extender	NE	10.35	$0.00	$0.00	$0.00
6. HUC	HUC	10.98	$0.00	$0.00	$0.00
7. Service assistant	SA	0.00	$0.00	$0.00	$0.00
8. Shift resource nurse	SRN	20.03	$0.00	$0.00	$0.00
9. Registry	REG	0.00	$0.00	$0.00	$0.00

Personnel Information:

Distribution of Time		Direct (%)	Overhead (%)	Non-nursing (%)	Other (%)
1. Nurse manager	NM	100	0	0	0
2. Primary I & II	RN	100	0	0	0
3. Primary III	III	0	0	0	0
4. Primary IV	IV	0	0	0	0
5. Nurse extender	NE	100	0	0	0
6. HUC	HUC	0	100	0	0
7. Service assistant	SA	0	0	100	0
8. Shift resource nurse	SRN	50	50	3	16
9. Registry	REG	0	100	0	0

Continued

Table 11.1 Continued

Personnel Information:
(Enter information per FTE)

Holidays per year: 0
Sick days per year: 0

		Vacation Days	Class Days	Orientation Days	Other ET Days
1. Nurse manager	NM	27.86	0	0	0
2. Primary I & II	RN	27.86	1.05	5.68	2.59
3. Primary III	III	0	0	0	0
4. Primary IV	IV	0	0	0	0
5. Nurse extender	NE	27.86	0	0	0
6. HUC	HUC	27.86	0	0	0
7. Service assistant	SA	27.86	0	1.74	0
8. Shift resource nurse	SRN	27.86	1.05	5.68	2.59
9. Registry	REG	27.86	0	0	0

Calculation of Salary with Benefits for Week Day Shifts:

		Week Day	Eve	Night
1. Nurse manager	NM	$25.99	$25.99	$25.99
2. Primary I & II	RN	$22.27	$22.27	$22.27
3. Primary III	III	$ 0.00	$ 0.00	$ 0.00
4. Primary IV	IV	$ 0.00	$ 0.00	$ 0.00
5. Nurse extender	NE	$12.42	$12.42	$12.42
6. HUC	HUC	$13.18	$13.18	$13.18
7. Service assistant	SA	$ 0.00	$ 0.00	$ 0.00
8. Shift resource nurse	SRN	$24.04	$24.04	$24.04
9. Registry	REG	$ 0.00	$ 0.00	$ 0.00

Burn/6810 Result: Skill Mix

	Direct (%)	Over-head (%)	Non-nursing (%)	Other (%)	Non-productive (%)	Total
Nurse manager	7.57	0.00	0.00	0.00	5.24	
Primary I & II	41.89	0.00	0.00	0.00	38.70	
Primary III	0.00	0.00	0.00	0.00	0.00	
Primary IV	0.00	0.00	0.00	0.00	0.00	
Nurse extender	45.25	0.00	0.00	0.00	31.32	

Continued

Table 11.1   Continued

	Direct (%)	Over-head (%)	Non-nursing (%)	Other (%)	Non-productive (%)	Total
HUC	0.00	66.16	0.00	0.00	7.17	
Service assistant	0.00	0.00	97.09	0.00	7.79	
Shift resource nurse	5.30	33.84	2.91	100.00	9.78	
Registry	0.00	0.00	0.00	0.00	0.00	
Position 10	0.00	0.00	0.00	0.00	0.00	
	100.00	100.00	100.00	100.00	100.00	
Avg HPPD	12.98	2.03	1.42	0.22	2.01	18.65
Weekday HPPD	14.04	2.02	1.41	0.22	2.12	19.82
Weekend HPPD	10.32	2.05	1.43	0.22	1.73	15.75

Burn/6810 Result: Annual Cost

	Direct	Over-head	Non-nursing	Other	Non-productive	Total
Nurse manager	$ 55,851	0	0	0	$ 5,976	$ 61,827
Primary I & II	264,990	0	0	0	37,839	302,828
Primary III	0	0	0	0	0	0
Primary IV	0	0	0	0	0	0
Nurse extender	159,614	0	0	0	17,079	176,692
HUC	0	$38,748	0	0	4,146	42,894
Service assistant	0	0	0	0	0	0
Shift resource nurse	36,152	36,152	$2,169	$11,569	10,325	96,366
Registry	0	0	0	0	0	0
Position 10	0	0	0	0	0	0
Total cost:	$516,606	$74,900	$2,169	$11,569	$75,364	$680,608
Avg $/hr:	$18.19	$16.85	$0.70	$24.04	$17.17	$16.67
Paid $/day:	$236.08	$34.25	$0.99	$5.29	$34.45	$311.06
Savings over base period:						($18,374)

Burn/6810 Result: Total FTEs

	Direct (%)	Over-head (%)	Non-nursing (%)	Other (%)	Non-productive (%)	Total (%)
Nurse manager	1.03	0.00	0.00	0.00	0.11	1.14
Primary I & II	5.71	0.00	0.00	0.00	0.82	6.53
Primary III	0.00	0.00	0.00	0.00	0.00	0.00
Primary IV	0.00	0.00	0.00	0.00	0.00	0.00
Nurse extender	6.17	0.00	0.00	0.00	0.66	6.83
HUC	0.00	1.41	0.00	0.00	0.15	1.56
Service assistant	0.00	0.00	1.44	0.00	0.16	1.61
Shift resource nurse	0.72	0.72	0.04	0.23	0.21	1.92
Registry	0.00	0.00	0.00	0.00	0.00	0.00
Position 10	0.00	0.00	0.00	0.00	0.00	0.00
	13.64	2.13	1.49	0.23	2.11	19.60

Problems occurred with the reconciliation process. The NCC tool could not accurately account for the complex differentials and staffing patterns. Thus, some of the information was averaged or rolled together and was not as accurate as the budgeting process, which separately delineated each alternative staffing pattern. A few units were never able to validate the NCC tool by comparing actual staffing patterns with current financial results. The analysts repeatedly raised concerns within the Analyst Committee, regarding the continued use of the NCC tool in OE without appropriate validation. Additionally, the analysts were concerned that not all of the managers' budgets reflected the current staffing on the unit when census was at budget.

Phase 2: Team Analyzing and Planning

Task forces within the division of nursing were established at the onset of Phase II and charged with the mission of brainstorming to identify any cost reduction ideas, sorting through any bright ideas submitted by hospital personnel not assigned to formal task forces, and quantifying those ideas considered feasible. Every idea that was quantified was also identified as high/low risk as it pertained to impact on patient care as well as hospital staff.

Task forces were set up to cover functional areas within the division of nursing. One team covered the perinatal areas and another covered patient flow within the patient's stay, from admission to discharge. This included areas such as billing, medical records, patient transportation, and medical social services. There was a team to cover all the administrative and support cost centers within the division of nursing, and finally, one to examine the basic model of care. The analyst's role during this time was to support the task forces by providing support to the task force leader in meeting structure (agenda preparation, meeting feedback) and guiding the members through the investigative and quantification processes.

In an effort to begin identifying savings, each nurse manager was asked to propose a modified staffing pattern. At this point, the managers were only aware that a partners-type model was being discussed. Communication was still limited between the managers and the Nursing Model Task Force. This further complicated the development of a new staffing pattern, since the conceptual framework was not complete.

Nevertheless, every nurse manager was asked to identify this new pattern. The process included identifying a leaner mix for each census level possible on the unit, for each shift. The new pattern was entered into the NCC tool, and the expenses associated with that pattern were compared with the current data to identify any potential savings. The only alterations made were in FTEs, as salaries remained the same for the purposes of comparison. Analysts' data from the NCC tool showed unrealistic savings, approaching 35 percent on most units. The analysts, managers, and directors questioned the validity of the NCC tool because the application of the identified savings into an actual unit budget seemed impossible and unrealistic. Continuous revisions and corrections were made to the information in the NCC tool by the analysts despite their reservations. The consultants continued to support the use of the NCC tool and believed the savings were appropriate.

Due to these concerns, a decision was made to test the analysis of the savings identified with the NCC tool by applying the modified plan of staffing for each unit into the current method of budgeting (manpower worksheet). This would validate for MVH if the savings were correct.

Each nurse manager was asked to complete a budget manpower worksheet as if the unit had the new staffing pattern in place. The analysts then compared that information with the current budgeted manpower to identify the savings. Frustrations were noted, since managers were asked to turn the manpower information around in 24 hours. The analysts then compiled the information and found that savings identified in this process were substantially less than those identified through the NCC tool. Thus, the decision was made to terminate use of the NCC tool. Therefore, the decision was made to proceed using the budget manpower worksheet as the base to calculate any savings related to a staffing model change; every effort was made to identify and correct all inconsistencies. The problems identified by the analysts included the following:

1. Overhead versus patient care time for the unit educators, clinical nursing specialists, and shift managers varied from unit to unit.

2. Depending on the alternative staffing plan category of RN FTEs selected for reduction, the savings varied. For example, deleting a staffing plan working three 12-hour shifts yielded different savings from that of a plan working two 12-hour shifts on the weekend (Table 11.2).

3. New roles and pay scales were not yet defined at the unit level.

Table 11.2

Personnel Worksheet

Titles	Current Actual FTEs	Adjusted FTEs	July Avg. Hourly Rate ($)	1992 Merit Increase (%)	1992 Avg. Hourly Rate ($)	1992 Paid Hours	1992 Salary Expense ($)
RN A	21.20	21.20	17.10	1.0500	17.96	44,160	792,886
Nurse manager	2.00	2.00	18.40	1.0500	19.32	4,166	80,487
RN B				1.0500	0.00	0	0
RN C				1.0500	0.00	0	0
RN D				1.0500	0.00	0	0
RN E				1.0500	0.00	0	0
LPN	1.00	1.00	11.20	1.0500	11.76	2,083	24,496
Agency	1.00	1.00	19.00	1.0500	19.95	2,083	41,556
PRN	2.00	2.00	21.00	1.0500	22.05	4,166	91,860
Support	0.50	0.50	23.00	1.0500	24.15	1,042	25,152
Shift resource nurse	1.00	1.00	24.10	1.0500	25.31	2,083	52,710
QA	0.40	0.40	17.10	1.0500	17.96	833	14,960
ED	0.20	0.20	17.10	1.0500	17.96	417	7,480
Clerical	2.80	2.80	9.50	1.0500	9.98	5,832	58,178
Attendant	2.00	2.00	8.00	1.0500	8.40	4,166	34,994
Trained attendant	4.00	4.00	8.40	1.0500	8.82	8,332	73,488
Student	1.00	1.00	5.95	1.0500	6.25	2,083	13,014
				1.0500	0.00	0	0
				1.0500	0.00	0	0
				1.0500	0.00	0	0
				1.0500	0.00	0	0
				1.0500	0.00	0	0
Total	39.10	39.10				81,445	1,311,262

4. Opinions varied regarding the use of the SA/host role in relation to the existing environmental service attendants/nutrition attendants currently on the unit.

5. Nurse managers had difficulty correlating a new staffing pattern with the existing positions in the manpower worksheet format.

Prior to beginning a new analysis, the directors of nursing identified standards of overhead versus direct patient care time as follows:

• Shift Managers: 20 percent fixed, 80 percent direct care
• Clinical Specialists: 80 percent fixed, 20 percent direct care
• Unit Educators: 60 percent fixed, 40 percent direct care.

All managers were to use these guidelines in their new staffing model plans.

In an effort to clearly identify the reduction of FTEs currently in the manpower worksheet, a tool was developed by the analysts to assist the nurse managers (Table 11.3). The nurse managers were asked to identify their budgeted staffing pattern and their proposed staffing pattern by category of employee (RN, LPN, NA, HUC, and SA) by shift. They were also asked to identify their specific use for the SA/host/hostess position and whether the unit would still have a need for current environmental services support.

The analysts then converted the number of personnel in each category to FTEs. This identified the number of FTEs in the original budget and the number of FTEs in the proposed staffing pattern by category. The difference for each category was calculated, and a new manpower worksheet was generated by simply subtracting this difference from the original manpower worksheet in the respective categories. For the category of RN FTEs, the nurse managers were asked to specify the type of RN most likely to be reduced (i.e., regular, in house per diem RN, etc.). This was necessary due to the complexity of the RN payment plans. This process was repeated several times with the nurse managers and analysts going over various assumptions regarding staffing pattern and census level. The role of the analysts again was merely of quantifying the different scenarios proposed by the managers and not judging whether there were appropriate resources being applied to the census levels.

The original worksheet salary expense and the revised worksheet salary expense were compared to calculate savings on the unit. Total net expense reduction was $1,900,000, or 5 percent of total labor dollars

Table 11.3

Staffing Pattern Worksheet

Cost Center Name _____ Cost Center Number _____

Average Census (1992 Budget) __34.95__

Original Budget

	Days	Evenings	Nights	Weekends	FTE
RN number	7	6	5	____	31.40 RN
FTE					
LPN number	0	0	0	0	0 LPN
FTE	–	–	–	–	
Extender number	4	3	2	____	12.55 WE
FTE					

Staffing Ratios (projected with model)

	Days	Evenings	Nights	Weekends	FTE
HUC number	5	5	0	____	2.73 Fixed
HUC FTE					4.89 HUC

Projected Budget (as per ADC)

	Days	Evenings	Nights	Weekends
RN number	5.5	4.5	3	same
LPN number	0	0	0	0
Extender number	5.5	4.5	3	same
HUC number	1.5	1.5		same

Staffing Ratios Provided in Nurse Cost Calculator (as per ADC)

	Days	Evenings	Nights	Weekends
RN number	5	4	3	same
LPN number	0	0	0	same
Extender number	5	4	3	same

Continued

Table 11.3   Continued

Number of (not FTEs) Service Associates Needed
Environmental

	WK			Weekend		
	D	**E**	**N**	**D**	**E**	**N**
	2	.65	.65	2	.65	.65

Hostess

	WK			Weekend		
	D	**E**	**N**	**D**	**E**	**N**
	1	.65	.65	1	.65	.65

Other _____

Did you include these service associates in your revised model budget?
No

Additional individuals/hours not in 1992 budget that need to be considered?

Describe nurse/patient ratio (including nurse extenders) for each shift.
• Days—RNs run with 7–8 pts with a Nurse Extender
• Eves—RN have 8–9 pts with a Nurse Extender
• Ngts—RN have 10–12 pts with a Nurse Extender
• The Nurse Extender would be a direct caregiver accountable for a specific
  group of pts with the RN. The NEs would have some basic ortho tech skills
  as outlined on the model position description.

(Tables 11.4 and 11.5). Additionally, worked HPDs and skill mix were calculated. Worked HPDs increased, reflecting the addition of the PCTs and SAs, while the RN skill mix declined (Table 11.6).

There was no salary expense for SAs in the original nursing budget–manpower worksheet due to the fact that environmental services was not unit based. Consequently, the salary expense of the SA/host role was calculated separately. Table 11.7 shows the calculations that were done separately to plan for the number of SAs needed for the new model of care.

At this time, the pay rate planned for SAs was the midpoint of their current range. The cost of adding the SA position was subtracted from the savings in RN/PCT skill mix change to calculate a final savings figure.

Table 11.4

Personnel Worksheet Before Model Changes

Titles	Current Actual FTEs	Adjusted FTEs	July Avg. Hourly Rate ($)	1992 Merit Increase (%)	1992 Avg. Hourly Rate ($)	1992 Paid Hours	1992 Salary Expense ($)
RN A	21.20	21.20	17.10	1.0500	17.96	44,160	792,886
Nurse manager	2.00	2.00	18.40	1.0500	19.32	4,166	80,487
RN B				1.0500	0.00	0	0
RN C				1.0500	0.00	0	0
RN D				1.0500	0.00	0	0
RN E				1.0500	0.00	0	0
LPN	1.00	1.00	11.20	1.0500	11.76	2,083	24,496
Agency	1.00	1.00	19.00	1.0500	19.95	2,083	41,556
PRN	2.00	2.00	21.00	1.0500	22.05	4,166	91,860
Support	0.50	0.50	23.00	1.0500	24.15	1,042	25,152
Shift resource nurse	1.00	1.00	24.10	1.0500	25.31	2,083	52,710
QA	0.40	0.40	17.10	1.0500	17.96	833	14,960
ED	0.20	0.20	17.10	1.0500	17.96	417	7,480
Clerical	2.80	2.80	9.50	1.0500	9.98	5,832	58,178
Attendant	2.00	2.00	8.00	1.0500	8.40	4,166	34,994
Trained attendant	4.00	4.00	8.40	1.0500	8.82	8,332	73,488
Student	1.00	1.00	5.95	1.0500	6.25	2,083	13,014
				1.0500	0.00	0	0
				1.0500	0.00	0	0
				1.0500	0.00	0	0
				1.0500	0.00	0	0
Total	39.10	39.10				81,445	1,311,262

Table 11.5

Personnel Worksheet After Model Changes

Titles	Current Actual FTEs	Adjusted FTEs	July Avg. Hourly Rate ($)	1992 Merit Increase (%)	1992 Avg. Hourly Rate ($)	1992 Paid Hours	1992 Salary Expense ($)
RN A	17.20	17.20	17.10	1.0500	17.96	35,828	643,285
Nurse manager	2.00	2.00	18.40	1.0500	19.32	4,166	80,487
RN B				1.0500	0.00	0	0
RN C				1.0500	0.00	0	0
RN D				1.0500	0.00	0	0
RN E				1.0500	0.00	0	0
LPN	1.00	1.00	11.20	1.0500	11.76	2,083	24,496
Agency	1.00	1.00	19.00	1.0500	19.95	2,083	41,556
PRN	2.00	2.00	21.00	1.0500	22.05	4,166	91,860
Support	0.50	0.50	23.00	1.0500	24.15	1,042	25,152
Shift resource nurse	1.00	1.00	24.10	1.0500	25.31	2,083	52,710
QA	0.40	0.40	17.10	1.0500	17.96	833	14,960
ED	0.20	0.20	17.10	1.0500	17.96	417	7,480
Clerical	2.80	2.80	9.50	1.0500	9.98	5,832	58,178
Attendant	2.00	2.00	8.00	1.0500	8.40	4,166	34,994
Trained attendant	8.00	8.00	8.40	1.0500	8.82	16,664	146,976
Student	1.00	1.00	5.95	1.0500	6.25	2,083	13,014
				1.0500	0.00	0	0
				1.0500	0.00	0	0
				1.0500	0.00	0	0
				1.0500	0.00	0	0
				1.0500	0.00	0	0
Total	39.10	39.10				81,445	1,235,149

Table 11.6

Cost Reduction Summary

			Skill Mix		H.P.D. (RN, NA, SA)		Savings
			Current	Proposed			
CC#	Unit	Type	(%)	(%)	Current	Proposed	($)
6100	3E/SE	Ortho	71.77	56.68	7.27	8.03	210,731
6130	4E/SE	Endo	67.21	57.84	6.91	8.16	10,632
6150	4NE	Renal	71.37	56.12	6.94	8.14	57,799
6160	5E/SE	Onc/Gyn	69.94	59.60	7.05	8.80	48,721
6200	5NW	M/S	73.02	60.29	6.88	8.40	58,830
6250	3NE	M/S	68.14	65.58	7.80	8.85	24,422
6292	6SE	Pain	100.00	100.00	4.94	4.94	0
6294	5NE	Onc	85.09	65.95	6.98	9.29	48,770
6730	BC1	BC1	69.52	56.68	6.64	7.78	58,232
6740	M3	M3	62.33	50.53	5.77	8.12	211,404
6400	2NW	CICU	94.94	86.38	17.63	19.17	12,172
6415	3NW	ICU	98.06	91.96	16.88	18.98	52,103
6500	NICU	NICU	94.93	65.79	13.40	13.91	568,301
6135	4W/SW	Neuro	79.43	62.67	9.22	9.95	222,685
6190	5W/SW	Telem.	73.73	64.53	8.50	9.28	108,388
6293	4NW	PM&R	72.62	51.79	7.64	8.60	146,803
6420	3W	Adv Care	85.00	68.15	11.54	13.58	21,452
6710	BC2/SC2	BC2/SC2	79.37	68.08	23.68	22.08	1,013,924
6810	3NW	Burn	74.60	57.57	15.74	17.09	56,278
6296	6NE	TNG PNT	53.66	48.31	6.00	6.47	53,298
6430	6W	Psych	71.91	59.27	9.41	9.50	206,640
			79.18	65.15	9.59	10.65	2,768,778

Less 46.49 additional service associates: 815,788

Total nursing model savings: ($1,952,990)

Each nursing unit manager has projected how the unit would run under the new model, producing a total of $1,952,990 annualized savings.

The total FTE, skill mix, HPD, and salary expense changes were presented to the OE Steering Committee for final approval. It was agreed that HPDs would increase since there would be more caregivers on the units; however, salary expense would decrease, since the mix of

Table 11.7

Service Associate FTE Summary

CC #	Unit	Type	Number SAs Presented to Steering Comm.	Nse. Mgr. Original Request	Add 8% PTO	Number SAs 93 Budget Request
6100	3E/SE	Ortho	6.02	6.02	6.50	6.80
6130	4E/SE	Endo	5.18	5.18	5.59	5.80
6135	4W/SW	Neuro	2.05	4.90	5.29	5.29
6150	4NE	Renal	3.36	3.36	3.63	3.62
6160	5E/SE	Onc/Gyn	8.40	8.40	9.07	9.07
6190	5W/SW	Telem.	9.13	5.60	6.05	9.47
6200	5NW	M/S	5.60	5.60	6.05	6.06
6250	3NE	M/S	2.38	2.38	2.57	2.35
6292	6SE	Pain	0.00	0.00	0.00	0.12
6293	4NW	PM&R	4.20	4.20	4.54	4.00
6294	5NE	Onc	5.04	5.04	5.44	5.44
6296	6NE	TNG PNT	1.40	1.40	1.51	
6400	2NW	CICU	3.10	2.80	3.02	4.20
6415	3NW	ICU	0.57	5.60	6.05	5.80
6420	3W	Adv Care	3.66	2.80	3.02	4.62
6430	6W	Psych	3.08	3.08	3.33	3.33
6500	NICU	NICU	4.49	4.20	4.54	1.80
6710	BC2/SC2	BC2/SC2	7.54	8.40	9.07	9.41
6730	BC1	BC1	3.34	6.30	6.80	6.81
6740	M3	M3	6.34	6.30	6.80	6.80
6810	3NW	Burn	1.61	1.61	1.74	1.52
		Totals	86.49	93.17	100.62	102.31
6780		ETR				4.50
6251		ATA				1.56

caregivers would have fewer numbers of RNs. The division of nursing was committed to the new patient care model. Once approved, the implementation phase of the project, known as Phase 3, began.

It should be noted at this point that the final savings figure presented to the steering committee for the division of nursing included other cost-saving ideas in addition to the model of care changes. Even though these were much smaller in their cost impact, they are worthy of note. They included such things as publishing fewer copies of the nursing newsletters; decreasing the cost of a variety of supply items by changing

Table 11.8
Attrition Data

		Before 92 Budget RN	After 92 Budget RN	Net Change	Historical RN Attrition Rate	Expected Annual Turnover	'92 Jun–Dec	'93 Jan–Jun	'93 Jul–Dec	93 Total
6100	Ortho	31.3	23.8	-7.5	19%	5	-3	-3.5	-1	-7.5
6135	Neuro	35.3	26.9	-8.4	20%	7	-3	-3	-2.5	-8.5
6430	Psych	24	18.4	-5.6	26%	6	-2.5	-1	-2	-5.5

		Before 92 Budget NA	After 92 Budget NA	Net Change	Historical NA Attrition Rate	Expected Annual Turnover	'92 Jun–Dec	'93 Jan–Jun	'93 Jul–Dec	93 Total
6100	Ortho	11.5	17.5	6.0	18%	2	2	2	2	6.0
6135	Neuro	6.1	13.1	7.0	65%	3	3	3	1	7.0
6430	Psych	0.5	3.3	2.8	33%	0	1	1	0.8	2.8

Clustering:

#5		#1		#2	
Ortho		Neuro		Psych	
-7.5		-8.4		-5.6	
-VG		Done		-TW	
-SM		Ready		-CK	
-LZ				-JS	
-CG				-JA	
-KH				-BC	
-NG				-BB	
-EF					
-JC					

vendors or changing quantity used; decreasing committee meeting times; critically evaluating administrative positions; moving staffing secretaries to a centralized area serving more than one unit; and eliminating alternative staffing plans by attrition, such as the Baylor plan in which RNs work 24 hours each weekend but are paid for 36 hours (Table 11.8).

Phase 3: Evaluation Based on Budget—Operationalizing the Changes

In March 1992, some errors were uncovered in the data, which had been presented to the OE Steering Committee and formed the basis of the cost savings calculations. The proposal approved by the OE Steering Committee assumed the SAs and PCTs, or nurse extenders, would be graded at a lower wage rate, thereby increasing the amount of savings attributed to the skill mix change. However, when HRD analyzed the specific jobs and assigned wage grades, which were one step higher than those projected, a portion of the projected savings was eliminated.

There was a shortfall of five SA FTEs to implement the model. This error was due to:

1. a transposition error
2. an outpatient unit that was overlooked
3. changing needs identified by the nurse managers
4. different consultants and analysts being responsible for different pieces of the proposal
5. turnaround time for data was measured in hours.

These errors point out the necessity to take enough time to thoroughly review and verify the accuracy of the final figures and assumptions as a whole before they are presented to a group like the OE Steering Committee for acceptance.

In April 1992, the finance department and management systems revised the 1992 budget to reflect the skill-mix changes and resulting cost saving that the division of nursing committed to achieving in OE. The revised budgets phased in the skill mix for the individual units was based on attrition. This was of some concern to the analysts because they knew that the Steering and Analysts Committees had just begun to organize their work and were not prepared to accept a timetable for unit implementation. Therefore, the revised 1992 budgets that were prepared in April would be inaccurate on an individual cost-center basis. There was concern that the managers and directors did not fully understand that each cost center would be either over or under budget for the rest of 1992 for monitoring purposes. The variance in monitoring implementation was not a priority at the time, since they were focused on the difficult task of implementation.

The Analyst Committee also had prolonged discussions regarding how to phase in the skill-mix change. Rather than use attrition, it made greater operational feasibility to phase in the change on a particular unit at one time. This enhanced the ability of the project managers to monitor the success of the change as well as enable the nurse managers and other unit leaders to prepare staff for the change in philosophy, as well as practice, and foster the introduction of the new roles of the PCT and SA. A change of this magnitude needed to be handled incrementally in order for improvements in the implementation process to be applied to other units implementing PACE 2000. It was determined that units should be clustered for the purposes of implementation. Two or three units would implement PACE 2000 every three months, which would enable classes to be scheduled for the staff affected and maximize the time availability of the educators.

Because the senior vice president determined that the achievement of the skill-mix change had been set as a goal for the division rather than for individual cost centers, the analysts focused on tracking and communicating divisionwide data rather than cost-center specific data. The analysts also spent time clarifying intent and terms used in Phase 2 of OE in order to assist the committees in moving forward with implementation plans for Phase 3.

Throughout the spring and early summer of 1992, the nurse managers and directors of nursing continued to refine the implementation of PACE 2000, including detailed requirements and job descriptions for the nurse extender roles based on feedback from the pilot unit. Directors, managers, and analysts met on at least six separate occasions to revise the 1993 budgets in order to meet the skill mix and expenditure reduction goals. The 1993 budgets also incorporated lessons learned regarding education and role clarification during the initial organizational process. This period was one of extremely high frustration for the nurse managers, directors of nursing, and analysts.

Assumptions were continually reexamined and revised, which made it difficult to keep track of the changes in the various budgets. One director further altered skill mix during this period, in effect buying additional PCTs with RN hours in order to more efficiently use the new role in particular units. This resulted in additional FTEs at no additional expense to the model. The decision to cluster the units for implementation purposes rather than implement on all units simultaneously via attrition led to implementation of the model more slowly than originally approved. Therefore, the draft 1993 budgets that were produced in July 1992 projected FTE usage in excess of levels that had been approved by the OE Steering Committee in February.

Once again, directors of nursing, nurse managers, and analysts felt under the gun to reconcile these differences, and another highly charged stressful period ensued. Different strategies were used to reconcile the 1993 budgets with the PACE 2000 projections. In some cases, the director met with the nurse managers and reviewed the assumptions used with the original model projections and elected to use those without alteration in the 1993 budgets. In other cases, directors met with the nurse managers and systematically had them build zero-based budgets, so they incorporated both the original PACE 2000 projections as well as changes in roles that had evolved from the implementation committees.

This process was a very good basic review for individuals who had made numerous incremental changes in their budgets in the ensuing four months but had not analyzed it as a whole. The manager started with the basic volume forecast of the average number of patients per day and used this to project the number of direct care givers needed for each shift for both weekdays and weekends. Added to this number were the fixed FTEs for SAs needed under the new patient care model. Additional fixed RN hours for such items as QA, education, orientation, and shift manager administrative time were also added. Then a standard percentage was applied to each employee category, based on each unit's history, for benefit time.

Eventually through the fall of 1992, a compromise was reached that allowed the division of nursing to implement the PACE 2000 model using the clustered implementation. Senior management determined that the slightly altered implementation timeline would result in a successful model while still yielding the cost savings projected.

Ongoing Monthly Monitoring

Accurate and timely financial and operational monitoring of the conversion to the new patient care model was essential to do the following:

1. Learn from the experience of the first cluster of nursing units who implemented the model to improve the successful implementation on successive units.

2. Determine when and where organizational support from other departments was to be required to achieve the model's objective. This needed to be communicated to those departments to enable them to structure their work to achieve the specific goals. For example, substantial HRD support was needed during various phases of the implementation in order to advertise, screen, hire, and orient personnel with specific qualifications. Other hospital departments affected were environmental services, information systems, and transportation.

3. Calculate the financial impact, if any, of variances from the proposed timetable of implementation. While some units moved forward on the timetable and others were deferred, the net impact may have been significant for any one monthly period but offsetting or negligible for year-to-date reporting purposes. This type of reporting served to focus energies where they were needed rather than unnecessarily spending time on minor fluctuations in the timetable.

4. Provide timely reporting of any unfavorable financial variances from the expected financial targets for the new patient care model. This would enable project managers and upper and middle management to determine what adjustments were needed to achieve the goals, or if any other switch in strategy or program focus was required, to attain the financial target on the completion of the project.

5. Track actual expenses attributed to the implementation of the patient care model. Any variance in implementation expenses had implications not only for the total expense of the model conversion, but the ongoing expenses associated with recruitment, orientation, and training necessary to sustain the new model in the future.

When MVH decided to implement the patient care model based on attrition of RNs from the various nursing units, an accurate monitoring tool to capture this data was essential. The analysts attempted to use the existing human resource system to track attrition via a report mechanism rather than create a new reporting structure. While this was ideal in theory, it was not practical because of the reporting of resignations in the systems to accommodate a manual payroll system. Therefore, the resignations were reported some time after the event had occurred and the manager had replaced the position. In order to receive timely attrition data, the analysts resorted to spot checks using the internal division of nursing database.

In retrospect, the provision of timely attrition data was not crucial due to the conservative attrition estimates used to project turnover and the actual RN turnover at MVH, which enabled most model conversions to proceed as scheduled. However if attrition had been significantly below projections, another tool would have been developed to provide this data on a more timely basis in converting units to the new model.

Variance reports, which the nurse managers produce every two weeks, were revised to add position data. This position data included positions on hold, position conversions, overhires, and conversion of alternative staffing plans to flexible staffing options (Table 11.9).

Once an implementation schedule had been established, there was now a point that could be measured against a baseline to see if skill mix had shifted toward the planned percentage and if labor dollars were indeed decreasing. An ongoing measurement process was designed with input from the senior vice president of hospital operations that was to track key success factors. It was believed that this information should be compiled for use at a fairly high level, that is, summarized for the division for use by upper management. The success factors that were selected first included salary expense per patient day (Figure 11.1). This certainly was a factor that needed to be monitored closely. At the same time, worked HPDs were always tracked on a biweekly basis (Figure 11.2). The tracking of paid HPDs was added (Figure 11.3). Average daily census was compared, actual to budget (Figure 11.4). Finally, the percentage of RN skill mix was calculated and shifted as units implemented changes (Figure 11.5).

Another monitoring tool was developed that reported the reduction in the number of Baylor plan positions via attrition from the organization on a monthly basis. This had to be tracked manually by the nurse managers and reported on the pay period–variance report (Table 11.10).

All of this tracking information was presented in a graph and was reported to upper level management at first, then eventually shared with individual nursing units, where interpretation and coaching came into play. Individual meetings were scheduled, especially during the budget season to review progress of the units and to discuss problems, issues, and concerns that were continually arising on the units.

Table 11.9

Variance Report

Inpatient Unit Pay Period Variance Report
Period: May 1, 1993

Cost Center   6135
Unit   4W/SW

	Units	x Weekend HPD x	Rate	= Total Worked Salary Expense
Budget	391	10.27	$13.85	$55,560
Actual	425	11.45	$13.91	$67,704
Variance	34	1.18	$0.06	$12,144
% Variance	8.8%	11.5%	0.4%	21.9%
Due to:	$4,891	$6,962	$291	$12,144

Explain any unfavorable weekend HPD and rate variance:

PNIII off the unit 20 hours teaching PCT classes, ACLS instructor and involved in trauma update presentation. PNIV involved in RN classes, therefore, the PNIII and PNIV were only able to work 52 hours clinical. 24 hours of shift manager office time—SM retreat orientation of new shift managers—16 hours of ACLS. Budgeted Medicus 0.9–1.30 range for this pay period equaled 1.40–1.72. Average hourly rate increased due to high acuity and increased need for rather than a PCT. 100 hours of transition duty incorrectly charged to us (we will investigate why). 144 hours of sitter with the 244 hours of sitter and transition duty actual HPD is 10.88.

Readiness Report

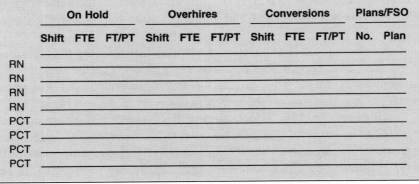

	On Hold			Overhires			Conversions			Plans/FSO	
	Shift	FTE	FT/PT	Shift	FTE	FT/PT	Shift	FTE	FT/PT	No.	Plan
RN											
RN											
RN											
RN											
PCT											
PCT											
PCT											
PCT											

Figure 11.1

Salary Expense per Patient Day
All Inpatient Units

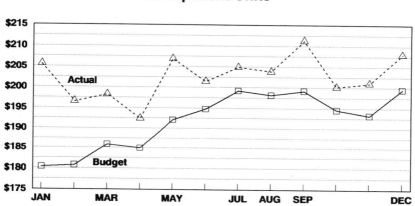

Figure 11.2

Worked Hours per Patient Day
All Inpatient Units

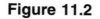
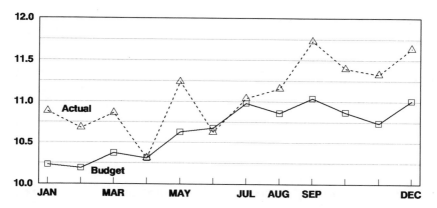

Figure 11.3

Paid Hours per Patient Day
All Inpatient Units

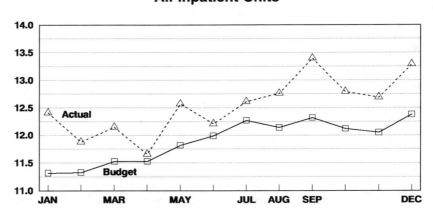

Figure 11.4

Average Daily Census
All Inpatient Units

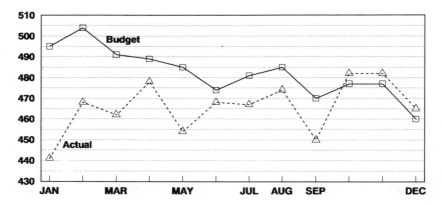

Figure 11.5

Skill Mix: Percentage of RNs
All Inpatient Units

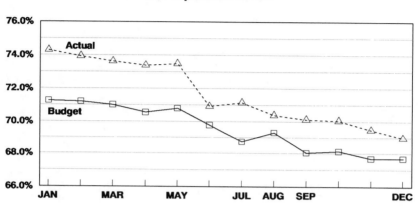

In addition to the information that the division of nursing chose to track, the hospital as a whole had a tracking mechanism in place for the overall OE Project. This consisted of monitoring general ledger line item adjustments by account. Appendix 11.A shows an example of a report generated from the OE database that illustrates the general ledger impact, not only by account, but by time frame (month, year, and dollar amount). Appendix 11.B then summarizes for a single cost center the rollup of various cost saving ideas and generates a total adjustment to a cost center budget. This proved helpful when multiple cost-saving ideas impacted a cost center. The division of nursing was primarily impacted by skill-mix ideas and changes, but other ideas such as automated medication dispensing; revised documentation to decrease duplication; block scheduling in surgery; altered span of control in nursing education, nursing administration, and orthopedic services; elimination of mandatory on-call in obstetrics; reduction of national RN recruiting; standardization of occular

Table 11.10

Alternative Staffing Plans

Tracking Alternative Staffing Plans
August 1992 year-to-date

	Plan 2		Plan 3		Plan 4		Plan 5	
	OE	ACT	OE	ACT	OE	ACT	OE	ACT
January	0	0	0	−1	0	0	0	−1
February	0	0	0	0	0	0	0	0
March	0	−1	−2	0	−1	0	0	−2
April	−1	−1	−1	0	−1	−1	0	0
May	0	−2	−2	−7	0	−1	0	0
June	−6	−1	−9	0	−2	−2	0	0
July	0	−10	0	−7	−1	0	0	−4
August	−1	−1	−3	0	−1	0	0	0
September	−1		0		0		0	
October	−1		−5		−3		−2	
November	0		0		0		0	
December	0		−2		0		0	
Total	−10	−16	−24	−15	−9	−4	−2	−7

lenses; glove supply consolidation; reduction in contract maintenance; and menu system computerization also contributed to individual cost-center savings.

Cost of Implementation: Committee Budgets

The implementation of a new patient care model introduced great changes to the staff, physicians, and patients at MVH. One of the best ways to facilitate this change included the provision of enough resources to effectively communicate with and train the staff. To ensure that resources to support this massive change were allocated, a separate budget to implement the PACE 2000 model was established.

The analysts first met with the chairs of the various subcommittees to solicit their estimates of resources to accomplish their individual tasks. Specific estimates of manhours, salary, supplies, other, and capital expense were then prepared and shared with the project leaders who proceeded to revise the estimates based on the changing calendar for implementation. Finally, the directors of nursing and the senior vice president reviewed the proposed budget and revised it to meet realistic time frame and resource constraints.

The PACE 2000 implementation budget for the first year was as follows:

- *Documentation*—$40,000 to revise, trial forms, and committee time.
- *Pharmacy*—$700,000 over two years to phase in hardware and software for an automated medication system, which was sold as an enabler for RN time.
- *Education*—$15,000 for educational materials, $5,000 for books and committee time.
- *Roles*—Committee time, $1,000 for training materials.
- *Training*—16 hours of training per RN, or 5.0 RN FTEs; 72 hours of training per PCT, or 6.23 PCT FTEs; 32 hours of training per SA, or .77 SA FTEs.
- *Clinical ladder*—Committee time.
- *Human resources*—Committee time.
- *Publication*—$5,000 to publish 4–6 issues of the newsletter, as well as stipends paid for editing and consulting fees.
- *Case management*—Committee time. Committee time generally consisted of 2–3 meetings per month at 2–4 hours each with an average of 10–12 participants.

As the year proceeded and the various subcommittees refined their plans, additional resources were required in the area of documentation, recruiting, and training outside hires for extender positions. Although there was the potential to have actual expenditures exceed the budgeted expenditures, since actual implementation of certain classes and bringing units up on the model lagged behind the initial calendar, the unanticipated expenses were more than offset.

Recommendations

From the analyst's perspective, OE and the development and implementation of PACE 2000 proved to be a positive learning process in many respects. One of the greatest areas of development noted was the refinement of the management team's budgeting skills. While nursing management had high-level budgeting skills prior to this process, the correlation of positions to budget was utilized. The relationship between staffing patterns and adjustments to those patterns and the overall operating expense became much clearer. This skill is one that continues to be refined and will be used in the future for annual budgeting, variance explanation, and evaluation of staffing patterns.

Another positive aspect of this process was the involvement of the staff. Rarely do staff have the opportunity to participate in work redesign of this magnitude. Their ability to have input into the restructuring of their work provided a framework for the change that continues to occur. Ground rules proved to be an asset to the process, since it facilitated an effective group of analysts and made the process clearer for those involved.

Finally, the presentation of information related to progress toward the target was very well received due to the use of aids such as graphing, which showed trends. The information was provided in a manner that was meaningful to the users and gave a visual summary of progress.

As with all processes, the analysts believe there were things that should have been done differently. Some of these items could not be identified until the particular phase was complete and, thus, could not be changed. Others were identified and corrected as appropriate. Following is a list of recommendations for the reader:

1. Thoroughly evaluate any prepackaged financial analysis tools for staffing patterns to ensure validity and accuracy. The NCC tool was found to be very time consuming and unable to calculate correct expenses associated with different staffing patterns. This was due to the inability of the tool to be user specific for MVH differentials and special pay policies. A great deal of the analyst's time was wasted compiling data that proved to be inaccurate.

2. Bring the management team into the process very early. The nurse managers were asked to identify specific staffing patterns for the new delivery of care concept very rapidly. This did not allow them time for extensive thought related to the logistics of the change. Their work would have been easier if they would have been included in the conceptual team.

3. Keep a detailed diary of all events, meetings, and decisions. The multitude of informal meetings, planning, and evaluating sessions was overwhelming. A diary of events would have been invaluable to reconcile issues.

4. Continuously clarify the analyst's role throughout the process. Although the role of the analyst was clarified at the beginning of the process to the analysts and administration, it became apparent that this was confusing to those individuals who were added after the start of the process. The main confusion stemmed from the perception that the analysts served to evaluate different staffing patterns for feasibility, rather than for financial impact to the hospital.

5. Utilize a zero-based budgeting approach from the onset. This proved to be a worthwhile exercise and would have saved project rework if it was utilized at the onset instead of at the end of the process.

6. Attrition calculations should not include a one-to-one replacement schedule for implementation and budgeting. Attrition data calculated by the analysts was based on historical data and assumed a one-to-one replacement schedule for nurses and PCTs. This schedule was then used to determine time frames of implementation and budget adjustments. This method did not account for the time needed for orientation and the adjustment of the staff to the new roles.

Summary

This chapter has described the processes that were put into place to monitor the impact of cost-containment efforts within MVH's Division of Nursing. To date, over $1 million has been reduced from the nursing budget.

Changes in the patient care delivery model (PACE 2000) began in 1992 and will conclude in late 1995. Over an eighteen-month period, the average hourly rate in the division of nursing has been reduced by $0.92 per hour. Though HPDs have increased, the skill mix has shifted from 79 percent RN to 70 percent with the integration of the PCT. Because implementation of the model is ongoing, the full benefit of all cost savings has not yet been realized.

Appendix 11.A

MVH Operational Excellence Idea Quantification Worksheet

IDEA DESCRIPTION:
Reduce skill in mix in cc 6136-Neuro Unit

SAVINGS

COST CENTER	MSA ACCT.#	DESCRIPTION	START MO/YR	ANNUALIZED $ SAVINGS
6135	5202005	1 RN	7-1-92	$37,968
9830	6805999	Compensation & Ben	7-1-92	$7,594
6135	5202005	1 RN	9-1-92	$37,968
9830	6805999	Compensation & Ben	9-1-92	$7,594
6135	5202005	1 RN	11-1-92	$37,968
9830	6805999	Compensation & Ben	11-1-92	$7,594
6135	5202005	1 RN	1-1-93	$37,968
9830	6805999	Compensation & Ben	1-1-93	$7,594
6135	5202005	1 RN	1-1-93	$37,968
9830	6805999	Compensation & Ben	1-1-93	$7,594
6135	5202005	1 RN	1-1-93	$37,968
9830	6805999	Compensation & Ben	1-1-93	$7,594
6135	5202005	1 RN	1-1-93	$37,968
9830	6805999	Compensation & Ben	1-1-93	$7,594
6135	5202005	1 RN	1-1-93	$37,968
9830	6805999	Compensation & Ben	1-1-93	$7,594
6135	5202005	0.4 RN	1-1-93	$15,187
9830	6805999	Compensation & Ben	1-1-93	$3,037

Total
$382,717

INVESTMENT

COST CENTER	MSA ACCT.#	DESCRIPTION	START MO/YR	ANNUALIZED $ ADDITIONAL
6135	5606123	1 Patient Care Tech	7-1-92	$18,916
9830	6805999	Compensation & Ben	7-1-92	$3,783
6135	5606123	1 Patient Care Tech	9-1-92	$18,916
9830	6805999	Compensation & Ben	9-1-92	$3,783
6135	5606123	1 Patient Care Tech	11-1-92	$18,916
9830	6805999	Compensation & Ben	11-1-92	$3,783
6135	5606123	1 Patient Care Tech	1-1-93	$18,916
9830	6805999	Compensation & Ben	1-1-93	$3,783
6135	5606123	1 Patient Care Tech	1-1-93	$18,916
9830	6805999	Compensation & Ben	1-1-93	$3,783
6135	5606123	1 Patient Care Tech	1-1-93	$18,916

9830	6805999	Compensation & Ben	1-1-93	$3,783
6135	5606123	1.05 Patient Care Tech	1-1-93	$19,864
9830	6805999	Compensation & Ben	1-1-93	$3,973

Total

$160,032

CAPITAL

A) Initial Outlay	
B) Useful Life (Yrs.)	
C) Salvage Value	
D) Future Outlay	
Budget Effect.Date	

Responsible: B. C.
Start date: 3-1-92
End Date   12-1-93

1992 TOTAL: $68,587
1993 TOTAL: $154,098

Appendix 11.B

Miami Valley Hospital Operational
Excellence Budget Adjustment Worksheet

COST CENTER: 6100

ACCOUNT	IDEA#	JAN	FEB	MAR	APR	MAY	JUN	JUL
5207251	12004357	0	0	0	0	0	0	0
5606123	12004357	0	0	0	0	0	$1,626	$1,683
5606123	12004357	0	0	0	0	0	$0	$0
5606123	12004357	0	0	0	0	0	$0	$0
5606123	12004357	0	0	0	0	0	$0	$0
5606123	12004357	0	0	0	0	0	$0	$0
5606123	12004357	0	0	0	0	0	$0	$0
ACCOUNT SUBTOTAL:		$0	$0	$0	$0	$0	$1,626	$1,683
5202005	12004357	$0	$0	$0	$0	$0	($3,224)	($3,337)
5202005	12004357	$0	$0	$0	$0	$0	$0	$0
5202005	12004357	$0	$0	$0	$0	$0	$0	$0
5202005	12004357	$0	$0	$0	$0	$0	$0	$0
5202005	12004357	$0	$0	$0	$0	$0	$0	$0
5202005	12004357	$0	$0	$0	$0	$0	$0	$0
5202005	12004357	$0	$0	$0	$0	$0	$0	$0
ACCOUNT SUBTOTAL:		$0	$0	$0	$0	$0	($3,224)	($3,337)
TOTAL EXPENSES:		$0	$0	$0	$0	$0	($1,598)	($1,654)
1217251	12004357	0	0	0	0	0	0	0
1616123	12004357	0	0	0	0	0	171	177
1616123	12004357	0	0	0	0	0	0	0
1616123	12004357	0	0	0	0	0	0	0
1616123	12004357	0	0	0	0	0	0	0
1616123	12004357	0	0	0	0	0	0	0
1616123	12004357	0	0	0	0	0	0	0
ACCOUNT SUBTOTAL:		0	0	0	0	0	171	177
1212005	12004357	0	0	0	0	0	(171)	(177)
1212005	12004357	0	0	0	0	0	0	0
1212005	12004357	0	0	0	0	0	0	0
1212005	12004357	0	0	0	0	0	0	0
1212005	12004357	0	0	0	0	0	0	0
1212005	12004357	0	0	0	0	0	0	0
1212005	12004357	0	0	0	0	0	0	0
ACCOUNT SUBTOTAL:		0	0	0	0	0	(171)	(177)
TOTAL LABOR HOURS:		0	0	0	0	0	0	0

Appendix 11.B   Continued

DIRECTOR: T. L.

AUG	SEP	OCT	NOV	DEC	92 TOTAL	93 TOTAL	94 TOTAL	95 TOTAL
0	0	0	0	0	0	($21,736)	($21,736)	($21,736)
$1,683	$1,626	$1,683	$1,626	$1,683	$11,610	$19,809	$19,809	$19,809
$0	$1,626	$1,683	$1,626	$1,683	$6,618	$19,809	$19,809	$19,809
$0	$0	$0	$0	$1,683	$1,683	$19,809	$19,809	$19,809
$0	$0	$0	$0	$0	$0	$16,604	$19,809	$19,809
$0	$0	$0	$0	$0	$0	$11,612	$19,809	$19,809
$0	$0	$0	$0	$0	$0	$7,281	$21,790	$21,790
$1,683	$3,252	$3,366	$3,252	$5,049	$19,911	$94,924	$120,835	$120,835
($3,337)	($3,224)	($3,337)	($3,224)	($3,337)	($23,020)	($39,275)	($39,275)	($39,275)
($3,337)	($3,224)	($3,337)	($3,224)	($3,337)	($16,459)	($39,275)	($39,275)	($39,275)
$0	$0	($3,337)	($3,224)	($3,337)	($9,898)	($39,275)	($39,275)	($39,275)
$0	$0	$0	$0	$0	$0	($39,275)	($39,275)	($39,275)
$0	$0	$0.	$0	$0	$0	($32,921)	($39,275)	($39,275)
$0	$0	$0	$0	$0	$0	($23,022)	($39,275)	($39,275)
$0	$0	$0	$0	$0	$0	($13,123)	($39,275)	($39,275)
($6,674)	($6,448)	($10,011)	($9,672)	($10,011)	($49,377)	($226,166)	($274,925)	($274,925)
($4,991)	($3,196)	($6,645)	($6,420)	($4,962)	($29,466)	($131,242)	($154,090)	($154,090)
0	0	0	0	0	0	(1,041)	(1,041)	(1,041)
177	171	177	171	177	1,221	2,083	2,083	2,083
0	171	177	171	177	696	2,085	2,083	2,083
0	0	0	0	177	177	2,083	2,083	2,083
0	0	0	0	0	0	1,746	2,083	2,083
0	0	0	0	0	0	1,221	2,083	2,083
0	0	0	0	0	0	696	2,083	2,083
177	342	354	342	531	2,094	9,914	12,498	12,498
(177)	(171)	(177)	(171)	(177)	(1,221)	(2,083)	(2,083)	(2,083)
(177)	(171)	(177)	(171)	(177)	(873)	(2,083)	(2,083)	(2,083)
0	0	(177)	(171)	(177)	(525)	(2,083)	(2,083)	(2,083)
0	0	0	0	0	0	(2,083)	(2,083)	(2,083)
0	0	0	0	0	0	(1,746)	(2,083)	(2,083)
0	0	0	0	0	0	(1,221)	(2,083)	(2,083)
0	0	0	0	0	0	(696)	(2,083)	(2,083)
(354)	(342)	(531)	(513)	(531)	(2,619)	(11,995)	(14,581)	(14,581)
(177)	0	(177)	(171)	0	(525)	(2,081)	(2,083)	(2,083)

12

Evaluation of Stakeholder Satisfaction

Jayne Lachey Gmeiner, Mary Lou Anderson,
Patricia A. Martin, and Kimbra Kahle Paden

PACE 2000 reflects an effort to achieve the work redesign, organizational restructuring, and patient-centered care at MVH for the next century. Indicators were established to monitor the progress and identify areas for improvement of PACE 2000 before the implementation process began. The CNO emphasized the need for continuous evaluation and monitoring to provide an environment that promoted positive change and did not result in settling for the status quo. The evaluation plan was based on the principles of total quality management, including assessing continuous improvement and benchmarking institutional goals/patient care outcomes internally and externally when possible (see Chapter 13). The evaluation plan, like PACE 2000, is focused on the needs of the patient, physicians, community, employees, and organization as a whole. The purpose of the plan is to provide a foundation for longitudinal evaluation yet remain flexible enough to assess short-term effects. Three major areas of consideration influenced the development of the plan including the following:

- The need to monitor the outcomes expected from the change, including (1) quality patient care; (2) improved satisfaction of patients, families, nurses, other direct caregivers, hospital employees, physicians, community, and; (3) cost-effective and efficient care.

- The time frame and budget for implementation and evaluation mandated a creative approach.
- Identification of personnel responsible for the evaluation activities, including data collection, data management, analysis, data interpretation, and development of implications from findings.

The first consideration that influenced the development of the evaluation plan related to three broad outcomes: quality patient care, improved satisfaction, and cost-effectiveness. Historically, baseline data have been collected about variables affecting these outcomes. A longitudinal study that began prior to PACE 2000 has been tracking nurses' responses to organizational dimensions, including work satisfaction, professional practice climate, autonomy, organization climate, centralization power, power orientation, and satisfaction with communication (Martin et al. 1993). This collaborative study between clinical nurses at MVH and nurse educators from Wright State University–Miami Valley School of Nursing occurs at least annually. In addition, a work excitement instrument has been used to evaluate nurses' feelings about daily tasks. The hospital has also been tracking employee job satisfaction and patient satisfaction for some time. The continued use of these measures will allow comparison to baseline.

The second consideration for developing an evaluation plan was the time frame. The time frame for implementation of the change was tight in relation to the time the evaluation plan was finalized. A deliberate effort was made to use existing evaluation indicators to avoid duplication of efforts and allow for preexisting data comparisons.

The third consideration included identification of personnel who would be responsible for the evaluation activities and report findings to appropriate personnel during the evaluation periods. Each indicator resulted in utilization of key personnel from a variety of departments as described later in this chapter.

The evaluation plan established in the summer of 1992 was based on the considerations of quality, satisfaction, cost-effectiveness, and maximum utilization of preexisting resources. The plan consisted of seven evaluation indicators, which are as follows:

1. Patient satisfaction

2. Patient outcomes

3. Employee satisfaction

4. Physician satisfaction
5. Community response
6. Cost-effectiveness
7. Clinical efficiency.

This chapter will feature detailed discussion of the evaluation criteria for each indicator identified. Evaluation occurred both concurrently and retrospectively for most indicators.

Patient Satisfaction

The number one goal, not only of PACE 2000 but also MVH, is patient satisfaction. Historically, patients have highly rated MVH and the care received. This information provides data comparison points to measure patients' perceptions of changes in care delivery over a period of years and will supplement the anecdotal information received from patients and families through consumer relations.

Sharing feedback from patients and their families with the individual caregiver is a very important part of the PACE 2000 effort. PACE 2000 encourages all comments received through consumer relations or other departments to be reported back to the caregivers through their nurse managers. Units, however, also proactively solicit patient views on customer service via unit-specific patient surveys. Survey results are then measured by the hospitalwide Quality Improvement Committee, while units note trends and develop appropriate action plans to address patient concerns. For example, the neuroscience unit attaches a patient questionnaire to its patient discharge summaries to monitor such indicators as the following:

- Did your nurse and other staff members identify their roles and responsibilities?
- Did your nurse address health care education needs or specific care instructions with you and your family during your hospitalization?
- Is there anything that could have been done differently during your hospitalization?

Each indicator response is evaluated quarterly, with the expectation that the needs will be met 90 percent of the time. The ultimate goal, however, is 100 percent.

Overall, the survey results have been above the 90 percent threshold. However, patient surveys have suggested some areas for improvement (e.g., reduction in noise and timely delivery of water and snacks). The neuroscience staff used this information to develop action plans that address these issues and shared the plans during monthly staff meetings.

Utilizing a nursing-specific patient satisfaction instrument was considered on a housewide basis, but the decision was made to use an existing marketing department survey. The marketing department coordinates evaluation of satisfaction through a national research firm. This report serves as a periodic measurement of the attitudes and perceptions held by past patients of MVH. Data are collected over a period of one year and analysis occurs between the months of January and August of the following year. Therefore, concurrent monitoring of patients' perceptions/feelings regarding care was an essential addition for this indicator. The objectives of the annual patient surveys include

- Determining the level of past patient satisfaction regarding the care, accommodations, procedures, and interpersonal relations at MVH
- Determining the level of return purchase inclination among past patients
- Examining the influences in past patient decisions to utilize the MVH for care on an inpatient basis
- Identifying the strengths and weaknesses of the hospital so that the hospital may capitalize and make corrective adjustments. (National Research Corporation 1993, 1)

The results are presented annually to the Marketing Department and hospital administration incorporating significant changes, trends, mean score summary tables, and verbatim comments. The mean rating summary table is based on patients answering questions on a five-point Likert scale. Sample sizes for the last three years have ranged from 1,500 to 2,300. Sample questions from the inpatient satisfaction questionnaire are provided in Table 12.1.

Implementation of PACE 2000 occurred in the fall of 1992 with the first set of cluster units. The implementation of PACE 2000 continued through the last quarter of 1993. Five patient care areas had implemented PACE 2000 by the last quarter of 1992. Random surveys were sent to a variety of patients who may or may not have been discharged from PACE patient care units. Therefore, data available from the 1993

Table 12.1

Longitudinal Inpatient Satisfaction Mean Rating Summary Table

Sample Questions	1988	1989	1991	1992	1993
My admission to Miami Valley Hospital was prompt and efficient.	4.38	4.49	4.37	4.36	4.39
Overall, I felt that the nursing care I received was excellent.	4.37	4.50	4.34	4.37	4.37
My room was kept clean.	4.27	4.49	4.36	4.32	4.33
My family and friends were treated well by the Hospital personnel.	4.42	4.50	4.48	4.50	4.49
My meals were served at the right temperature.	3.93	4.13	4.00	3.94	4.01
I would choose this hospital again.	4.45	4.59	4.49	4.50	4.47

Note: Based on 5-point Likert scale response.

survey cannot be used to measure differences in perceptions of care as attributed to changes in care delivery, but can continue to serve as baseline information for 1994 survey results, which at this time are pending. The goal of the PACE 2000 implementation team and MVH is to strive to meet the needs of the patient and family while maintaining quality and promoting cost-effectiveness. The CNO, directors of nursing, nurse managers, unit councils, and PACE 2000 project leaders will assist with monitoring the data provided by the marketing department on a long-term basis.

Patient Outcomes

Patient outcome information is measured by several methods and monitored by the division of nursing, nursing quality assurance/improvement (QA/I), hospital QA/I, and risk management. Quality improvement (QI) data, including fall rates, medication errors, and procedure errors, were selected to serve as measures of quality patient outcomes. No additional expense is incurred to monitor these outcomes because the indicators were already included in the nursing QI program. Each patient care unit established indicators based on hospital criteria and the patient population it serves. The goal is to monitor patient outcomes by tracking existing QA/I data and intervening if negative trends occurred. Rates of medication errors, patient falls, and procedural error rates have not changed over the last two years.

Patient outcomes are also addressed through benchmarking efforts described in Chapter 13. Merging of the care delivery system, case management, and the benchmarking efforts are processes resulting in shorter lengths of stay and cost-effective care. The potential for improvement is quite promising and should stimulate creative change to facilitate expert care in a variety of patient populations. The benchmarking efforts are supported by the hospital QA/I department, which supplies case mix, cost, and reimbursement data. Evaluation criteria will be established for each individual patient diagnosis and monitored by a multidisciplinary benchmarking team.

Employee Satisfaction

The PACE 2000 care delivery system has impacted every department of MVH. Another goal of PACE 2000 is to maintain and improve employee satisfaction in the midst of integrating job roles and responsibilities and redesigning work. Training and support have been offered to increase the employees' development in the areas of consistency, collegiality, mutual respect, and empathy for the patient as well as each other during the PACE 2000 classes. Still, issues involving trust, delegation, respect, and scheduling inconsistencies have been cited as concerns for the RNs and PCTs working in the new system.

Overall, employee attitude surveys are administered at scheduled intervals by the HRD. This survey was conducted again in the spring of 1994 and should give a total analysis of employees' perceptions regarding all aspects of the environment. Open meetings have been conducted by the CNO on an as-needed basis to monitor feelings, perceptions, and satisfaction during the transition to the new care delivery system. These meetings were scheduled to maximize the employees' opportunity to respond. Meetings were held three to six months after implementation for the first three clusters. Special emphasis has also been given to the roles of the SA and PCT through open meetings and through a survey designed by the PACE 2000 Analyst Committee. The surveys were created to assess work perceptions and time spent performing specific responsibilities of the SA and PCT. The time spent in different aspects of the job description is described in Figure 12.1. This analysis is compared between the Main Hospital SAs and those employed in labor and delivery. The Main Hospital SA spends approximately 53 percent of time with environmental aspects compared with approximately 45 percent of time in labor and delivery. The labor and delivery SA spends much more time stocking and supplying carts between deliveries, which is unique to this area and delineates the uniqueness of adapting the SA role to the needs of the patient care unit. Tables 12.2 and 12.3 describe sample questions and responses of PCTs and SAs as described by Cluster One unit employees six months after implementation on their particular units.

Open communication has been effective and has promoted an overall positive environment for change. Growth at MVH is greatly enhanced by the creativity of the employees of the institution.

Registered Nurse Formal Evaluation

The group most affected by the PACE 2000 care delivery system is the nursing staff. From the beginning, evaluation of the nurses' perceptions to the changing care delivery system has been given high priority. A review of the literature indicated that few organizations obtained baseline data prior to implementing similar changes. However, organizations have addressed turnover and burnout. A classic study by Herzberg, Mausner, and Snyderman (1959) demonstrated that factors such as recognition, advancement, growth, achievement, and responsibility are thought to contribute significantly to job satisfaction and motivation. However, the absence of these factors does not necessarily lead to job dissatisfaction.

Concept of Work Excitement

In order to better understand the component of RN evaluation, a brief overview of Lillian Simms et al. (1990) work excitement research is presented here. According to the literature, employees are influenced by a sequence of events, including work redesign, which causes them to become dissatisfied with their jobs and leads them to search for alternative employment (Simms et al. 1990). The influence of work group culture is seen as increasingly important in understanding the phenomena of turnover, burnout, satisfaction, and motivation. Simms

Figure 12.1

Cluster One SA PACE 2000 Survey Results

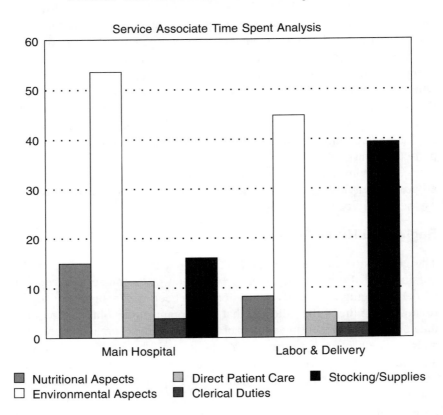

Service Associate Time Spent Analysis

Legend: Nutritional Aspects · Direct Patient Care · Stocking/Supplies · Environmental Aspects · Clerical Duties

et al. (1990) chose to examine these phenomena from a different perspective. The concept of *work excitement* was identified using a modified grounded theory approach. Work excitement was defined as "the personal enthusiasm and commitment for work evidenced by creativity, receptivity to learning, and ability to see opportunity in everyday situations. Work excitement is influenced by individual (personal) factors and work (organizational) factors" (Simms et al. 1990, 178). From this concept, the authors developed the work characteristics instrument (WCI), which identifies those aspects of work that are the most interesting, exciting, frustrating, time consuming, meaningful, and exhausting for nurses. The

Table 12.2

Cluster One PCT PACE 2000 Survey Results (Spring 1993)

Response Summaries

Sample Questions	Very Satisfied	Satisfied	No Change	Dissatisfied	Very Dissatisfied
1. How satisfied are you with your role as a Patient Care Technician?	50%	50%			
	Always	Usually	No Change	Rarely	Never
2. Does your RN partner appropriately delegate tasks that you can perform?	75%	25%			
3. Do you feel that patient call lights on your unit are answered in a timely manner?	66%	25%	8%		
4. Do you feel you have the skills to perform your job at the level expected by your RN partner?	Yes: 100%	No: 0%			

Table 12.3

Cluster One PACE 2000 Shift Manager Survey Results (Spring 1993)

Sample Questions	Response per 5-Point Likert Scale
1. Do you feel patient flow has improved?	3.8
2. Does the unit/patient rooms appear "tidy"?	4.0
3. Do you feel patient lights are reduced at mealtime?	4.4
4. Do you feel patient lights are reduced overall?	4.16
5. Do you feel the trays are passed to patients in a timely fashion?	4.2
6. Do you feel snacks get passed in the evening?	4.16
7. Has the SA been integrated into the Patient Care Team?	Yes: 75% No: 0% Somewhat: 25%
8. Are supplies readily available at the bedside?	Yes: 83% No: 0% Sometimes: 20%

5 = strongly agree, 1 = strongly disagree.

forced choice questionnaire was designed to collect information regarding nurses' perceptions of their work. Content validity was established through the grounded theory approach described earlier. Cluster and factor analysis were used to identify the structure of the items included in the questionnaire. Cronbach's alpha was used to assess internal consistency of the questions. The individual factors themselves were found to have reliability coefficients ranging from 0.61 to 0.86. The WCI is copyrighted by Simms and Erbin-Roesemann of the University of Michigan (1989).

The WCI was utilized to survey 168 staff nurses and head nurses in two teaching hospitals and one home health care agency (Simms et al. 1990). Results from the initial study revealed that only 35 of the

168 respondents described themselves as very excited about their work. Those nurses who described themselves as very excited were 30 to 39 years old, worked 40 to 49 hours per week, were baccalaureate prepared, and viewed themselves as direct care providers. In addition, these nurses worked the day shift on a unit utilizing primary nursing, had been in nursing from 5 to 15 years and in their current position from 1 to 9 years.

In terms of work setting, the home care nurses reported significantly higher levels of work excitement than those who worked in the areas of critical care, general care, or rehabilitation. In addition, flight or aeromedical nurses were statistically more excited about their work than nurses in critical care, general care, or rehabilitation.

Further analysis of the findings from the early study identified four factors to be significant predictors of an individual's work excitement. These include work arrangements, growth and development or learning, variety of experiences, and working conditions. The factor of work arrangement includes the variables of inappropriate staffing, understaffing, and the issues of sufficient time to get work finished. Work arrangement was identified as being negatively related to work excitement, thereby identifying the impact of these stresses on the nurses' perception of their work (Simms et al. 1990).

The factor of growth and development or learning includes the variables of challenging problems or projects, solving problems or accomplishing these projects, and participation in the growth and development of other nurses (mentoring). Growth and development or learning was positively related to work excitement, identifying the importance of providing opportunities for nurses to meet their growth and development or learning needs.

The factor of variety of experiences includes the variable of variety and was positively related to work excitement. This correlation suggests that variety in a job contributes to work excitement. The nurses who had higher levels of work excitement were overall less negative about their jobs and identified fewer activities as being exhausting. The findings from this study support the need to evaluate all components of nurses' work and to identify those that are the most interesting, exciting, frustrating, time consuming, meaningful, and exhausting. With this data in place, one can then redesign work to help alleviate those activities that are frustrating, time consuming, and exhausting, while enhancing those that are interesting, exciting, and meaningful.

Measurement of WCI at MVH

The concept of work excitement was identified as useful to evaluate perceptions of nurses at MVH. Lillian Simms was contacted for permission to use the tool and modify the instrument. More Likert scale options and fewer open-ended and other type responses were utilized to ease the processing of data (Paden and Martin 1992).

After permission was granted and the revisions were completed, a pilot project was planned on four different medical-surgical units. The primary purpose of the pilot study was to trial the modified WCI for ease of use and identify any needed changes. The pilot units included a 44-bed orthopedic unit, a 15-bed urology unit, a 27-bed medical-surgical unit, and a 12-bed ambulatory treatment area. The 15-bed urology unit had previously undergone some basic work redesign in 1991 and was included in the pilot for this purpose. The ambulatory treatment area by nature had a different job design and was included because of its difference from the other three units. The orthopedic and medical-surgical units had not made any changes toward work redesign at the time of the pilot study. All four units had different skill mixes and very different atmospheres.

The staff members from these units were approached in staff meetings regarding the project. Participation was voluntary and withdrawal from the study at any time was without penalty. Completion of the modified WCI signified consent to participate in the project. No names nor identification numbers appeared on the instrument, however, data were analyzed by work area. A convenience sample of the RNs working on the units was utilized. The questionnaires were placed in all RNs' mailboxes along with a cover letter identifying instructions for completion and return of the questionnaire. A 26-question demographic sheet was also included with each questionnaire. Questionnaires were returned to a secured envelope on each unit over a two-week period. All responses were handled in a confidential manner. A total of 51 nurses returned the questionnaires, representing a response rate of 82 percent.

On the average, the questionnaire took 30 minutes to complete. Very few suggestions were made regarding the instrument and these were primarily related to the length of the questionnaire. Each of the characteristics in the modified WCI were examined for reliability. Their normal consistency was measured using the Cronbach's Alpha Coefficient. The values for this test were as follows: interesting, .9226; exciting, .9078;

frustrating, .9288; time consuming, .7953; meaningful, .8976; good day, .8791; and exhausting, .9386. A data base was then designed to allow ease of data entry. The specific results of the pilot study will not be shared because a larger housewide study will be described. One conclusion was that the majority of the nurses reacted very positively to the study and were pleased to be given the opportunity to voice their perceptions regarding their jobs. The use of the modified WCI prior to the PACE 2000 project implementation provided valuable information and the basis for a longitudinal study utilizing this instrument.

The longitudinal study utilizing the modified WCI began in August 1992, concurrently with the first PACE 2000 educational series. The WCI evaluation plan, sampling methods, and frequency were established by the CNO and PACE 2000 project managers. The modified WCI was established as the formal evaluation tool for the RN work group. The instrument was distributed for completion prior to each PACE 2000 educational series. The PACE 2000 RN educators described the intent of the study and its goal to evaluate nurses' perceptions of their work environment over the implementation and monitoring phases of the PACE 2000 project.

To date, the only units who have not implemented PACE 2000 are the ICU, the coronary intensive care unit (CICU), and the neonatal intensive care unit (NICU). These units are in the transition phase, in preparation for the final implementation of PACE 2000. Preimplementation data, using the modified WCI has been done for all units, including the ICU, CICU, and NICU. Postimplementation data has been collected on three units from the first PACE 2000 cluster (a medical-surgical unit, the burn unit, and the neuroscience unit). In April 1994, postimplementation data collection occurred on all of the remaining units that had implemented PACE 2000. A third data collection will also occur at this time on the previously mentioned medical-surgical unit, the burn unit and the neuroscience unit.

Analysis of the preimplementation data for the first three clusters has been completed ($N = 531$). Demographic composites of these three clusters are congruent with those of the MVH nursing population as a whole. An outline of the demographics for these three clusters can be seen in Table 12.4.

Each of the WCI's individual questions for the three clusters were also analyzed ($N = 519$, 12 missing data cases). When asked "to what extent are you excited about your work?", 216 individuals (41.6 percent)

Table 12.4
Demographic Composites

Demographics	Options	Number
Age range	Under 20 years	1
	20–29 years	153
	30–39 years	220
	40–49 years	89
	50 years or greater	53
Basic nursing education	ADN	180
	Diploma	174
	BSN	157
	Other	7
Highest nursing degree	ADN	152
	Diploma	140
	BSN	195
	Master's	19
	Other	5
Length of MVH employment	Less than 6 months	28
	6 months to a year	17
	Over 1–3 years	116
	Over 3–5 years	68
	Over 5–10 years	120
	Over 10 years	169
Employment status	Full-time	317
	Part-time	141
	Support	61
Years on current unit	Less than 1 year	85
	1–4 years	201
	5–9 years	129
	10–15 years	59
	Over 15 years	35
Average hours worked per week	Less than 20 hours	86
	20–39 hours	249
	40–49 hours	175
	Over 49 hours	8

responded with "moderately" excited, 197 (38 percent) with "very" excited, and 23 (4.4 percent) with "extremely" excited; a total of 66 individuals (12.7 percent) responded with "somewhat" excited. Only 17 individuals (3.3 percent) stated that they were "not too" excited or "not at all" excited about their work. The PACE 2000 Analyst Committee were very pleased with the responses to this specific question.

The remaining WCI questions were specifically related to interesting, exciting, frustrating, time consuming, meaningful, exhausting components and activities of the individuals' work. These questions had Likert scale options. Each of the options were given a corresponding score with 0 = "not applicable," 1 = "not at all," 2 = "seldom," 3 = "moderately," and 4 = "very." A mean score for each characteristic was then calculated by totalling the scores and dividing by the number of responses.

The question relating to a "good day" asked the individuals to identify how often they could use any of the 17 options to describe their good day. A Likert scale was also used for this question with 1 = "never," 2 = "seldom," 3 = "often," and 4 = "always." A mean score for this question was also calculated using the technique previously described.

Figure 12.2 shows a comparison of the mean scores per question for each of the three clusters. There were no significant variations between any of the clusters on any of the characteristics. Thus, further data analysis was done on all three clusters cumulatively (N = 531).

Ranking of the mean scores for all three clusters provided some very interesting information (Figure 12.3). Those characteristics that had the highest mean scores were meaningful, interesting, good-day descriptors and exciting, respectively. These characteristics carry with them a positive connotation. The characteristics of time consuming, frustrating, and exhausting were ranked the lowest. These three characteristics have a more negative tone.

Additional analysis of the characteristics and demographics was done using simple linear correlations. Table 12.5 shows those correlations that were statistically significant. Correlations of data from future clusters will be done to further validate these findings.

The modified WCI asked the participants to identify three activities (per characteristic) that they believed were the "most" consuming, "most" exciting, "most" frustrating, "most" time consuming, "most" meaningful, and the "most" exhausting. The activities were analyzed for frequency. Preimplementation information for the first three clusters can be found

Figure 12.2

Work Characteristics Study—Means per Question, by Cluster

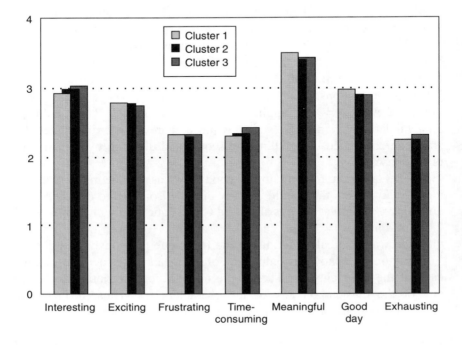

Note: Cluster 1 *N* = 154; Cluster 2 *N* = 233; Cluster 3 *N* = 144.

in Table 12.6. Postimplementation data analysis for these questions has not been completed yet. It is interesting to note that many of these activities were impacted by the PACE 2000 changes. Further analysis of the postimplementation data will identify the impact of PACE 2000 on these activities.

A comparison of the preimplementation and postimplementation data from the three Cluster One units has been done (a medical-surgical unit, the burn unit, and the neuroscience unit). A total of 164 individuals participated in the postimplementation data collection for these three units. Because of changes in the units' composition over the last year and the poor postimplementation return rate, the number of matched pairs were only 35. This made it impossible to draw any real conclusions from

Figure 12.3

Work Characteristics Study—Initial Data Collection Means for Each Characteristic

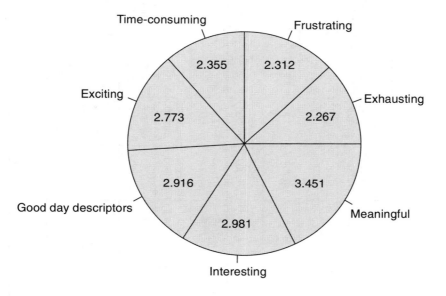

N = 531 (Likert scale of 1 to 4).

the data. Although none of the data was significant (Table 12.7), a slight increase in the mean scores for interesting, exciting, and frustrating was noted. A slight decrease in mean scores was seen for time consuming, meaningful, good-day descriptions, and exhausting. Future data collections will provide more matched pairs with which to analyze.

The study results are limited to the MVH population at this time. Analysis of future data collections will allow for the identification of trends or themes. It is recommended that a replication of the study be done at other similar hospitals to increase the data base and allow for comparisons of the findings.

The PACE 2000 Analyst Committee is anxious to review further findings of this longitudinal study. These findings will assist the committee in fine-tuning the model to better meet the needs of the nurses, while contributing to the overall goals of PACE 2000 and MVH.

Table 12.5   Correlation of Characteristics to Demographics

	Age	Basic Education	High Education	Years Employed	Hours Worked	Status	Years Licensed	Years as RN	Years on Unit
How excited				−.1266 $p<.004$					−.1319 $p<.003$
Interesting									
Exciting				−.1055 $p<.016$	+.1459 $p<.001$	−.1538 $p<.000$			
Frustrating				+.1033 $p<.019$	+.1183 $p<.007$	−.1729 $p<.000$			
Time-consuming				+.0984 $p<.025$	+.1960 $p<.000$	−.2270 $p<.000$			+.0976 $p<.028$
Meaningful				−.1038 $p<.018$	+.0897 $p<.041$	−.0932 $p<.034$	+.0940 $p<.035$	−.0940 $p<.035$	
Good day descriptors									
Exhausting	−.0932 $p<.034$		−.1024 $p<.020$			−.2129 $p<.000$	+.0894 $p<.045$	−.0894 $p<.045$	

Clusters 1, 2, and 3 (*N* = 520).

Table 12.6

Work Characteristics Study

Three most exhausting aspects of work
- Increased patient load
- Decreased staff
- No time for breaks or lunches

Three most interesting aspects of work
- Rewarding, fulfilling work; feel I make a difference
- Interesting and exciting work
- Stimulating, motivating, challenging environment

Three most exciting aspects of work
- Taking on challenging projects or problems and accomplishing or solving them
- Seeing and assisting patients to improve and leave unit
- Seeing and participating in the growth and development of other nurses

Three most frustrating aspects of work
- Nonnursing functions
- Defective equipment
- Lack of supplies

Three most time-consuming aspects of work
- Charting, paperwork activities
- Care of high acuity patients
- Documentation, care plans, discharge planning

Three most meaningful aspects of work
- Giving comfort to a patient or family
- Seeing patient improve
- Stabilizing a critical patient

An additional RN evaluation instrument was developed by the PACE 2000 Analyst Committee. The tool assesses levels of satisfaction with nursing care, delegation skills, partnerships, environmental issues, physician relationships, and overall role changes resulting from PACE 2000.

Initial responses to this survey are summarized in Table 12.7 and describe in percentages perceptions regarding satisfaction and delegation

Table 12.7

Comparison of Means Pre- and Post-Implementation

Question	Mean Pre-Implementation	Mean Post-Implementation	Single T-test	p Value
Interesting	2.984	3.042	−1.352	0.185
Exciting	2.818	2.829	−0.054	0.957
Frustrating	2.197	2.199	−0.042	0.967
Time-consuming	2.422	2.389	0.426	0.673
Meaningful	3.544	3.532	0.123	0.903
Good day descriptors	3.022	2.935	1.213	0.234
Exhausting	2.367	2.293	1.218	0.232

For Cluster 1 only, N = 35 (from 164 cases).

of tasks. Due to the small sample size responding to the initial RN survey, these results were not able to be generalized. As evident from the survey, the majority of the RNs were satisfied with the care delivery and were delegating tasks to the PCT/LPN. The RNs (73 percent) also found patient needs were anticipated prior to the use of the call light.

Physician Satisfaction

Incorporating physician ideas and input into the PACE 2000 Care Delivery System resulted in a positive transition from primary nursing to the new care delivery system. Historically, primary nursing promoted collegiality between the physician and the nurse by reporting of patient variances while making rounds with the physicians. MVH supports active collaboration between all caregivers and provides mechanisms to enhance communication within different work groups/specialities. This relationship was extended during the PACE 2000 planning and implementation phases by active participation and membership on a variety of committees. Physician evaluation has been accomplished through three methods, including

- Formal marketing surveys conducted in a similar format to the patient satisfaction survey
- Open meetings held on an as-needed basis

• Direct reports to shift managers, nurse managers, directors of nursing, and the CNO.

The marketing department assesses physician opinions annually and reports information and analysis directly to hospital administration. Sample questions relate to a variety of topics and are analyzed based on historical baseline information. One section of the survey asks questions about the nursing staff. The medical staff study is conducted by a national firm and focuses on the following general categories:

• Nurses attitudes and behavior toward patients
• Communications between nurses and physicians
• Quality of patient care delivered
• Quality of professional relationships between physicians and nurses
• Quality of nursing unit management
• Adequacy of nurse staffing on the unit
• Overall performance of nursing staff.

These questions are based on mean ratings on a four-point Likert scale with 4 being excellent and 1 being poor. The comparison mean ratings are then analyzed and results are compared in several ways, including annual comparisons, unit-unit comparisons, service comparisons, and Dayton area hospital comparisons. This information is utilized to assist with assessing areas to improve services, communication, and relationships with physician groups. The results released in 1993 were based on 1992 data collection and would have not been impacted by PACE 2000 Implementation.

In addition, the hospital board and administrators developed a primary care physicians project (PCPP) in 1991 to establish an ongoing commitment to promote positive physician interaction. The PCPP Committee comprises multidisciplinary work groups whose main emphasis is to improve physician relationships within the MVH environment. Another physician focus-group study was conducted late in 1993 to assess overall opinions and perceptions about many aspects of hospital functioning and resources. This study was conducted by verbal interviews by an outside independent agency, and the care delivery system was just one component of the session. Responses from the focus groups are still pending; action teams will be developed to analyze issues, develop plans to solve problems, and implement new ideas. Hospital administration has served as the support system and administrator of this project.

In summary, MVH is committed to maintaining and enhancing physician satisfaction for over 1,000 physicians who admit and care for patients within this environment. Physicians have been integral team members for the PACE 2000 project as well as for other changes impacting the patients, environment, or institution as a whole.

Community Response

Community response to changes in the care delivery system is an important aspect to monitor during the implementation and evaluation phases. The communication and marketing departments have served as the main monitoring stations for community perceptions. Overall, the response has been favorable, with many patients writing letters of praise regarding their stay at MVH.

The PACE 2000 program managers have been dedicated to responding to questions and concerns from the academic institutions in the community. The Education and Clinical Ladder Subcommittees membership consisted of representatives from the local associate degree and baccalaureate nursing programs to obtain feedback and strengthen communication bonds from the beginning.

Concerns regarding shifting from a primary nursing concept to a partnership concept were usually verbalized directly to the PACE 2000 program managers, but sometimes concerns were discovered in an indirect method such as the rumor mill. The main concern of some academic institutions is the fear that the demand for nurses would decrease in future years as more institutions decreased skill mix and introduced nonprofessionals into the work force. The other issue was the concern for the patient and the overall potential to affect quality if some aspects of care were delivered by nonprofessional personnel. Presentations of the care delivery changes and the PACE 2000 concepts to adjunct faculty who utilize MVH as a clinical site began in the fall of 1992. The PACE 2000 program managers emphasized the goal to expand the professional responsibilities of RNs and enhance their ability to direct and plan patient care through utilization of the nursing process. Time was also spent educating faculty in relation to developing RNs with abilities to be flexible in a very changing health care environment. Lectures have also been presented at local universities to both nursing and health care administrator classes per request of faculty and students.

The other interesting community response was from local, regional, and national hospital institutions. Initially, the local hospital administrators and educational personnel responded that the new care delivery system deviated from normal RN practice. Their vision for professional RN practice was not congruent with PACE 2000's and resulted in discomfort. After the analysis, planning, and implementation phases, requests for numerous consultations, verbal feedback, and questions indicated definite change in the community perspective.

A national conference was planned and implemented in the fall of 1993 to provide colleagues with information regarding the care delivery system and other care delivery systems nationally. The conference was well attended and promoted networking for institutions locally, regionally, and nationally.

In summary, the PACE 2000 implementation team constantly strives to promote a positive image of MVH to the community and the customers it serves. This image is consistent with the organization's goals and mission.

Cost-Effectiveness

The goal to provide care in the most cost-effective manner became a dual responsibility between administration and care providers during OE and PACE 2000 processes. This responsibility changed dramatically during the past three years and resulted from empowering employees to think creatively and solve problems as they occurred. Unit councils with strong membership and abilities to solve problems together have resulted in methods to become increasingly cost-effective. The CNO, directors of nursing, nurse managers, and staff recognize the need to find continued opportunities to promote cost-effectiveness. The impact of the cost-containment efforts of PACE 2000 are outlined in Chapter 11.

Clinical Efficiency

The goal to promote clinical efficiency is measured not only by costs in relation to delivery of care, but is also evaluated by patients' lengths-of-stay, readmission rates, mortality rates, and service indicators (e.g., numbers of laboratory tests, x-rays, antibiotic utilization, etc.). The goal is twofold: (1) to promote maximum efficiency of partnerships through establishment of comfort with one another, resulting in the ability to handle differing acuity levels or number of patients and (2) to continue to develop interdisciplinary plans, pathways, and streamline care to maximize utilization of resources and promote the best possible care in the shortest amount of time. Chapters 11 and 13 focus on financial monitoring and benchmarking efforts. The future must also include methods to extend the walls of the corporate health care institution into the community to meet the needs of patients on a continuum once they are discharged.

Recommendations

In the process of analyzing the evaluation methods for the transition to a new care delivery system, several recommendations for process improvement have been recognized, which are as follows:

- Schedule a quarterly meeting between departments participating in the evaluation (marketing, infection control, risk management, quality management, customer relations, and communications) to bridge communication between all disciplines
- Encourage more RN staff currently enrolled in graduate programs to participate in research studies regarding different aspects of the evaluation methods. To date, two graduate students have studies pending utilizing aspects of the evaluation plan
- Improve communication in regards to the fact that this process is never complete and requires ongoing commitment similar to any continuous quality improvement project
- Establish a better method to determine how nurses spent their time before and after implementation of changes in the care delivery system; the survey completed by the staff may be reflective of the opinions of the day and not a true picture
- Develop a method to maintain enthusiasm, positive energy, and initiative
- Develop a longer timeline.

Summary

Evaluation of the PACE 2000 care delivery system has been a very involved process managed by many departments within MVH. The PACE

2000 Program Managers report directly to the CNO to provide a method of direct communication during this ongoing continuous quality improvement process. Evaluation of project management was continuous with feedback from the CNO, directors of nursing, staff, physicians, and all departments of MVH. To date, the feedback received has deemed the program successful, but opportunities for improvement are recognized and pursued constantly. Patient outcomes have remained consistent in regards to mortality rates, infection rates, medication administration errors, and patient falls throughout the change. Data continues to be collected and analyzed from all consumers. Changes continue to be made from the feedback received. The teamwork established by the OE process and extended during the PACE 2000 effort has resulted in open communication between all departments and positively impacted the ability to function as an institution. MVH has been successful as a quality institution, recognized by physicians and patients in the community and the region as an institution committed to the provision of excellence. In 1991 and 1994, MVH received official commendation by JCAHO in recognition of overall hospital excellence.

References

Herzberg, F., B. Mausner, and B. Snyderman. 1959. *The Motivation of Work.* New York: John Wiley & Sons.

Martin, P., J. Corron, L. Cox, T. Gustin, G. Jordan, T. Lupo, D. Mals, and P. Risner. 1993. "Organizational Dimensions of Hospital Nursing Practice." Unpublished raw data. Dayton, Ohio.

National Research Corporation. 1993. *Inpatient Study*: 1, Lincoln, NE: The Corporation.

Paden, K. K., and P. A. Martin. 1992. "Modified Work Characteristics Instrument." Unpublished paper, Dayton, OH.

Simms, L. M., and M. Erbin-Roesemann. 1989. "The Conceptualization of Work Excitement." Unpublished manuscript, Ann Arbor, MI.

Simms, L. M., M. Erbin-Roesemann, A. Darga, and H. Coeling. 1990. "Breaking the Burnout Barrier: Resurrecting Work Excitement in Nursing." *Nursing Economic$* 8 (3): 178.

Part V

Future Directions

Part V, Future Directions, includes a discussion of case management and clinical benchmarking. Chapter 13 explains the organization's commitment and history of case management. Chapter 14 details the relationship between case management, continuous quality improvement, and clinical benchmarking. Benchmarking steps are explained and an example of the interdisciplinary process is provided with process flow charts for the pharmacy and clinical laboratory processes used for pneumonia (DRG 89) benchmarking. This section concludes with an epilogue about making it successfully through the change to the new PACE 2000 Partners in Practice model of patient care delivery.

13

Case Management

Margaret Eigler, Catherine G. Hall, Marjorie Mahle,
Carol Lynn Miller, and Kathy A. Tilton

This chapter describes the process of MVH's journey toward the ultimate
goal of case management implementation and integration into the PACE
2000 initiative. The chapter begins with a discussion about the theoretical
background of case management, followed by a brief history of the concept at MVH. Next is the description of three committees that addressed
the concept. The Case Management Committee reviewed the process and
care/case manager role. The Quality Assurance Subcommittee analyzed
case types and the process for integrating QA and case management. The
Documentation Subcommittee developed critical paths (care maps) and
related documentation. The chapter concludes with a discussion of future
directions for case management at MVH.

Background

There have been monumental changes in the health care system over the
past decade. Technology has continued to grow along with health care
cost. Restructuring of the payment system for health care led to measures that impacted reimbursement for services. Hospitals were forced
to decrease length of stay in order to comply with third party payers
and to maintain financial stability. Although many measures have been

instituted to control costs, society is dissatisfied with the health care system (Bowers 1988).

The restructuring of health care reimbursement to date has limited consumers' choices about health care. Consumers have not always chosen their preferred physician or hospital, although consumers have become more financially responsible for health care expenses. Consumers have started to pay additional premiums for health insurance and have higher deductibles and co-pays. At the same time, health care providers have become frustrated with the responsibility of managing complex, higher acuity patients and external forces dictating clinical practice.

Managed care is defined as the controlled balance of cost and quality while meeting the needs of society, the reimbursement system, and the health care systems (Zander 1988). The concept of managed care in the acute care setting was pioneered at the New England Medical Center in 1988 by Karen Zander. Case management is a method to achieve managed care. Case management is the actual "utilization, monitoring, and rationalization of the resources that patients use over a course of illness" (Zander 1988).

The original term for managed care was second generation primary nursing (Zander 1988). The focus of health care delivery changed from nursing care being the product of nursing service to outcomes as the product of the nursing service. In an outcome-oriented nursing service, efficient use of resources and decreased length of stay became major benefits (Zander 1988). Zander's managed care system was developed by nurses with physician collaboration. Collaboration with other health care disciplines was not a major focus of Zander's model.

MVH History

Case management at MVH began as a formal commitment within the division of nursing in 1988. Committee membership included nurse managers, nurse educators, and staff nurses.

The purpose of the committee was to investigate case management, determine case management's role within MVH, and plan the future direction and goals of case management. It was initiated with unit-based managed care where the primary nurse followed a previously established unit diagnostic treatment plan, incorporating diagnostic related groupings and established lengths of stay. The development and utilization of critical paths with monitoring of cost-effectiveness and quality assurance followed.

Strengths and Weaknesses of Early Attempts

Key strengths of the prior efforts were the success of the educational plan, the support of nursing administration, clear united goals and implementation plans, and the talent and creativity of the committee members. The major weaknesses were the lack of an interdisciplinary focus, minimal plans beyond the initial trials, lack of involvement by the division of finance in evaluating cost and length of stay components, and lack of clarity regarding accountability and authority for implementation. Also, the additional work to develop managed care without adjustments in staff work expectations contributed to waning enthusiasm over time.

Operational Excellence

OE was a project initiated by Hospital Administration to increase the efficiency of services provided by the hospital. Structure and processes were intricately analyzed within the institution, and suggestions for improvement were made. PACE 2000 was a program developed for changing the nursing care delivery system at the completion of the OE project. OE became an institutionwide commitment with employees throughout the institution actively involved in committees that analyzed and developed proposals. Case management concepts were frequently suggested by various committees during the OE process, and the decision was made to reactivate and restructure the Case Management Committee as a part of PACE 2000. The OE process created a positive environment for case management by validating the following institutional expectations:

1. OE facilitated the concept of interdisciplinary teamwork and problem solving. For example, issues were examined as patient care issues rather than nursing or respiratory care issues. By utilizing the interdisciplinary approach, the OE process was able to examine an issue and identify factors that impacted decision making. This was regarded as a natural platform for case management. All disciplines needed to be included in the process to affect efficient utilization of resources and decrease length of stay.

2. Case management was identified by many of the OE subcommittees as a means to improve efficiency of the care delivered. A variety of disciplines became aware of the benefits of case management. Physicians who participated on committees became aware of the strengths of case management. The implementation of case management became an identified strategic goal of the institution. These factors increased momentum and validated the credibility of the case management concept.

3. The professional staff quality assurance department, with a change in leadership and recommendations from OE, provided data that previously had been difficult to access. Utilization and financial data were available and could be accessed in a timely manner.

PACE 2000 Case Management Committee

The first meeting of the interdisciplinary Case Management Committee under the new PACE 2000 structure occurred April 1992. The committee was composed of representation from a variety of disciplines: nursing, medicine, respiratory therapy, physical therapy, nutrition, social services, finance, information systems, professional staff quality assurance, and utilization review.

The newly structured Case Management Committee reviewed the process of case management, as well as the care/case manager role.

Case Management Process

During this time frame, in conjunction with a financial analysis, the decision was made to develop a method to implement case management within the institution. After brainstorming, a flow map for implementing case management at the unit level was developed (Table 13.1).

The first step is to identify and analyze the patient population of the organization. This information can be obtained from the department of finance. The second step is to evaluate the potential for case management to see if it can affect a decrease in length of stay and a cost savings for the institution. Key participants are listed. The third step is to conduct a small random chart review to identify common problems and common standards of care for a certain patient population. Steps four, five, and six are components that should be included into the development of the

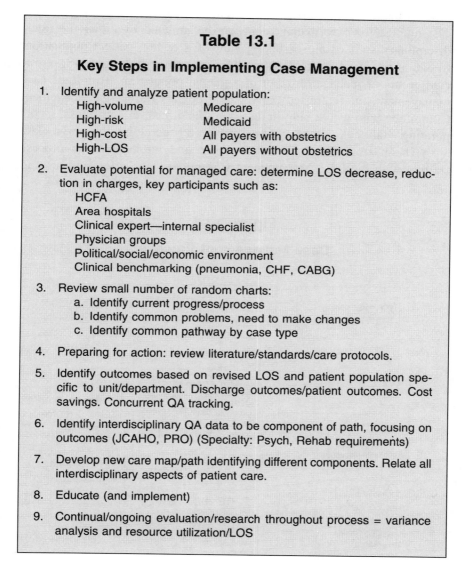

Table 13.1

Key Steps in Implementing Case Management

1. Identify and analyze patient population:

High-volume	Medicare
High-risk	Medicaid
High-cost	All payers with obstetrics
High-LOS	All payers without obstetrics

2. Evaluate potential for managed care: determine LOS decrease, reduction in charges, key participants such as:

   HCFA
   Area hospitals
   Clinical expert—internal specialist
   Physician groups
   Political/social/economic environment
   Clinical benchmarking (pneumonia, CHF, CABG)

3. Review small number of random charts:
   a. Identify current progress/process
   b. Identify common problems, need to make changes
   c. Identify common pathway by case type

4. Preparing for action: review literature/standards/care protocols.

5. Identify outcomes based on revised LOS and patient population specific to unit/department. Discharge outcomes/patient outcomes. Cost savings. Concurrent QA tracking.

6. Identify interdisciplinary QA data to be component of path, focusing on outcomes (JCAHO, PRO) (Specialty: Psych, Rehab requirements)

7. Develop new care map/path identifying different components. Relate all interdisciplinary aspects of patient care.

8. Educate (and implement)

9. Continual/ongoing evaluation/research throughout process = variance analysis and resource utilization/LOS

critical path. Step seven is the actual development of the pathway. Steps eight and nine are the implementation and evaluation of the process.

A flow map describing the process for development, approval, and implementation of a critical pathway was developed (Figure 13.1). The process begins at the top of the flow map with the initiation pathway. The interest for case management can be initiated by either the interdisciplinary staff or nurses taking care of a certain patient population. Initiation of case management can be accomplished by the CNS, physician group, or manager/director of a patient population. To initiate case management, the interested party would contact the Case Management Committee who would help in data analysis of cost-effectiveness, incorporating quality assurance and establishing a general timeline and a plan.

The next phase is the development and implementation process starting with the Case Management Committee, who after analysis and

Figure 13.1

Case Management Process

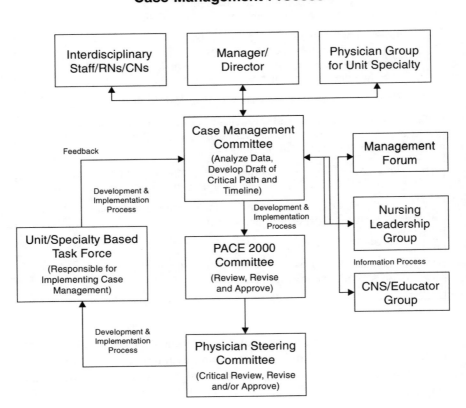

drafting of a plan, presents to the PACE 2000 Committee to obtain support for the pathway and also for critical review of its components. After revisions, the pathway is presented to the Physician Steering Committee, or the physician group that initiated the plan, for approval and critical review.

After support has been obtained, a unit or specialty patient population interdisciplinary task force is formed. This group will be the core group for that patient population in implementing case management. They will be responsible for the key steps in implementing patient care management (see Table 13.1), especially steps five through nine. This group will also be responsible for incorporating the quality assurance reporting process (Figure 13.2) into the pathway development. This group reports back to the Case Management Committee and utilizes the committee for assistance and support as needed.

The feedback loop and evaluation of progress takes place within the development process. Evaluation of the pathway is an ongoing process and involves the members of the Case Management Committee, PACE 2000 Analyst Committee, Physician Steering Committee, and the unit/specialty-based task force.

The information process is initiated by the Case Management Committee. The main function is to keep all of the leaders of MVH informed of the progress, cost savings, and patient satisfaction of the established or forming pathway.

The finishing point occurs after the task force completes a critical pathway. A pathway is always open to improvement and reviewing as the environment changes.

Case Manager

The Case Management Committee had originally planned for the development of a case manager subcommittee to examine the role of the case manager and to determine the education the case manager would need to acquire to successfully complete the components of their positions. The Case Manager Subcommittee was never actually developed due to the unresolved issue of ultimate accountability for the implementation of case management. Issues requiring attention included authority for follow-up with individual practitioners when unacceptable variances occurred and the institution's philosophy specific to interdisciplinary plans of care.

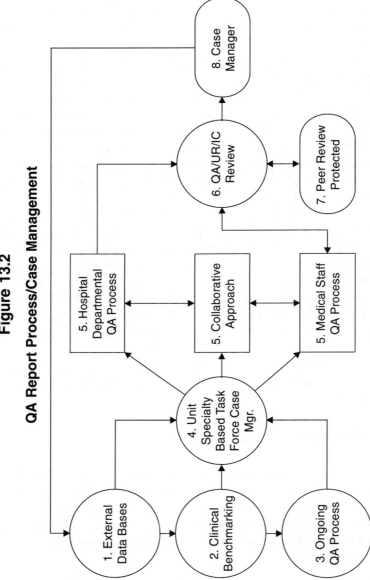

Figure 13.2

QA Report Process/Case Management

The Case Management Committee did research the role of case manager in the literature and discussed key issues regarding implementation of the case manager role. The first question addressed was who will perform the role of case manager? The literature demonstrated a variety of disciplines as case managers. Professional nurses were the dominant discipline utilized as case managers in the acute care setting. The Case Management Committee concluded that the case manager in this particular setting could be performed by a variety of disciplines within the institution. The committee believed the case managers would require education in a variety of processes to become effective in their roles. The topics recommended were reimbursement, negotiation, benchmarking, total quality assurance, assessment skills, resource utilization, and patient/family education.

There has been no further development of the case manager role to this point. The case type or benchmarking process will likely identify who the case manager will be and their specific responsibilities (see Chapter 14).

Quality Assurance Subcommittee

The initial goal of the Quality Assurance Subcommittee was to recommend which case types would be the most appropriate to trial for case management. Appropriateness was based on the financial and political environment, as well as the ability of a specific unit to adapt.

Initially, the most frequent 15 Medicare DRGs were analyzed. This information was obtained from the department of finance. The process for establishing these diagnoses is to select the top diseases from each category as follows:

- Major diagnostic category (MDC). There are 25 MDCs (e.g., MDC 5: Circulatory System).
- DRG. There were 492 DRG groups as of 1992 (e.g., DRG 107: coronary artery bypass graft (CABG) without catheterization).
- International classification of diseases (ICD-9). There are thousands of classifications (e.g., ICD-9 414: coronary atherosclerosis).
- Diagnosis (1–6) and procedures (1–6). Classifications are then broken down into the top six diagnoses and procedures per patient for payment purposes.

From the top 15 Medicare DRGs admitted to MVH, the 50 most frequent Medicare ICD-9s were analyzed. Comparisons were drawn between MVH's and the Health Care Finance Administration's (HCFA) length of stay and cost data. HCFA is a federal agency that monitors health care finances. The focus of the case management group was to examine case types in which 50 percent or greater were reimbursed on a per-case basis, which provided the most cost savings per admission. Medicare and Medicaid are examples of payers who reimburse on a per-case basis, which is the rationale of why those DRGs were investigated first.

The top 50 Medicare diagnoses (ICD-9s) were reviewed and sorted in descending order by number of discharges, patient days, average length of stay, and total charges. The top ten Medicare diagnoses were then reviewed to identify which had the greatest variance in length of stay and total charges. The decision was made to do a histogram on length of stay and identify outliers in these particular diagnoses. This analysis provided data identifying high volume, high risk, high cost, and possible managed care populations. Analyses were completed on the top ten Medicare diagnoses: congestive heart failure, chest pain, pneumonia, coronary atherosclerosis, cerebral artery occlusion, intermediate coronary syndrome, chemotherapy, hypovolemia (volume depletion), hyperplasia of prostate, and atrial fibrillation.

An analysis of the top 20 Medicaid diagnoses (ICD-9) was also performed. Most were related to the area of obstetrics. Again, these diagnoses were reviewed for case types that could be priority candidates for case management development. The case types chosen were uncomplicated cesarean sections and uncomplicated vaginal deliveries. For future reference, also identified were the top ten admission diagnoses (ICD-9) for MVH, which were not Medicare and Medicaid related. This included younger populations who utilize MVH (e.g., trauma).

Quality assurance report process

After examining a number of factors, the Quality Assurance Subcommittee decided to pilot two separate groups in the case management system incorporating quality assurance concepts. Obstetrics was the first group with a focus on uncomplicated vaginal births and cesarean sections. The second group was pulmonary disorders with a concentration on the pneumonia population. The decision to include pulmonary was influenced by the favorable environment for change, because it was also the target group for the first benchmarking analysis at MVH (see Chapter 14). Also because pneumonia was undergoing benchmarking, it would have the very important component of physician support. Obstetrics was placed on hold for development because there was difficulty in establishing physician support. The major issue in obtaining physician support was specific to divergent philosophies of the obstetrical groups.

The decision to incorporate quality assurance into the case management process involved a discussion of the feasibility of linking clinical indicators into critical pathways. The ultimate goal was to weave all quality assurance into the critical path, thus decreasing fragmentation and cost while improving quality and utilization of data results. After several revisions, a flow map for the quality assurance report/case management was developed (Figure 13.2).

The quality assurance report process starts with (1) an external database, (2) clinical benchmarking, and (3) ongoing quality assurance. The external database includes resources that are utilized in the formulation of quality assurance indicators, required or optional, such as JCAHO, or other regulatory agencies (e.g., Commission on Accreditation of Rehabilitation Facilities (CARF) and American College of Surgeons (ACS)).

Clinical benchmarking is a continuous quality improvement quality assurance tool used to evaluate processes based on a comparison of best practices to improve outcomes. Ongoing quality assurance uses internal indicators to identify areas requiring improvement.

The next step identified is the formation of a Unit/Specialty-Based Task Force. The task force consists of an interdisciplinary membership focused on the quality and outcomes related to the care of this patient population. A case manager serves as chairperson/coordinator of this committee. The task force utilizes the flow map for implementing patient case management (Figure 13.1) to develop case management for a case type. Utilizing the external database, clinical benchmarking, and ongoing quality assurance variances, the committee develops a global plan for quality improvement. Identified indicators are incorporated into each department's quality assurance important aspects of care, and all variances are reported to the appropriate quality assurance departments (hospital and medical staff) based on case type. The Hospital Quality Assurance Committee includes different departments, while the Medical Staff Quality Assurance Committee is exclusively focused on medical issues. The proposed collaborative approach combines medical staff and hospital quality assurance, with the focus being total quality improvement. If variances cross several quality assurance sections, then results are reported to appropriate quality assurance departments. The information specific to quality assurance is filtered through the Quality Assurance/Utilization Review/Infection Control area for the purposes of peer review protection. Peer review protection is utilized as an avenue to report quality assurance deficiencies or improvements, but the information is protected from legal review or legal action.

After peer review protection, the information would be routed to the case manager, who is responsible for the development of indicators, data collection, analysis of information, and distribution and reporting of information specific to the case type. The case manager has accountability for the development of action plans promoting quality improvement. The case manager is also given responsibility for obtaining feedback from different departments and disseminating the information back to the external database, benchmarking, and the quality assurance specialty group.

Documentation Subcommittee

The primary objective of the Documentation Subcommittee was to identify the methodology for development of critical pathways (care maps) and other related documentation. Additional objectives for the subcommittee were to develop a generic format for the interdisciplinary care map, to review the potential for automation of the care map, and to assist in the formation of specific care maps.

Critical Path Format

Brainstorming sessions enabled the Documentation Subcommittee to agree on general characteristics of the care map, which included

1. One general format for the hospital
2. A format that allowed for individuality of patients and/or hospital situation
3. A format that complied with regulations and standards
4. A format that was interdisciplinary in nature
5. A format that was an integral and useful component of the medical record (every day documentation)
6. A format that could eventually be automated

7. A structure that would include problem areas, treatment areas, and outcomes.

The subcommittee was aware that individual nursing units and/or programs at MVH had already developed and were successfully using care map type tools. It was decided to review these, compare format styles, and then evaluate practical application of these tools. Tools that were reviewed included

1. Open heart surgery/coronary artery bypass graft (CABG) valve guidelines
2. Inpatient rehabilitation interdisciplinary treatment planning process forms
3. Total knee replacement and total hip replacement managed care guidelines
4. Tissue plasminogen activator medical nursing quality assurance for Emergency Department/CICU
5. HIV assessment tool.

Each of these guidelines was unique to the area in which it was developed and utilized. The guidelines that were most successfully utilized in patient care were those that were useful and pertinent in everyday care. The open heart surgery/CABG guidelines and the inpatient rehabilitation interdisciplinary treatment planning process forms were a permanent part of the patient's medical record.

The subcommittee then began developing a generic format, which was tentatively entitled, *MVH Managed Care Guidelines* (Table 13.2). The generic format can be specific to a diagnostic group or program so the title incorporates both the diagnostic group/program and the assigned DRG (where applicable).

The generic format lists both actual and potential patient problem areas that can then be addressed through treatment interventions. The patient problem areas identified are inclusive of those problems and/or potential problems that are addressed during the patient's hospitalization. Those areas include the following: physiologic assessment, diagnostic studies, nutrition/swallowing, psychosocial, self-care/activity/communication, discharge plans, and teaching.

The generic format allows for the documentation of projected problem resolution in the column entitled outcomes. Outcomes are intended

Table 13.2

MVH Managed Care Guidelines

Problem Areas	Time Frame Interventions	Outcomes

1. **Problems identified through nursing assessment**
   Skin
   Pulmonary
   Neurological
   Cardiac
   G.I.
   Musculoskeletal
   G.U.
   Endocrine
   E.E.N.T.

2. **Diagnostic studies**
   Lab work
   X-rays

3. **Nutrition/swallowing**
   Weight
   Appetite change
   Special diet
   Feeding route

4. **Psychosocial**
   Social cognition
   Coping, support system
   Economic status
   Spirituality
   Sexuality

5. **Self-care/activity/communication**
   A.D.L.s
   Ambulation
   Verbal vs other

6. **Discharge plans**
   Resources
   Placement
   Equipment
   Referrals

7. **Teaching**
   Patient
   Other

to be projected early in the patient's stay, and usually are planned to occur at or before the DRG limit (as applicable).

Interventions to resolve problems and/or potential problems are written in time frames that are most useful to the specified diagnostic group/program. It was decided that no one time frame (hour, shift, day, or week) is practical for every patient care area at MVH. These time frames are decided by the team members developing the individual care maps.

Format Trial

The subcommittee decided to trial the format incorporating existing guidelines into the generic format. The cardiac clinical nurse worked with the subcommittee to place the telemetry nursing guidelines into the subcommittee's generic format. Trialing the format enabled the subcommittee to determine that the generic format would meet practical needs of documentation in the medical record.

A second trial was recommended by the subcommittee and was completed by an interdisciplinary team working with a specific diagnostic population. An inpatient rehabilitation interdisciplinary team that worked with lower-extremity amputees volunteered to trial the format. This team consisted of occupational therapy, physical therapy, rehabilitation, nursing, social services, and psychology. Charts of patients who had been discharged following amputations were reviewed. Each intervening discipline recorded services provided, the patient's functional status each week and the patient's functional status at discharge.

Information from these discipline-specific chart reviews was compiled by two subcommittee members. The average length of stay was determined and utilized in calculating the time frame in which interventions would typically be completed.

The problem areas and/or potential problem areas were determined by identifying those areas for which treatment interventions were working to resolve. Treatment interventions and the patient's status were obtained from the team's chart reviews. The time frame of a week was chosen for this inpatient rehabilitation care map due to the team's previously established method of reviewing patients' cases on a weekly basis.

Outcomes were established with team members and were intended to be the patient's projected status at discharge in relation to the initially described problem and/or potential problem areas. Appendix A identifies specific problem areas and then projected outcomes for a lower extremity amputee patient.

Alternative Documentation Styles: Documentation by Exception

The subcommittee identified the need for clarification of the sequence to complete critical path documentation formulation and implementation. The recommended sequence was proposed for approval (Figure 13.3). The sequence includes the development of general hospitalwide guidelines that apply to all patients who are treated at MVH. These would serve as the basis for unit-specific guidelines that can be developed as necessary. These MVH consumer care guidelines were developed from the MVH mission statement (Exhibit 13.1).

Care guidelines can then be developed for selected patient populations that operationalize the general hospital guidelines to those selected

---

Exhibit 13.1

Consumer Care Guidelines
(MVH Mission Statement, 1992)

I.   The Consumer shall be able to access coordinated comprehensive health care services and information.
     (Mission Statement Nos. 1, 6, 8)

II. The Consumer shall receive services from medical staff and employees who are competent and current in their practice.
     (Mission Statement Nos. 2, 6, 7, 9)

III. The Consumer shall receive services that are generally directed and evaluated by a quality management plan.
     (Mission Statement No. 5)

IV. The Consumer shall have access, to the extent possible, a safe and supportive environment.
     (Mission Statement Nos. 3, 6, 9)

V.   The Consumer shall receive care in compliance with the Patient's Bill of Rights.
     (Mission Statement Nos. 2, 4, 6)

Figure 13.3

Case Management Documentation Recommended Sequence

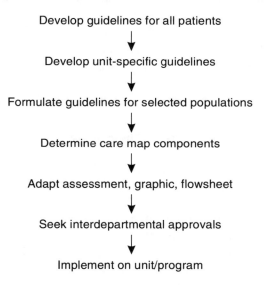

Develop guidelines for all patients

Develop unit-specific guidelines

Formulate guidelines for selected populations

Determine care map components

Adapt assessment, graphic, flowsheet

Seek interdepartmental approvals

Implement on unit/program

patient populations. Critical path components summarize the patient's entire treatment plan, including projecting the patient's status at discharge. Assessments, graphic sheets, and flow sheets are developed to facilitate the documentation of pertinent information related to patient care. Interdepartmental participation and approval are required prior to implementation on units and/or programs.

To facilitate communication and use of the critical path among disciplines involved in care of the patient and to expedite documentation, the subcommittee briefly discussed different options for computerization of the critical path map and flowsheets. The concept of charting by exception (CBE) was also reviewed as one method to include necessary information and to decrease the amount of time that disciplines would spend in documenting the patient's status. The discussion helped the group visualize a simpler system that may eventually replace the current manual system. The hospital is currently in the process of reviewing existing systems in relation to the needs of the hospital and is planning appropriate changes.

The critical path format is now at the point of being trialed. The Pneumonia Task Force used the critical path format to document the pneumonia (nonventilator) critical path. The subcommittee was involved in suggesting format changes and in recommending potential trial sites. These decisions have not yet been finalized.

The subcommittee's role at this point is one of resource. The trial will occur on the clinical level and will be overseen by designated members of the Pneumonia Benchmarking Task Force. The subcommittee will assist as necessary as concerns regarding the format may be raised. The subcommittee may also be involved as other critical paths are developed.

Future Directions

The Case Management Committee is currently evaluating, in conjunction with the Pneumonia Benchmarking Task Force, the future of case management implementation at MVH. There are still unanswered questions as to whom will be ultimately responsible for the implementation of case management at MVH. It is possible that a Case Management Committee will no longer exist and instead the expertise will be utilized as an implementation team for the benchmarking processes, which have been identified as a priority at MVH due to new systemwide changes with a new patient care delivery system.

Summary

A background for the initial development and implementation of case management at MVH has been reviewed. Strengths and weaknesses of this process were identified. The Case Management Committee structure was addressed with suggestions for implementation of documentation and total quality assurance.

References

Bowers, K. 1988. *Case Management by Nurses*. Kansas City, MO: American Nurses' Association.

Zander, K. 1988. "Nursing Case Management: Resolving the DRG Paradox." *Nursing Clinics of North America* 23 (3): 503–20.

Appendix 13.A   Interdisciplinary Treatment Plan: Lower Extremity Amputee

Problem Areas	Week 1	Week 2	Week 3	Outcomes
1. Systems A. Skin	1. Stump will be assessed for infection and level of skin breakdown. 2. Individualized treatment implemented.	1. Stump will be assessed for infection and level of skin breakdown. 2. Individualized treatment implemented.	1. Stump will be assessed for infection and level of skin breakdown. 2. Individualized treatment implemented.	1a. Patient's stump will be free of infection on discharge. 1b. No skin breakdown present on discharge.
B. Endocrine	Diabetes will be assessed as to type and controlled.	Diabetes will be treated as ordered.	Diabetes will be treated as ordered.	Diabetes will be controlled on discharge.
2. Diagnostic Studies				
3. Nutrition/ Swallowing	Nutritional needs and problems are evaluated and care plan formulated and initiated. Education needs are assessed.	Nutrition education/teaching initiated. Patient participates in appropriate education programs. Assessment of nutrition adequacy of intake completed.	Reinforcement of diet teaching. Evaluation of expected compliance. Discharge summary. Follow-up plans.	Patient/family can plan diet to meet patient's nutrient needs (regular versus modified).
4. Psychosocial	Rehab orientation/interview by social service. Amputee support group information given. Discussed discharge options. Education and support counseling.	Team conference #1: Information discussed with patient and family. Patient and family to participate in family/team conference. Discuss discharge options, transportation, education, support, and counseling.	Team conference information discussed with patient and family. Discuss discharge plans, transportation, education, support, and counseling.	Patient and family aware of amputee support. Patient and family aware of support systems available. Patient and family aware of potential community resources and services available.

Continued

Appendix 13.A Continued

Problem Areas	Week 1	Week 2	Week 3	Outcomes
	Invite family and patient to family team conference. Initial evaluation by psychologist in areas of cognitive intactness and psychosocial situation.	Discuss therapeutic leave of absence/independent living apartment. Patient will meet with psychologist weekly. Patient will participate in cognitive group and advance cognitive testing as needed. Relaxation techniques for pain.	Patient will meet with psychologist at least weekly and participate in cognitive group as appropriate.	Patient's emotional status will not affect program in therapy. Patient's behavior—allows effective participation in program. Patient will demonstrate positive level of adjustment to his or her disability.
5. Self-Care Activities and Communication Dependent in following: *Self-Care* A. Feeding B. Grooming C. Bathing D. Dressing: Upper Body E. Dressing: Lower Body F. Toileting G. Application Ace/Shrinker/Prosthesis	Occupational Therapy evaluation & Physical Therapy evaluation. Self-Care instruction initiated: A. Independent B. Independent C. Mod supervision D. Mod independent E. Total-mod independent F. Total supervision G. Not using/total-mod independent	A. Independent B. Independent C. Min-mod independent D. Mod independent E. Max-mod independent of dressing F. Mod supervision G. Not using/max and independent	Occupational Therapy discharge summary and Physical Therapy discharge summary. A. Independent B. Independent C. Min-mod independent D. Mod independent E. Mod-mod independent F. Min-mod independent G. Not using/mod-mod independent	Completed and in medical record. Safe self-care skills: A. Independent feeding B. Independent grooming C. Safe with bathing min-mod independent D. Mod independent upper body dressing E. Min-mod independent less dressing F. Min-mod independent toileting G. If using—safe application of stump

Mobility Transfer:	Transfer training initiated:			Safe transfers:
H. Bed, chair, wheelchair	H. Bed, chair, wheelchair (Total-mod indep)	H. Bed, chair, wheelchair (Max-mod indep)	H. Bed, chair, wheelchair (Mod-mod indep)	H. Bed, chair, wheelchair (Mod-mod indep)
I. Toilet	I. Toilet (Total-sup)	I. Toilet (Max sup)	I. Toilet (Mod-mod in)	I. Toilet (Mod-mod indep)
J. Tub, shower, car, floor	J. Tub, shower (Total-sup)	J. Tub, shower (Total sup) Car transfer instruction (Mod-sup)	J. Tub, shower (total-mod indep) Floor transfer instruction (Max-sup)	J. Tub, shower (Toilet-mod indep) Car (Mod-sup) Floor transfer (Max-mod indep)
K. Walk/wheelchair	K1. Wheelchair training initiated (Mod-mod in)	K1. Wheelchair training (Min-mod indep)	K1. Wheelchair training	K1. Functional wheelchair mgt. (Min-mod indep)
	2. Walking/standing initiated (Mod-mod in)	2. Walking training continues	2. Walking training continues	2. Functional wheelchair mobility and/or walk (Min-mod indep)
		3. Step management instructed.		3. Functional step mgt.
L. Community mobility	L. Community mobility (Total-mod indep)	L. Community mobility initiated (Min-mod in)	L. Community mobility instructed (Min-mod indep)	L. Functional community mobility (Min-mod in)
M. Homemaking	M. Homemaking (Total supervision)	M. Homemaking (Mod-mod indep)	M. Homemaking (Mod-mod in)	M. Functional homemaking (Mod-mod indep)
6. Discharge Plans				
A. Equipment	1. Adaptive ADL equipment assessed/issued.	1. Bathroom equipment assessment.	Equipment issues resolved, equipment obtained, in process.	Necessary equipment issues finalized successfully ILA/TLOA stay.
	2. Wheelchair assessment.	2. Walking equipment assessment.		
	3. Stump equipment modifications.	3. Stump equipment assessment.		
B. Discharge Situation	Team Conference #1			Discharge situation finalized successful ILA/TLOA.

Continued

Appendix 13.A   Continued

Problem Areas	Week 1	Week 2	Week 3	Outcomes
C. Follow-up		1. Family/Team Conference #1. 2. Home assessment information completed. 3. ILA/TLOA completed.	Team Conference #3. Therapy follow-up needs identified social service referral for follow-up.	Therapy follow-up recommendations completed. Comprehensive follow-up identified.
7. Teaching				
A. Skin/Stump Care	Patient and/or significant other (SO) will participate in basic education of skin/stump care.	Patient and/or SO will explain signs & symptoms of skin breakdown and infection.	Patient and/or SO will do stump care correctly and assess skin for potential breakdown areas.	Patient and/or SO will perform skin/stump care and be knowledgeable about signs & symptoms of breakdown & infection
B. Medication	Patient will participate in Stage I self-medication program.	Patient will participate in stage II self-medication program. SO will obtain medication information as needed.	Patient will participate in Stage II self-medication program. SO will obtain medication information as needed.	Patient and/or SO will be knowledgeable of medication and correctly administer.
C. Bowel and Bladder	Patient and/or SO will participate in bowel and bladder educational program.	Patient and/or SO will verbalize bowel and bladder program.	Patient and/or SO will participate in bowel and bladder program.	Patient will be continent of bowel and bladder.
D. Exercise	1. Instruction in UE exercise (Min-Mod assistance). 2. Instruction in stump exercise (Min-sup assistance).	Exercise continues (Min-sup)	Exercise continues (Min-mod indep). Exercise continues (Sup-mod indep).	Mod indep with exercise program.
E. Patient/ Caregiver Instruction	Patient/caregiver observes nursing/therapy.	Patient/self-care, wheelchair, caregiver instructed in transfer, ambulation care transfer	Patient/caregiver review as necessary.	Patient/caregiver safely assists with transfers, self-care, ambulation and equipment.

14

Clinical Benchmarking

Karen L. Davis and Jayne Lachey Gmeiner

This chapter describes the background about MVH's decision to bench-mark and the subsequent steps taken to fulfill this goal. Related project findings and results will also be discussed.

Background

One of PACE 2000 goals was to empower the primary nurse to manage the overall care provided to the patient. Efforts were made through the Case Management Subcommittee to integrate previous case management initiatives used in isolated specialties into PACE 2000 plans. These initiatives had first been developed in 1990, with interdisciplinary drafting of two care guidelines, one coronary artery bypass surgery graft (CABG) and the other for total joint replacements. Although these two guidelines met with success, efforts to broaden this approach failed due to lack of data support and the perception by some ancillary services and physicians that this process was nurse-driven and controlled.

Following the success of an organizationwide cost-reduction pro-gram, a paradigm emerged that encompassed a case management fit with the hospital mission and goals. The incentive was to politically inte-grate streamlined case management into the overall PACE 2000 patient care delivery model. Interdisciplinary participation would be enhanced utilizing the continuous quality improvement (CQI) process in a strong, collaboratively driven environment.

CQI was the paradigm that integrated organizational change with accountability into the culture at MVH. CQI is a model that focuses on the concepts of customer, process, teamwork, measurement (monitoring quality), and continuous improvement (preventing and innovating) (Organizational Dynamics 1991).

CQI transcends the organization as a managerial philosophy. The desire by many clinicians to focus on quality outcomes, associating costs with these gains, arose after initially concentrating on reduction of costs. Continuous quality improvement tools such as benchmarking can naturally lead to case management (Figure 14.1). Case management is an outcome-driven collaborative model of patient care delivery that positively affects quality of care, length of stay, and cost containment. Case management team providers establish critical pathways for specific case types that integrate standards of care and institutional variables to map, track, evaluate and adjust the patient's care and achievement of outcomes (Zander 1988). The case management model can incorporate results of the benchmarking process.

Benchmarking is a tool in the CQI process to measure performance against best-in-class organizations. The subsequent process analysis is done to determine how best-in-class organizations achieve superior per-

Figure 14.1

Relationship Among CQI, Clinical Benchmarking, and Case Management

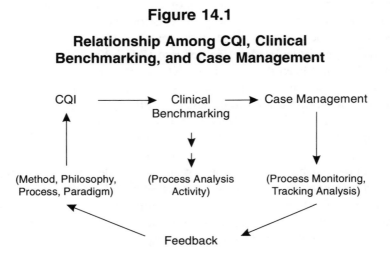

formance levels. Independently contracted consulting firms with external data bases can be used to compare information from best-in-class hospitals such as Medis Group or Mediqual. At MVH, the Mediqual–Medis Group comparative national data base was used for these benchmark comparisons. The data base contains information such as key clinical findings, length of stay (LOS), mortality and morbidity rates, and charges. This information is then used as the foundation for internal strategies to meet or surpass organizations with superior outcomes.

Clinical benchmarking activities progress to completion with developed action plans, while case management allows for a consistent monitoring of patient care and follow-up. Progressive monitoring and tracking lead to planned feedback loops in which process improvements can be philosophically challenged. These challenges produce additional process improvements through the benchmark process analysis that can be incorporated into case management. Case management becomes the conduit whereby improvements and appropriate patient care utilization are managed.

Benchmarking Steps

In general, specific steps are taken to prepare and perform benchmarking activities. MVH utilized these steps in its benchmarking process.

1. *Planning:* In the planning phase, the objective is to identify what area of improvement is to be benchmarked. Comparable data bases are then chosen, and a data collection method is determined.

2. *Analysis:* In the analysis phase, the gap in performance is determined through analysis and comparison of processes. Future performance levels are then assessed and projected.

3. *Integration:* During the integration phase, benchmark findings are communicated for the purpose of gaining acceptance. Goals are then established in order to improve the process.

4. *Action:* In the action phase, plans are implemented with specific monitoring and tracking mechanisms to assess progress.

5. *Maturity:* During maturity, benchmark performance is recalibrated, as an opening objective to continually improve and maintain superior performance. (Camp 1989)

Planning

The most critical element in getting started is the acquisition of physician guidance and leadership. Two to three physicians should be identified for each specific case type to be benchmarked. It is imperative that the physician leader have an opportunity to review all internal and external data related to the selected case type. This may include sex and age distribution, type admission, nursing unit distribution, and key clinical findings. Attention focuses on specific case types evidencing high volume, high variability, and the opportunity for improvement in quality outcome.

Once the physician leader feels comfortable with the quality of information provided, the team composition is collaboratively determined. The objective is to include all necessary ancillary and hospital departments in the process analysis. The membership for the pneumonia benchmarking effort included the following MVH representatives: respiratory medical director, associate director of Medical Education, medical director of the Emergency and Trauma Center, chairman of Medical Staff Quality Assurance/chief of staff, respiratory administrative director, Microbiology director, two nurse project managers of PACE 2000, Management Engineering personnel, Infection Control nurse, ICU registered nurse, representatives from hospital-based quality improvement/utilization management, and a consultant from Mediqual Systems. The membership for the pneumonia effort was expanded with small focus groups as the need arose. For example, a multidisciplinary antibiotic subcommittee was developed to closely examine antibiotic usage and implement an antibiotic biogram. The biogram suggests appropriate antibiotic utilization based on microorganism analysis with cost differentiation. Another multidisciplinary subcommittee was formed to develop the pneumonia case protocols and the final critical path to be utilized for DRG 89.

These physician leaders must be the communicators of patient care process improvements at a peer level. Chosen physician leaders should be well respected among the medical staff and show great interest in and understanding of quality improvement concepts.

Medical staff buy-in to this process is not difficult when process improvements are approached in a scientific, research-based manner utilizing appropriate data. Individual physician practice patterns become a nonissue when the entire patient care process is addressed. MVH selected the diagnosis of pneumonia, DRG 89, as the first case type to be benchmarked for the following reasons:

1. MVH was contacted by Mediqual to participate in the benchmarking effort as a test site for the pneumonia (DRG 89) benchmarking process.

2. A pulmonary specialist at MVH demonstrated strong physician leadership qualities.

3. The pulmonologists' physician leader verbalized willingness to evaluate care of the DRG 89 (pneumonia) patient population, which was the third highest Medicare admission diagnosis at MVH.

4. The team composed of the physician leader and the Quality Management Department had an established history of positive group work promoting positive outcomes.

5. The physician leader could assess the entire initial benchmark process during each phase and make recommendations to facilitate positive outcomes for future endeavors (i.e., congestive heart failure, cesarean sections, and vaginal deliveries).

Analysis

In the initial phase of pneumonia benchmarking, hospitals with more than 200 pneumonia (DRG 89) cases per year over the past three years, with a severity adjusted mortality rate statistically superior at the 95 percent confidence level, were used to form the benchmark for DRG 89. This benchmarking indicated that MVH already achieved favorable outcomes compared with institutions in the data base. It was believed, however, that further refinement of internal processes could result in even better outcomes and improved efficiency. The decision to continue led to a microanalysis of the processes of (1) pharmacy notification of allergy documentation, (2) ETC documentation of antibiotic administration, (3) sputum collection and screening, (4) antibiotic usage, and (5) DRG coding.

The process analysis phase is when the total process of care was examined by the multidisciplinary team. CQI tools used for process analysis included flow charting and brainstorming. The team diagramed the process of care delivery for DRG 89 from arrival in the acute care setting to discharge. Key players in pneumonia patient care were interviewed. Sample chart reviews were conducted to verify the process flow (see Figures 14.2 and 14.3 for pharmacy and laboratory process flow). It was also in this phase that opportunities to improve patient care were identified.

Integration

The results from the analysis phase led to the identification of several opportunities for improvement. The areas for improvement focused on communication of patient allergies to the pharmacy department, documentation of antibiotics administration in the ETC, collection of sputum specimens, appropriate utilization of antibiotics, and correct DRG grouping of pneumonia. Opportunities for improvement were communicated to appropriate hospital and medical staff departments. For example, pneumonia improvements were communicated to the medical staff departments of internal medicine and family practice. Details of the pneumonia improvements are outlined in the following section. Findings were also discussed with the hospital departments of pharmacy, laboratory, respiratory care services, nursing services, and the ETC. At this point, each department assisted with the resolution to the identified problems.

Action

The input received from each department was shared by the interdisciplinary benchmark committee. Action plans addressing each problem were designed and approved by the committee. Action plans for each problem are outlined as follows:

1. *Notification of Pharmacy Regarding Known Drug Allergies*—Allergy information is asked of patients by nursing, the ETC staff, and physicians, but it was rarely communicated in a timely manner to the pharmacy dispensing the antibiotic. A proposed information systems upgrade is planned to correct this issue. The information systems improvements will include an integrated communication system between pharmacy and nursing. The HUC will enter known allergies in the Nursing Information Module (NIM), and this information will be directly communicated to pharmacy via computer (Pharmakon). If an allergy is not entered at the time of admission, the pharmacy will print out a record of data gaps for known allergies and return this to the

Figure 14.2   Miami Valley Hospital Pneumonia Clinical Benchmarking

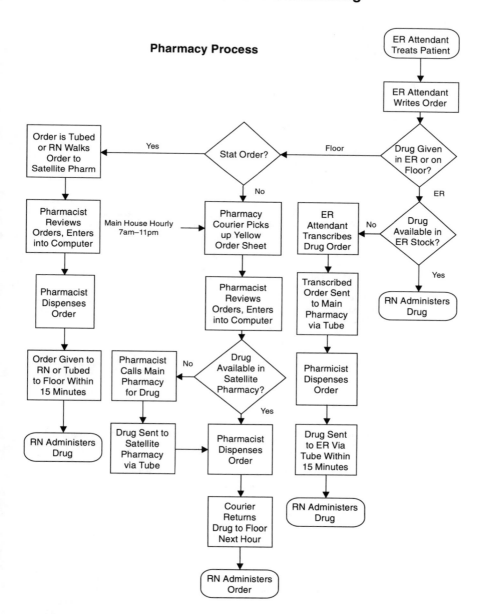

Figure 14.3   CompuNet Clinical Laboratories Micro Lab Process

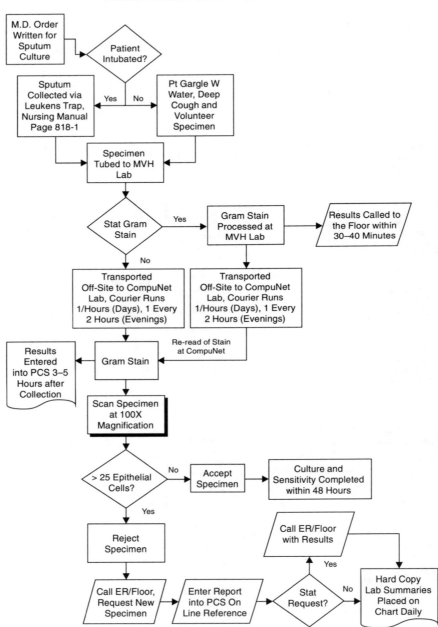

nursing unit for completion. The goal of this process is to have 100 percent of allergies reported to the pharmacy before antibiotics are administered. The major yield from the information systems upgrade will be a reduction in potentially harmful incidents to the patient, potential liability, and an increase in HUC productivity.

2. *Emergency and Trauma Center Documentation*—A review of cases and process flow revealed that antibiotics in the ETC may be documented in any of five different locations in the medical record. These five different areas may include medication administration record (MAR), nursing notes, physician order sheet, ETC face sheet, or parental fluid sheet. The lack of consistency in documentation practices made it difficult for health professionals outside of the ETC to determine when antibiotics had been administered. Final resolution of a uniform location for the documentation of medications in the ETC was determined by the ETC unit leadership group. A simplified method of documentation will occur as follows:

- If the antibiotic is ordered by the ETC physician, the medication will be documented on the ETC face sheet.

- If the antibiotic is ordered by an attending physician and is written on the physician's order sheet, medication will be documented on the MAR.

3. *Sputum Samples*—The rejection rate for sputum samples was 25 percent, compared with an average of 12 percent for the four hospitals with benchmark performance in pneumonia. Rejection primarily occurred due to the sample being saliva rather than sputum. The task force recommended that the respiratory therapist collect all specimens and obtain specimens using ultrasonic nebulizer treatments as indicated. Accurate processing of these samples to identify the correct microorganism determines the DRG grouping and subsequent reimbursement. Monitoring the effectiveness of this new procedure for sputum collection will occur.

4. *Antibiotic Utilization*—In the sample (36/301 = 12 percent) used for detailed analysis, the clinical pharmacists determined that 30 different high-cost antibiotics, many in combination, were used on those 36 patients. This issue is related to the problem addressed in poor sputum samples but also is reflective of uncertain practice patterns. An in-depth study was conducted by the multidisciplinary Antibiotic Subcommittee and presented to the Pharmacy and Therapeutics

Committee. Recommendations for appropriate antibiotic utilization in the treatment of pneumonia were made. An antibiotic biogram has been developed as a reference point for physicians who admit patients under the diagnosis of pneumonia.

5. *DRG Grouping*—Correct grouping of pneumonia is primarily dependent on identification of the microorganism causing the illness. The difference in reimbursement between DRG 89, simple pneumonia and pleurisy, and DRG 79, respiratory infections and inflammations, is $1,837.99 per case, with DRG 79 being the higher. This difference stems from precise identification of the more virulent microorganisms, such as pseudomonas in DRG 79 versus pneumococcal in DRG 89. Six incorrectly coded patients were found in the 36 sample population. The charts were coded for pneumonia (DRG 89) and should have been coded for DRG 79, indicating a loss of $11,028 in reimbursement for these six cases. Generalizing this incorrect rate (16 percent) to the average 300 cases of DRG 89 results in an annual yield of $91,900 in increased reimbursement.

Two inservice programs were provided to address the DRG grouping issues. *Coders* in medical records were educated about accurate identification of microorganisms in the chart, and two pulmonologists provided inservice programs to the Departments of Internal Medicine and Family Practice regarding appropriate antibiotic orders based on sputum results.

One additional step in the action phase is analyzing the impact of the cost of quality. Cost of quality estimations will be assigned to each action plan with the assistance of the department of management systems.

The goal of the action plan for notification of pharmacy regarding known allergies and the action plan for the ETC documentation will be measured by QI and reduction in harmful incidents to the patient. Productivity gains are expected in areas of notification of pharmacy regarding known allergies and collection of sputum specimens. More substantiated financial gains are expected with the action plan for sputum collection and specimen processing, antibiotic utilization, and DRG grouping.

Cost of quality estimates were made for decreased LOS using a critical path or managed care guideline, which stipulates an average of 5.0 days LOS. The 1991 average LOS was 9.2 days for Medicare patients at MVH and 8.9 days for all payers, with 7.0 days being the HCFA mean LOS for DRG 89 in 1993. In addition, no cost of quality estimate has been given for mortality reduction, although in comparison to Dayton regional hospitals, this is a clear opportunity for the lower-risk category of pneumonia. Data analysis provided a mortality rate of 2.0 percent for benchmark hospitals with low-risk pneumonia patients and 3.3 percent for MVH low-risk pneumonia patients. In comparison, the mortality rates for higher-risk pneumonia patients for benchmark hospitals is 15.7 percent, and 13.4 percent for MVH.

Maturity

This phase involves the periodic monitoring and evaluation of the action plans. The process improvements are compared with patient care outcomes. For example, the improvement in organism identification through better sputum collection protocols could be related to reduction in the sputum rejection rate and the initiation of the most appropriate antibiotic. These interventions should contribute to a shorter LOS and reduce the mortality rate.

The benchmarking process concludes with the institution once again comparing itself with the data base institutions. The institution is compared with best-in-class organizations to determine if the actions taken actually resulted in the desired outcomes (i.e., reduced LOS). For example, pneumonia group data will be analyzed to determine if there has been change from the benchmark with respect to LOS, mortality, and readmission rate. Once the results are known, the institution will determine where it stands in relation to the current year's benchmark statistics. An assessment of the need for further improvement will also be addressed.

Recommendations

As the group worked through the benchmarking process, we learned lessons that will stimulate future benchmarking activities. The following are issues that should be addressed with any benchmarking process:

- Keep group size small. Generally seven to ten people are an appropriate group size. Other departments/expertise should be called upon on an ad hoc or as-needed basis.
- Revisit flow process/brainstorming issues for opportunities to improve when the benchmarking proceedings become stagnant. This will help refocus the entire group.
- Reinforce keeping an open mind when barriers to change are presented. This will hopefully stimulate a reduction in turf battles.

- Explore creative methods to overcome barriers that may produce patient care improvements. Even though it may have never been done before should not preclude the exploration of new and innovative ideas.
- If applicable, include pathway development in the benchmarking process. This will eliminate redundant work in the future.
- Develop clear parameters for future measurement (quality indicators).
- Identify, establish, and nuture relationships with major physician stakeholders related to the process.
- Recognize timelines need to be flexible from process beginning through implementation.
- Be patient.

Summary

In summary, the CQI process improvements are notable considering favorable outcomes prior to benchmarking. Improvements in the care of pneumonia patients should result in significant financial gains because DRG 89 (pneumonia) is the third highest volume Medicare DRG at MVH.

Future plans consist of continued, focused interdisciplinary clinical process improvements such as those experienced with pneumonia. Included in these plans are benchmarking for congestive heart failure, cesarean section/vaginal delivery, and coronary artery bypass graft. Pneumonia will be monitored and then reevaluated later.

References

Camp, R. C. 1989. *Benchmarking: The Search for Industry Best Practices that Lead to Superior Performance*. Milwaukee, WI: ASQC Quality Press.
Organizational Dynamics, Inc. 1991. *The Quality Advantage*. Burlington, MA: Organizational Dynamic.
Zander, K. 1988. "Nursing Case Management: Resolving the DRG Paradox." *Nursing Clinics of North America* 23 (3): 503–19.

Epilogue

Patricia Sue Fitzsimons

Three years have passed since the initial vision was developed by the nursing leadership that resulted in the redesign of nursing work called PACE 2000. At this time all inpatient units have implemented the new care delivery paradigm; many are evaluating the original assumptions and are reworking their original models.

Numerous changes have occurred since PACE 2000 was designed. LOS has continued to decrease across DRGs. There has been a continued shift of inpatient to outpatient care, and the penetration of managed care has increased with an increasing focus on utilization and system issues. All of these changes have created the need for ongoing evaluation of how care is delivered. Additionally, the focus on overall health care reform and a capitated system has focused increasing attention on the cost of care.

As this institution continues to look forward and strategically plan for its future, the benchmarking projects that began a year ago are moving into planned implementation phases. We have discovered that interdisciplinary planning for care changes based on data is very effective and is the best approach to achieve buy-in from different professional groups. Analyzing best practices and monitoring the impacts of planned changes in care as well as improving the system have proved to be very helpful in moving proactively forward to improve care. We have also discovered that these efforts are very resource intense and time consuming when done well; the institution can only complete two to three of these major efforts annually.

Improving continuity of care into the community has been an additional benefit of the benchmarking efforts. We have learned that we need to ensure a smooth transition to the community for patients and develop mechanisms that ensure that patients have the necessary information and resources to prevent readmission. Exciting projects involving nursing students in the community have developed as a result of some of our learning in these projects.

The design of the clinical ladder has been completed. This huge undertaking was especially difficult since the institution already had a ladder in place; there was great threat in getting rid of what was known and comfortable. At this point, there appears to be enthusiasm for the new system, and it will be implemented in 1995.

The vision we developed three years ago created an environment where staff are highly involved in system changes. With health care reform on the horizon and the role of the nurse and the acute care setting changing dramatically, this philosophy of having to change to survive is very powerful. No one assumes that what we know today and do today will be the care delivery system of tomorrow. Another benefit is the cooperation among disciplines to participate in patient outcome efforts.

We are here for the benefit of patients. However, all too often the professional needs and identities superimpose themselves on what really is the best for our patients. As a system, we have made major strides in this positive direction.

Patient care at this institution is very different in 1994. We are still struggling with it and what it should be. Roles continue to be defined and redefined. Our goal of 65 percent skill mix is not yet realized; we did achieve 68 percent mix as of year end 1993. Given our case mix of patients, not many more changes can be made to decrease that further. However, that is today's thinking. We are not sure what the impact of new methodologies and wisdom yet to be learned will have on our system.

The past three years have been very hard work and have resulted in great learning and great rewards. The process has resulted in increased collaboration with all parts of the institution and changes in care delivery that would have been very difficult if not impossible to achieve five years ago. We have successfully changed how people view work and focused attention on the true mission of the organization—patient care.

Additionally, we did indeed change our skill mix through thoughtful planning and restructuring the role of the nurse.

Many individuals have emerged as true leaders in this process. Their development and contributions to the system have been a real reward for me as the identified leader of this change. Their commitment and enthusiasm have never wavered; they deserve the real recognition for the success of this effort. My heartfelt thanks goes to them all.

List of Contributors

Mary Lou Anderson, RN, MS, is nursing projects/transition manager at Miami Valley Hospital and serves as co-program manager of PACE 2000. Her clinical area of expertise is critical care nursing.

Mary E. Benson-Landau, MSN, RNC, is manager of Management Development in the Human Resources Department at Miami Valley Hospital. She held the position of nurse educator in the Center for Nursing Excellence during the implementation process.

Nancy L. Breidenbach, RN, is a clinical nurse educator on the Advanced Care Unit at Miami Valley Hospital. She has been a clinical instructor for Miami University in Oxford, Ohio for several years. She has 16 years of experience in critical care nursing.

Sally Clements, RN, is currently employed at Miami Valley Hospital in the Emergency and Trauma Center.

Bonnie Coalt, RN, MS, is director of Nursing Services at Miami Valley Hospital. She holds a master's degree in Nursing Administration from Wright State University in Dayton, Ohio. Her experience includes 25 years in the areas of critical care nursing.

Connie Curran, RN, EdD, FAAN, is national director, Patient Care Services, APM Incorporated.

Rebecca J. Czachor is nurse manager of a Neuroscience Unit at Miami Valley Hospital, and was co-chair of the Roles Subcommittee. She obtained her nursing education in Cambridge, England and midwifery education in Scotland. She has worked in a variety of fields and roles since moving to the United States in 1981.

Karen L. Davis, RN, MBA, was manager of Concurrent Quality Assessment and Improvement, Utilization Management, and Infection Control at Miami Valley Hospital. She is currently director of Quality Assurance, Utilization Management, and Risk Management at Healthspring Medical Group in Dayton, Ohio. She graduated in nursing from Spalding College of Louisville, Kentucky and holds an MBA from the University of Louisville.

Jennifer L. Eddlemon, RNC, served as cochair of the Roles Subcommittee during Miami Valley Hospital's transition to the PACE 2000 concept. She is currently on the staff of Miami Valley Hospital's Birthing Center and Perinatal Intensive Care Unit.

Margaret Eigler is clinical coordinator of Physical Therapy Rehabilitation and Outpatient Services at Miami Valley Hospital.

Debra K. Fearing, PharmD, is clinical manager of the Department of Pharmacy Services at Miami Valley Hospital.

Patricia Sue Fitzsimons, RN, PhD, is senior vice president of Hospital Operations at Miami Valley Hospital and is past president of the Ohio Chapter of the American Organization of Nurse Executives.

Jayne Lachey Gmeiner, RN, MS, CCRN, is co-program manager of PACE 2000 at Miami Valley Hospital. She has a clinical background in critical care nursing and previously held the position of clinical nurse specialist on the telemetry unit.

Catherine G. Hall, RN, MS, is nurse manager of the Emergency and Trauma Center at Miami Valley Hospital. She holds a bachelor's degree in Nursing and a master's degree in Nursing from Wright State University.

Keith A. Lakes, AAS, RRT, is manager of Critical Care for the Department of Respiratory Care Services at Miami Valley Hospital.

Therese C. Lupo, RN, is director of Nursing Services at Miami Valley Hospital. She holds a bachelor's degree in Nursing from the College of St. Catherine, St. Paul, Minnesota and a master's degree in Nursing Administration from the University of New Mexico—Albuquerque.

Marjorie Mahle, RN, MS, is the Trauma clinical nurse specialist at Miami Valley Hospital, which is a Level I Trauma Center.

Deborah Mals, RN, MS, is currently the director of Perinatal Services at Miami Valley Hospital. Her professional experience includes 11 years of managerial/administrative experience in both the critical care and perinatal areas.

Patricia A. Martin, RN, PhD, received her bachelor's degree from the College of Nursing and Health, University of Cincinnati; her master's degree with a nursing major from Wright State University; and her doctorate with a nursing major from Case Western Reserve University. She has worked as a staff nurse in Maternal Child Nursing, as nurse researcher at Miami Valley Hospital, and as faculty in a variety of nursing programs. Her research in organizational dimensions of hospital nursing practice and experience in program evaluation were key to her participation in development of an evaluation plan for PACE 2000. Currently she is director of Nursing Research at Wright State University—Miami Valley College of Nursing and Health.

Carol Lynn Miller is clinical nurse specialist of the Coronary Intensive Care Unit and the Cardiothoracic Surgical Intensive Care Unit at Miami Valley Hospital.

Kimbra Kahle Paden, RN, MSN, is a medical-surgical clinical nurse specialist for Orthopedics at Miami Valley Hospital. She received her bachelor's degree in Nursing from Eastern Kentucky University at Richmond and her master's degree in Nursing from Wright State University, Dayton, Ohio.

Maribeth Richwalsky is manager and senior engineer of the Department of Quality Management at Miami Valley Hospital.

Candace Skidmore, RN, BSN, is program manager of CareFlight Air Ambulance Service at Miami Valley Hospital.

Victoria A. Studebaker, MS, MT(ASCP)SBB, is the administrative director of CompuNet Clinical Laboratories, Inc., the provider of laboratory services for Miami Valley Hospital.

Kathy A. Tilton, RN, MS, CCRN, is nurse manager of a rehabilitation unit and pain unit at Miami Valley Hospital.

Christine L. Tipton, RN, CCRN, is a staff nurse on the Intensive Care Unit at Miami Valley Hospital. She has ten years of experience in critical care nursing.

Linda S. Welin, RN, MS, CCRN, is clinical nurse specialist on the Telemetry unit at Miami Valley Hospital and adjunct faculty at Wright State University–Miami Valley College of Nursing and Health. She has 25 years of experience in critical care nursing and seven years of teaching experience at Wright State University.

John K. Wiley, MD, FACS, is in private practice of Neurosurgery and is associate clinical professor of Surgery at Wright State University, Dayton, Ohio. He is also chief-of-staff elect at Miami Valley Hospital.

Arlon Zabel, MPA, is business manager of the Division of Nursing at Miami Valley Hospital.

About the Editors

Phyllis Baker Risner, PhD, RN, is an associate professor at Wright State University–Miami Valley College of Nursing and Health. Her teaching areas of expertise are nursing administration, research, and community health. She has published textbook chapters about nursing diagnosis and journal articles about health promotion research.

Claire Blust Rodehaver, MS, RN, ONC, is employed as the Bone Marrow Transplant Program Manager at Miami Valley Hospital. She has held various clinical and leadership positions over the past 11 years. Most recently, she was the oncology clinical nurse specialist of the David L. Rike Cancer Center at the hospital. She has published a textbook chapter about collaboration and the staff nurse role and journal articles in *Oncology Nursing Forum* and *Nursing Clinics of North America* about various clinical issues.

Robin G. Bashore, MS, RNC, is the perinatal clinical nurse specialist at Miami Valley Hospital. Her clinical expertise is in high-risk and critical care obstetrics. Robin has published in *Critical Care Clinics of North America* and the *Journal of Perinatal/Neonatal Nursing* about clinical obstetrical topics.